Nightclub

Nightclub

Bouncers, Risk, and the Spectacle of Consumption

GEORGE S. RIGAKOS

McGILL-QUEEN'S UNIVERSITY PRESS | Montreal & Kingston • London • Ithaca

ISBN 978-0-7735-3361-5 (cloth)
ISBN 978-0-7735-3362-2 (paper)

Legal deposit second quarter 2008
Bibliothèque nationale du Québec

Printed in Canada on acid-free paper that is 100% ancient forest free
(100% post-consumer recycled), processed chlorine free.

This book has been published with the help of a grant from the Canadian Federa-
tion for the Humanities and Social Sciences, through the Aid to Scholarly Publications Programme, using funds provided by the Social Sciences and Humanitites
Research Council of Canada. Research for this book was supported by the Social
Sciences and Humanities Research Council (grant 410-2000-0145).

McGill-Queen's University Press acknowledges the support of the Canada Council
for the Arts for our publishing program. We also acknowledge the financial support
of the Government of Canada through the Book Publishing Industry Development
Program (BPIDP) for our publishing activities.

Library and Archives Canada Cataloguing in Publication

Rigakos, George
Nightclub : bouncers, risk, and the spectacle of consumption / George S. Rigakos.

Includes bibliographical references and index.
ISBN 978-0-7735-3361-5 (bound). ISBN 978-0-7735-3362-2 (pbk.)

1. Bouncers. 2. Nightclubs–Social aspects. 3. Consumption (Economics)–Social
aspects. 4. Risk–Sociological aspects. 5. Private security services–Case studies.
I. Title.

TX911.R44 2008   302.3'3   C2007-905861-2

Illustration concept by D'urban Design Illustration. Art by Bao Phan.
This book was designed and typeset by studio oneonone in Garamond 11/13

Contents

Acknowledgments

I am deeply indebted to the many people who have made this book possible. Thank you first of all to the dozens of Halifax doorstaff, Halifax police officers, and RCMP members who participated in this study. I am grateful to you for opening up your minds to the research process. Your candid commentary about nightclubs is now the core of my analysis, and I hope I have done your thoughts justice. Thanks especially to "Monster" Joe Baldwin (now retired) for orienting me to the Halifax nightclub scene. Much of the ethnographic and interview data that appears in this book was collected by Andrew Dunn and David MacDonald, both former students at Saint Mary's University, who despite telling me that getting paid to hang out in nightclubs was the best gig they could have ever hoped for, have wisely moved on to greener pastures. Two other research assistants, Neera Datta and Jillian Cameron, also conducted interviews. Their amiable natures made it easy for research subjects to speak freely, and this is repeatedly evident in the data. Thank you also to Sandi Cole-Pay and Lindia Smith for transcribing sometimes muffled and indecipherable interview data with diligence and care. Stephen Perrott of Mount Saint Vincent University gave me access to his invaluable expert knowledge on measuring police culture and in-group solidarity as well as practical assistance with making sense of our jointly collected data.

When I moved to Carleton University, I met Jake Lindsay, a fourth-year student who did a fantastic job of legal research on the topic of bouncers and liability. I was also lucky to meet Alan Blunt, whose keen statistical eye probably saved me from embarrassment. I owe him a particular debt of thanks. For looking over sections of this book, thanks to

Logan Atkinson, Joanna Pozzulo, Doris Buss, and Alan Hunt. For listening to me go on about nightclubs, thanks to all of my students in the fourth-year seminar "Policing and Social Surveillance" and graduate seminar "Crime, Law and Social Order" at Carleton University and even the students who sent me emails after my presentation at the Surveillance Group seminar series at Queen's University. I would like to also thank the anonymous reviewers of previous versions of this manuscript and the staff and editor of McGill-Queen's University Press for their professional support. For moral support and intellectual stimulation, thanks to John McMullan, Wendy Chan, and Jean-Sebastien Rivard. Finally, thanks to my family, the bedrock of my life: Mom, Dad, Peter, Sandy, little Steve, Gabriella, and of course my wife, Andie, who is my wisest critic, most enthusiastic supporter, and the love of my life.

For Andie and Lucas

Nightclub

You know what happens in clubs? Nothing. Nothing happens. A few thousand people stand around and get fucked up. Sometimes, they go back to the bathrooms to take leaks. Other times, they go back to the bathrooms to do coke or get blowjobs. Afterward, they go back to where they were, and they stand there for a few more hours. Occasionally, they dance. The men look like retards when they dance. The women don't, so the men follow them around and try to encourage *the sex*. A mating ritual ensues. This ritual has made me realize that the people I'm dealing with at the club are several steps down on the evolutionary scale. The women shake their tail feathers. The men strut and preen. Sometimes they fight over women. Animals do this too.

From "Clublife," an on-line journal of the nightly nonsense endured by a bouncer at two of New York's most popular nightclubs, http://standingonthebox.blogspot.com (accessed June 2006)

Pleasure always means not to think about anything, to forget suffering even where it is shown. Basically it is helplessness. It is flight; not, as is asserted, flight from a wretched reality, but from the last remaining thought of resistance. The liberation which amusement promises is freedom from thought and from negation.

Adorno and Horkheimer 2000, 15.

1

Introduction

It's almost 2 A.M. I've now been sitting at the bar for over two and a half hours. My back is sore and my bladder is full of Mexican beer. For the last half hour or so I've been watching a muscular young man in a red T-shirt. He looks familiar. Perhaps he's a university student? He walks around the perimeter of the dance floor, stopping intermittently to talk to acquaintances and generally eyeing other men with scowls of discontent. He's not happy. His steps are exaggerated as he moves slowly about the bar. Already he has intentionally bumped into three other men. I'm convinced he's looking for a fight. I've been inside Halifax nightclubs long enough to identify a prospective pugilist as he fuels himself with alcohol, and I'm sure the bouncers have noticed him too.

Sure enough, two burly doormen begin to creep towards him. Their timing is impeccable. The angry young man has strutted his way onto the dance floor and bumped, jostled, and nearly knocked over another three revellers. He also hasn't put down his beer, which is a dance-floor violation.

The doormen don't stop to explain their actions to their intended target. They immediately seize him by both arms and begin dragging him towards the door. One of the bouncers actually manages to pull his pint of beer away and set it on a table. The man in the red T-shirt seems stunned and compliant as he is dragged away. He was taken by surprise. Some of his "friends" notice but only slowly move over to watch. They are intercepted by another bouncer and an animated discussion ensues. One of the group throws up his hands and shakes his head, smiling as he talks to the bouncer and pats him on the back. It looks like his associates are distancing themselves from any involvement in the fracas.

By the time the bouncers pull the young bodybuilder to the door, he begins to kick and wrench away, trying to fling himself from their grasp. He succeeds in getting his right arm free and flails his fist wildly at the bouncer holding his left arm. He gets off two punches ... In the meantime two other bouncers have come across the dance floor to assist. One of the bouncers, a shorter fellow, crashes into the fray with an elbow to the head of the young man. "Calm down!" he orders through his clenched jaw.

Another bouncer, who is also holding onto him, adds his own admonition: "I told you, we're not putting up with your shit anymore!" as he wrenches back the young man's right arm with force.

The melee is next to the exit, so the majority of the nightclub crowd hasn't a clue what is happening, obliviously hopping and swaying to the Go-Go's "We've got the beat, we've got to beat, we've got the beat, yeah, we've got the beat ..."

I slide wearily off my sweaty bar stool and slowly make my way over to the exit following the tangled pack of doormen now completely smothering the red T-shirted man from my sight. Closing time is at hand, and I know there is more of this to come. (fieldnotes)

The original purpose of this book was to examine the subculture and surveillance practices of nightclub doorstaff as an addition to the expanding literature on private policing. After all, bouncers are the last vast unregulated, unsupervised, and pugnacious form of security provision in North America. For social scientists and policing theorists, bouncers lurk in the nighttime shadows as the state and respectable civil society slumber (Melbin 1978, 210–18). More and more, city centres are inviting this form of transgressional nighttime consumption towards creating a twenty-four hour urban buzz (Hobbs et al. 2003, 19–36). It made sense, therefore, to view bouncing and its concomitant safety concerns through the lens of security provision. What forms of surveillance are in operation? How are populations being ordered? What are the technological manifestations of these surveillance practices, and how are these resisted? Good questions, I thought, and I make every effort to answer them in this book. But my experience in the Halifax nighttime economy and numerous observation sessions in Toronto, Ottawa, and Montreal opened my eyes to broader issues about the overall maintenance and effect of nighttime culture: those who inhabit it, those who police it, and the way these two facets interlink to make nightclubs important sites of consumption.

So, while this book is still very much about security, surveillance, and the organization of risk in the nightclub setting, it is more importantly about coming to terms with how a nightclub operates as a site of consumption. Specifically, I establish a theoretical nexus between "consumption," "security," and "risk" in order to comprehend the dynamics of order, desire, and surveillance in nightclubs. This is the fundamental theoretical contribution of this book: establishing through empirical analysis and observation the consumption-security-risk nexus for understanding the nightclub as a site of aesthetic and experiential production in late capitalism.

In urban and cultural studies there is often a tendency to embrace the liberating, the transgressional, and the edgework (e.g., Lyng 2005) that surround the urban nighttime economy and rave scene (Malbon 1999), within a celebratory understanding of spectacle and "carnival" (Presdee 2000). Nightclubs are seen as spaces of transcendence – usually fuelled by drugs like Ecstasy – opening up the night to sensual and freeing expression, even if in the form of violence (e.g., Thomsen 1997). Indeed, one current of thought suggests that the nighttime economy somehow breaks the bonds (the everyday habitus) of daytime order, risk management, and policing (see Ferrell 2004; Jackson 2004; Palmer 2000). This is to an extent undoubtedly true, since the forms, directional flows, and rhythms of population and order maintenance start to change after the sun sets.

What I discovered, however, also challenges this rather cheery postmodern rendition of nocturnal movements. Albeit bleary and sexually voyeuristic, the panoptic eye remains vigilant well into the night. This is one aspect of difference between the objectives and theoretical arguments of this book and other literature on nighttime consumption.

Another point of divergence – in this case with the majority of private policing studies – is my critique of this literature's limited engagement with the fundamental aspects of capitalist relations. Up to now it has seemed largely sufficient to state that private policing provision is on the rise (Jones and Newburn 1995; Sanders 2003; Swol 1999), that private security employees serve clients in spaces that are part of burgeoning tracts of mass private property (Jones and Newburn 1999; Shearing and Stenning 1983), and that state fiscal planning under neoliberal regimes has caused a crisis of policing (South 1984; Spitzer and Scull 1977). Rarely have analysts turned their attention to understanding the specific dynamics behind how security is sold (Loader 1999), commodified, and valorized (Rigakos 1999a; Spitzer 1987), and how seemingly chaotic spaces are made to look ordered for the purpose of translating ephemeral, immaterial security labour into a tangible, marketable consumable (Rigakos 2002b). In the context of a nightclub, such analyses become indispensable, because in their absence we would be embroiled in a endless spiral of uncertainty trying to catch up with the latest in subcultural capital (see especially Jensen 2006; Thornton 1995), free-floating signifiers, music genres, and beats per minute. These are all intriguing facets of the nightclub in and of themselves, but we would risk misapprehending the experiential lustre of the nightclub as a site of production and profit that is actually manufactured through the negotiation of security. I argue, in fact, that security provision most obviously manifested in the presence of the bouncer actually helps *produce* the nightclub.

By now it is hardly an exaggeration to say the concept of risk has become an important part of the analytic lexicon of many social scientists in fields ranging from psychology to philosophy. It is a ubiquitous idea, multifaceted in its application, but nonetheless directly connecting to the problem of order, government, and even "knowing" the social world, at least in an instrumental sense (Mythen 2004). For criminologists and sociologists, risk has played an increasingly important role in theorizing about all aspects of social relations ranging from everyday morality (Hunt 2003) to governmental thinking (O'Malley 2004) and even world ecological disaster (Beck 1999). But with few exceptions (e.g., Chan and Rigakos 2002; Coleman 2004; Engel and Strasser 1998; Hannah-Moffat 1999; Mythen 2005; Rigakos and Hadden 2001; Rustin 1994), the deployment of risk as an analytic concept has been uncritical and disengaged from the capitalist production process. And in certain cases, risk theorists have even deliberately exorcized notions of class, gender, and race from their analyses (Beck 1997; O'Malley 2001) or have purported that risk thinking now transcends these rather dated modernist notions. Deploying a Marxian perspective, the concept of *risk markets* reveals rather than obfuscates the connections between risk and axes of race, class, and gender within the context of the nightclub setting. It is through this sensibility that we may have a concrete and realistic grasp of the complexities of potential violence mediated by representational strategies that make a nightclub possible. Nightclubs attract populations based on whatever form of material, social, or subcultural capital they are able to muster, inviting certain people in while vetting out dangerous populations. Those who are in circulate the unquenchable desire to be desired, to be included; those who are out actually spatially reinforce this desire, this exclusivity.

Methods of Inquiry

This project employs multiple methods in an attempt at triangulation: a methodological notion (Denzin 1978) that seeks to analyze as many sources of data as possible about the same object of analysis. If one source of data is deficient or is able to capture only a particular "angle" or part of the lived experiences and setting of those it seeks to understand, then data gleaned from other sources can help round out, indeed amend, our understanding. This book is based on an ethnographic analysis of the nightclub setting, a standardized survey of fifty-five bouncers, and in-depth interviews with twenty-six bouncers employed by over half a dozen nightclubs in downtown Halifax.

Given that the intended focus of this project was to examine bouncers, the largest of the nightclubs operating in downtown Halifax were strategically selected because they typically employed the highest concentrations of security personnel. I use the terms *doorstaff, bouncers*, and *security personnel* interchangeably in this book. Most nightclubs in Halifax (and elsewhere in Canada) also use these terms interchangeably, although *bouncer* was sometimes seen as a derogatory term. In cities such as New York, some nightclubs make a formal distinction between doormen and bouncers. The former deal with patrons, lineups, and VIPS – a form of nightly public relations – while the latter deal with violence. Like my respondents, I make no such distinction. Bouncers, therefore, are paid by nightclub owners to conduct access and egress control, protect VIPS and other persons in the nightclub, ensure nightclub policies are enforced, and use force or the threat of force to foster compliance by removing or threatening to remove unsuitable, disorderly, drunken, threatening, or violent patrons. Moreover, they help produce the nightclub insofar as they act as guarantors of its social makeup, ambience, and aesthetic.

The minimum requirements for selection were that the research sites employed six or more doorstaff and that the bar had been in operation for at least three years. Not only did this allow me to focus on the more densely populated nighttime spots but it also ensured that there was a stable management team in place so that I was able to query both staff and managers about their past personal experiences and general developments in the downtown Halifax urban nighttime economy. Six nightclubs in downtown Halifax qualified and agreed to participate in the overall research project. These clubs allowed me access to their security personnel so that standard questionnaires could be administered and their doorstaff interviewed. Two nightclubs declined to participate, despite my attempts to negotiate their inclusion. In both cases these clubs had recently undergone managerial changes.

There are no gay or lesbian bars included in the sample. This is the case for three reasons: first, because only fleeting familiarity confirms that these sites are markedly different in their organization, level of violence, and security procedures from the rest of the Halifax nightclub scene. Second, and relatedly, these clubs did not employ the minimum number of six bouncers for inclusion. Third and finally, when we did approach the manager of one gay bar in downtown Halifax, she declined to participate because the club had recently changed management and because, as she put it, "We don't have those types of security concerns here." Thus, it is important to keep in mind that the sites of analysis included in this study are actually large, heterosexed, Halifax nightclubs in existence for three or more years and employing six or more doorstaff.

From these six nightclubs a subset of another three nightclubs were chosen for comprehensive observational research. As part of my negotiation with managers for access, I promised confidentiality for their place of business, employing the pseudonyms the Galaxy, the Mansion, and the Beacon.[1] Generally speaking, while it is true that each of these three sites had something distinctive to offer by way of the provision of security, aesthetics, music played, and types of clientele frequenting them, they are drawn on interchangeably and do not govern the organization or arguments in this book. In-depth descriptions of each club would easily compromise confidentiality and potentially expose their identity to most Haligonian readers, so in order to honour my agreement with proprietors, I am careful not to specifically refer to where acts of violence or other illicit activities took place. Moreover, in my attempt to establish a general theoretical understanding of nightclub operations from a risk markets perspective, it is far more useful to think about and discuss nightclubs generally while making use of specific aspects from each.

The primary source of data for this book, shaping most of my theoretical insights, is a long-term two-staged observational study: first, of a structured ethnography of Halifax area nightclubs between February 2001 and 2002, and second, additional intermittent visits to nightclubs in Halifax, Toronto, Ottawa, and Montreal up until January 2004. The second phase of the observational research, unlike the first, was largely unstructured. I did not employ research assistants, made no prior arrangements with nightclubs I visited, and did not conduct interviews or collect other data beyond natural observation. While it would be tidy for me to report that this second phase was part of my general research plan, I would be disingenuous in doing so. These additional natural observation sessions were for the express purpose of rounding out the theoretical notions I had developed based on the Halifax field research. It was simply useful to visit additional venues as the scope of my project developed, and I aimed to produce a more generalizable analysis of the spectacle of the nightclub beyond the localized analysis of Halifax nightlife.[2] Despite my many trips to nightclubs in other Canadian cities, it is nonetheless important that the reader understands that the nightclub clients I encountered were predominantly white, current or former university or college students in their twenties, with all the liminal, transgressional, and coming-of-age sensation-seeking that such a group would be culturally expected to embrace. Any theoretical elucidations I make or future research that may find such theorizing useful must keep this context in mind.

Ethnographic study is perhaps the most basic, unfettered, yet nuanced form of data collection (Lofland 1974). I utilize a critical ethnographic approach that centres power and its associated dialectics of social control (Thomas 1993) as a focal point from which to understand social relations. I undertook the initial Halifax phase of the project with two research assistants[3] trained to look for certain aspects of nightclub security and surveillance and its organization. I supplied my research assistants with an observation template they referred to as they made observations and took copious notes in the field. I accompanied both of these ethnographers on their first few visits to the nightclub and gave them additional instruction. Of course, as field research continued, all of us relied less and less on the template as we became familiar and practised with the instrument and because the objectives of this study grew to encompass more than bouncers, risk, and surveillance. In the end, this book relies on over 250 hours of observational study, producing over two hundred pages of typed reports from fieldnotes.

On any given Saturday night in downtown Halifax, there are approximately one hundred doorstaff working in various pubs, nightclubs, and bars. We interviewed twenty-six bouncers, six of them supervisors or managing security operators for the nightclubs. All but three were men. Indeed, we made a particular attempt to seek out as many women who were working as bouncers as we could, because they would add insight into the bouncer culture and how gender, and particularly masculinity, might play a role in their negotiation of occupational tasks.

The interviews were conducted early on in the research process by a team of research assistants[4] under my supervision. Once again, I accompanied each of them during their first interview and provided them with feedback immediately thereafter. I conducted key interviews with respondents (mostly managers) who had been working in the Halifax nightclub scene for some time. The interviews were semi-structured, and respondents were encouraged to discuss their experiences as they saw fit. A series of open-ended questions focused on (1) general workplace and personal experiences of violence; (2) perceived attitudes towards bouncers by members of the public, police, media, friends, etc.; (3) relations with nightclub managers and police; (4) negotiation and use of electronic surveillance; and (5) connection to fellow bouncers and bouncer culture. Towards the end of the interview, respondents were urged to give their own account of their jobs, any concerns they might have about the future, their career goals, and generally what they liked and disliked about being a bouncer.

Interviews ranged from twenty-five minutes to over an hour and a half in length. In one case, I had to return to complete an interview the following day because one particular respondent was such a rich source of information. Of course, as in all interview situations, some respondents preferred monosyllabic answers and had to be cajoled repeatedly to add further insight.

An important part of the interview process was making ourselves known to potential respondents for the later survey and ethnographic work. My previous experience with conducting research on policing agencies – public or private – confirms much of the established ethnographic wisdom that advises researchers to spend some time in the field before presuming they are getting at the most candid representation of reality possible. Social groups of all sorts are reticent to allow outsiders into their inner circle, and bouncers are no exception. Indeed, two of my research assistants complained that some respondents were being evasive and needed to be re-interviewed. On more than one occasion the gender of the interviewer played a role. In some cases female interviewers were not taken seriously or were kept waiting for up to an hour, yet in other cases they managed to get some fascinating accounts of workplace violence. I suspect both of these tendencies could be attributed to what I will later consider as macho posturing and the masculine subculture of bouncers. In another case a male interviewer had difficulty with some bouncers because of his own history in the nightclub culture. Wherever possible these tensions were avoided by either substituting research assistants or conducting the interview myself.

The interviews allowed me to map out the social terrain before deciding on what sites were best for more in-depth observational study. Moreover, in order to save time and money, we took the opportunity of meeting with security managers and bouncers during interviews to introduce quantitative surveys that were distributed to fifty-five doorstaff. This procedure yielded quite a remarkable rate of return, given that there are approximately one hundred doorstaff working in a downtown Halifax nightclub scene.[5] Indeed, after some initial reservations, most respondents were quite energetic about participating. Managers and bouncers were concerned about their depiction, especially after recent media reports had portrayed them in an unflattering light. Managers and doorstaff were able to put a face to the research project; we also provided those who completed the survey with five dollars in cash.

The survey consists of a few demographic questions followed by a series of standardized scales related to interpersonal conflict at work (Spector and Jex 1998), job affective well-being (Van Katwyk et al. 2000), job satisfaction (Spector 1985), work locus of control (Fox and Spector 1999), right-wing authoritarianism (Altmeyer 1988; Altmeyer 1996); belief in a just world (Rubin and Peplau 1975); and alienation (Perrott 1991; Perrott and Taylor 1994; Perrott and Taylor 1995). Most importantly, for this section of the project, Perrott and Kelloway (2006) administered identical scales to other occupational groups during the same data collection period under a reciprocal data-sharing arrangement. In chapter 3 I discuss these quantitative findings and relate them to the general observational and interview data as well as comparing downtown Halifax bouncers to RCMP and Halifax regional police officers across these measures.

Organization of This Book

This book is organized into nine chapters, including this introduction. Chapter 2 sets up a theoretical lexicon from which to understand the nightclub as a site of consumption, security, and risk. Each of these concepts is considered in light of their common usage in the sociological and criminological literatures, how these ideas might best be deployed from a critical standpoint, and finally, how we might make sense of these concepts within the project of understanding the operations of a nightclub. Thus, chapter 2 outlines my notion of the nightclub as a risk market – a site saturated by aesthetic labour, consumption, competing subcultural capitals, and the negotiation of risk identities relating to race, class, and gender.

In chapter 3, "Policing and Bouncing," I begin my analysis of the role of bouncers in the nighttime economy in the context of private policing and its relationship to public law enforcement. This is done not only at a conceptual and theoretical level but also through analyzing comparative data on police officers and bouncers across standardized measures such as workplace violence, job affective well-being, and even right-wing authoritarianism. I provide empirical evidence that bouncers experience statistically significantly more workplace violence than local police officers and go on to compare this with other facets of public policing responsibility. Having set up conceptual and theoretical overlaps between public and private policing in the nighttime economy, the remainder of the chapter is devoted to a legal analysis of the status of the bouncer. General citizens' powers of arrest and detention and legal notions of trespass, defence of person, and defence of property are scrutinized through an analysis of judicial decision-making in both criminal and civil litigation relating to bouncer violence.

The theme of violence and its consequences is carried into chapter 4, which offers a systematic deconstruction of bouncer culture. The chapter relies heavily on observational research and interviews in order to glean how bouncers understand their work world and each other, and how this constitutes their awareness of risk, danger, violence, and masculinity in the nightclub setting. There are similarities and differences between bouncer culture and the general private security and public policing occupational cultures. These are discussed within the context of the central tasks of doorstaff, what I term *sentry-dataveillance*, and how this relates not only to the formation of bouncer culture but also the formation of the nightclub itself as a production process.

Chapters 5, 6, and 7 connect the theoretical and conceptual analysis provided up to this point to a three-stage chronological examination of the nightclub. Chapter by chapter, I ask the reader to consider the nightclub in three successive steps: getting in (chapter 5), getting noticed (chapter 6), and getting home (chapter 7). I utilize extended use of observational data and interview responses as well as careful consideration of the surveillance, enforcement, and vetting practices employed by bouncers. In chapter 5, we come to understand bouncers as part of the aesthetic production of the nightclub in their basic deployment as instruments of exclusion and inclusion and the vetting of undesirable populations based on risk identities that predictably bond to axes of age, class, race, and gender. It is in the process of "getting in" that material and social capital is tirelessly displayed to gain access, negotiate identity, and establish hierarchy. Chapter 6 deals with the internal dynamics of the nightclub as an engine of sex, desire, masculinity, and danger within the unceasing, unrelenting eye of surveillance. The panoptic impulse within the nightclub, I argue, is symbiotic with pleasure – it is voyeuristic – a veritable *synoptic frenzy* of seeing and being seen, which is intimately linked to the provision of security and the maintenance of risk management yet is essential

to the creation of the nightclub as a site of consumption and the promise of the indulgence of desire. In chapter 7 I invite the reader along on
the long walk home. It is at this moment, at "closing time," that the private spectacle of consumption, the synoptic frenzy, becomes translated
into a public nuisance, and the predictable flows of population in the
Halifax nighttime economy begin to organize themselves. Police vans idle
outside the nightclub, revellers stagger towards the city's infamous "pizza
corner" – all predictable developments within the scripted expectations
of the consumption-security-risk nexus. The urban landscape becomes
reanimated by staggering steps and unintelligible groans and yelps. Thus,
it is within these three chapters that the orientation I outline at the beginning of this book becomes most directly linked to the empirical data
collected in the field.

The conclusions (chapter 8) focus on tying together the arguments
made throughout the book, looking ahead to further research and making sense of the empirical findings presented in light of existing theory
on surveillance and policing. I also include an epilogue (chapter 9) that
I wrote long before the book was finished. This may sound like a strange
practice but I hope it is understandable after one reads through it. Having written it in the form of an analytic *confessional*, I titled it "Confes-
sions of a Playa Hata," because it captures my sense of unease conducting
research on groups that I wanted to understand but towards which I was
increasingly developing an antipathy. Obviously, this may have been a serious impediment to my analysis that needed to be addressed – if not entirely overcome, then at least considered reflexively. I include it because
I hope it may be useful to graduate students or other analysts interested
in these normative aspects of the research process.

2

The Nightclub as a Risk Market

We cannot comprehend, in a critical manner, the sense of space (Lefebvre 1991) that a nightclub represents without understanding the nexus between consumption, risk, and security that constitutes the nightclub as a site of aesthetic production in late capitalism. The way in which these terms are utilized here is often different than their typical usage in the social sciences. In a contemporary theoretical context, this is especially so, given that notions of race, class, and gender are often overlooked or intentionally hived off from our understandings of governmental reasoning, urban consumption, or insecurity. The reasons given by some for this analytic decision ranges from simple investigative emphasis on other matters (O'Malley 2001) to meta-theoretical claims of inconsistency between their projects and the universalizing notions that realist categories elicit. Indeed, when the spirit of these postmodern tendencies are coupled with cultural analyses of crime, the nighttime economy, and especially club culture, there is almost a celebratory disengagement with materialist and structural understandings of the social world to a point where "the sensual intensity of clubbing generates an alternative body in which the structuring framework of the habitus is temporarily erased" (Jackson 2004, 4–5; Malbon 1999; Thornton 1995). Perhaps so, but in the spatial dynamics of the nightclub, escapism, transgression, and liberation are also part of an ordered régime – sensuality, sexuality, expressive freedom, nightly drama, and elation merge with formats of security, risk aversion, and an endless array of consumables. Nightclubs, rather than liberating spaces of resistance, may very well be the ultimate manifestation of the drive towards the well-ordered commodification of everything *including* cultural expression and sociality. Hierarchies are reinforced, not obliterated. Gender roles are reified, not transcended. Violence and risks are amplified, not forgotten. Racialization is rampant, not held in abeyance. And expressive subcultural cliques are co-opted by a relentless "cool-hunting" global monoculture (Klein 2000: 63–86). Rather than slumbering, the panoptic eye is actively immersed within the making of the spectacle of partying. Of course, resistance is *not* futile but while hundreds of partiers in unison may defiantly pogo, throw up their fists, and recite, "Fuck you, I won't do what you tell me!" to the chorus of *Killing in the Name*,[1] you can safely bet they will probably not practise what they preach. In fact, within the risk market of the nightclub, they are far more likely to follow a predictable and compliant script – they will most likely "go with the flow."

This chapter is organized into four sections dealing with (1) consumption, (2) risk, (3) security, and finally (4) the nightclub as a risk market. Given the multiple uses and overlapping meanings that the first three of these terms have come to occupy in the sociological, criminological, and general social scientific literatures, it is important to spell out how I deploy these theoretical concepts.

Consumption

To suggest the nightclub is awash in consumption is admittedly a banal observation. Everybody knows that nightclubs are profit-oriented enterprises selling action, ambience, and alcohol. What more can be said? I think we can understand both consumption generally and its specific application to nightclubs in a more comprehensive, systematic way, and by doing so can build a theoretical model for analyzing nightclub consumption and its relationship to security and risk. Consumption is nothing more than the ingestion or use of the products of human labour. Under industrial capitalism, this means that the creation of material commodities for exchange can be equated with productivity as a capitalist accrues surplus value from the unpaid labour of workers. In a supposed post-industrial society, this must now include the productivity of sensate, non-material commodities for exchange, ranging from the sizable contract service sector economy to the type of aesthetic production evinced by moving bodies in a nightclub. For most analysts of club culture, raves, and the nighttime economy, the specific dynamics of consumption in nightclubs have been almost entirely overlooked. In fact, the general study of consumption has largely been positioned as a countervailing movement against macro-economics and political economy (e.g., Baudrillard 1981). And for good reason: historically, the broad theoretical orientations of economic approaches simply shrugged off the problem of "accounting for taste" or took refuge behind a universalizing model of rationalistic man. The classic economic assumption still remains that people simply buy what they need. But of course, "need" is a rather malleable thing. Marketing firms may have largely replaced ritual and custom in driving what becomes essential, but in either case, economists have little to say about how these needs arise and how they are manifested in changing social relations. The western notion of the rational consumer existing across time and space is not only an economic and social construction but, when viewed at the level of everyday social interaction, is also an obfuscating fallacy that hides far more than it reveals.

We need not go further than the pub itself to illustrate how understanding the culture of consumption provides insights that general macro-economics simply cannot offer. Take, for example, the anthropological study of an isolated coal-mining community in West Yorkshire, England (Dennis, Henriques, and Slaughter 1969). Most of the men in this working-class community earned a good living. Despite the fact that the market for coal was high and the local economy was booming, there was little in the way of social differentiation based on consumables. Indeed, there was no community expectation that homes be improved, that investments be made into a higher standard of consumption, or that savings be accrued against inevitable lean years ahead (see Douglas and Isherwood 1996, 124). For all intents and purposes the community appeared to the outsider as a rather homogeneous, self-recruiting, and stable working-class town. Nonetheless, important differences in wages existed, particularly between those who made a "day-wage" and more senior contract coal miners. But the miners seemed to keep a close watch on each other in order to identify any deviations from accepted norms of consumption. Expensive tobacco, home improvements, or even savings were viewed as "posh" or anti-social.

The pub played a significant role as a social institution and as an economic stabilizer, since the level of domestic consumption was kept low through the draining off of surplus by drinking. This maintained social solidarity and ensured that class cohesion was preserved. It is still an accepted custom today that when friends visit a pub, they take turns buying beer – each purchasing a round in turn. But in a potentially economically stratified working-class community such as Ashton, that simple rule of reciprocity was amended: high wage earners bought more rounds, low-wage earners and pensioners bought fewer rounds. It was customary and expected for high earners to buy eight pints for the members at Christmas, Easter, and other holidays as well as to regularly contribute to official town institutions.

Economists viewing the distribution of wages in the community from a life-cycle perspective would likely be baffled that differences in income did not produce a higher propensity to either save for the future or spend on durable household commodities and improvements. Given that toiling in the coal mine was considered "a job for life," and expected income was stable and predictable over a worker's career, we should expect higher savings for bigger purchases such as new homes and even some indulgence in cheaper luxury items. Differences in income, however, did not result in differences in basic consumables such as housing or even luxury items such as tobacco, since this would have being viewed as "putting on airs." An anthropological understanding of the social mores of the community thus proves a far more powerful analytic tool in understanding consumption than generalized political economy.

Not only does our coal-mining town example provide empirical evidence of the limits of macroeconomic theory and the important role of understanding social context and custom for analyzing consumption, but it nicely centres pubs and drinking as one pivotal space for understanding social structure. Indeed, it has long been observed by ethnographers that even the act of physically consuming (drinking) a pint of beer becomes a socially structured activity. In the 1930s, researchers in the Mass Observation group reported that drinkers in pubs tended to consume their beer at the same rate, with rarely more than a quarter of an inch difference in the depth of liquid in the glasses of a group of drinkers (Mass Observation 1943). Researchers noted that uniformity of consumption increased at the halfway point of drinking a pint within each group and that members moderated their consumption so that they would finish almost simultaneously. They also noted that this even applied to one case of a group of blind men who sat at a round table and ordered pints. Their synchronous drinking centred on the duration of time the beer glass stayed on their lips and the size of their gulps. This also resulted in less than a quarter-inch difference in their rate of consumption.

The regulation of consumption in this context is based on the need to take turns buying rounds. A fast drinker would have to wait patiently as others finished around him in order to get another beer. He might agitate his friends by buying a round before they were ready. A slow drinker whose turn it was to buy might upset the company even more so by having them wait until he himself had finished. One obvious conclusion we can cull from the Mass Observation research in Bolton and Blackpool –

largely echoed in social pub drinking today – is that the average drinker does not go at his or her own pace but rather regulates consumption based on social context. Another conclusion is the potency of specific symbolic meanings that are attached to consuming in any given group activity such as pub-going.

Understanding meaning, ritual, social context, and the symbolic importance of commodities is how both cultural anthropologists and social theorists of consumption begin their critique of macroeconomics. Jean Baudrillard, whose work I consider in more detail shortly, is perhaps the best-known contemporary critic of political economy, arguing that we need to untether our notion of things having some intrinsic value outside their contextual, symbolic, and relational meaning (Baudrillard 1983; Baudrillard 1996). He counterposes his work on consumption not only with foundational conservative economic formulations but also the critical political economy of Karl Marx (1976), whom he assails for making no clear substantive break from classical theorists such as Smith (1937) in his notion of value (see the review by Leadbeater 1985). Baudrillard wants us to substitute "symbol" and "consumption" for "material" and "production." He argues that Marx uncritically accepted conservative economic notions of value by imbuing use-value with some implicit, inherent, natural, or "true" value outside human apprehension of a given object.[2]

But before Baudrillard, cultural anthropologists interested in consumption were already well aware that the simplistic notion of the rational individual within economistic theorizing simply could not account for, indeed intentionally eschewed, the issue of taste. Moreover, without immersion into the everyday realities of human exchange at the cultural level, they argued, we can have no comprehensive understanding of how value is conferred by human judgment, since nothing has value by itself: one shoe is useless without the other, a comb has no value for a bald head. Value must have some relational significance to other objects, to symbolic meaning; it must communicate as if it were a label (Douglas and Isherwood 1996, xxii). So, rather than being of secondary significance, consumption may very well determine large-scale economic trends that have absolutely nothing to do with rational calculation. On an imaginary island inhabited by luxury-loving consumers, high value would be placed on goods involved in feasting, song, and dance. However, should a visiting missionary manage to convert these islanders to a life of prayer, fasting, and penance, then surely resources formerly spent on partying would now pour into church construction. Masons would do quite well, while the sale of meats and exotic foods would surely wane. Thus, a presumed unintended consequence of political economy's detachment from everyday consumption is its complicity with libertarian macroeconomic theory. The new item, the hot new addition, the larger icebox, the colour television – these are seen as obvious in their own right *post facto*. Without them we would have technological regression, primitivism, a lower standard of living. But let's put aside the rather profound historical problematic of progress and production for a moment to get back to the core of Baudrillard's difference with Marx.

We must reckon with Baudrillard's rejection of Marx for one very important reason: in order to avoid a false theoretical break between materialism and production on the one hand and symbolism and consumption on the other. It is quite clear that we must move beyond broad material theorizing based solely on productive forces in order to adequately account for the (g)local complexities and importance of consumption. It is also clear that classic economics negates the relevance of taste, desire, distinction, historical practice, and local custom in deference to a rather unsophisticated adherence to the notion of a universal rational consumer. But should we have to choose between analyzing material structures and ephemeral symbols? Or, to put it more accurately, between the structures of symbols versus the structures of the real? We have seen that consumption practices in pubs, as elsewhere, can be deeply conditioned by external, material, and structural forces or simply the necessities of custom and convention.

Thus, if Baudrillard and his contemporaries (e.g., Sahlins 1976) are correct, Marxism is a rather perilous base upon which to erect a critique of consumer culture, consumption, or the culture of the nightclub, because it is at odds with understanding the circulation of symbolic meanings in the realm of goods. Marx is thus guilty of unnecessarily mystifying fetishism by reserving it for the realm of exchange instead of applying it to the very nature of meaning we imbue in all objects.[3]

However, the only way that Marx circumscribes use-value through reference to natural properties is by simply acknowledging that objects have finite properties. Because an object is not at the realm of exchange, it cannot be said to be productive because it is not a commodity. But this does not mean Marx meant it was static in its interpretive value: "The usefulness of a thing makes it a use-value. But this usefulness does not dangle in mid-air. It is conditioned by the physical properties of the commodity, and has no existence apart from the latter" (Marx 1976, 126). Indeed, Marx's apprehension of the variability of "use" is evinced by how he gave voice to his commodities: "if commodities could speak, they would say this: our use-value may interest men but it does not belong to us as objects" (Jhally 1990, 40; Marx 1976, 176). Thus there seems to be no persuasive theoretical basis for Baudrillard's (mis)characterization of Marxian notions of value.

What this means for setting up an analysis of nightclub consumption is that we need not get bogged down in artificial dichotomies such as production-consumption or material-symbolic. Both the material productive processes that directly affect the way patrons relate to one another through processes of alienation (Mandel and Novack 1970) and the way in which we come to view others as a conglomeration of symbolic cues based on wardrobe, style, deportment, body type, and so on are inextricably linked.

The basis for applying labels (Goffman 1959) for inclusion or exclusion is made possible by the freedom of marketing agencies to spend exorbitant resources on associating feelings with brand names. The valorization of the realm of the *symbolic* (Jameson 1984) is made possible by the relentless spread of *material* capitalism to "developing economies" or local urban sweat-shops staffed by exploited proletarian nomads (Hardt and Negri 2001, 210–18) such that corporate distinction can bombard the consumer, the nightclub, the pub reveller in a way that was heretofore impossible. The budgets for large brand names are now almost entirely made up of marketing and advertising (Klein 2000, 11, table 1.1 and pp. 16–26). The way things are made and where they are made become even more mystified – the designer shirt becomes even more fetishized because we are divorced completely from its production and because it is laden with associated symbolism made possible by the valorization of global capitalism and the availability of cheaper international labour. Thus, the freedom and power of corporate symbols link directly to the commodifying tendencies and proliferation of global capital. Distinction is a ruse, as it increasingly transforms into corporate differentiation and a relentless tendency towards a regressive global monoculture. The more production is hidden or mystified, the more commodities become imbued with symbol, the more commodity fetishism becomes a salient basis for analysis. "In the advanced sectors ... social space is being blanketed by stratum after stratum of commodities ... alienated consumption is added to alienated production as an inescapable duty of the masses" (Debord 1995, 29). Knowledge about goods is a form of cultural capital (Bourdieu 1986, 243–8). Brand names need only be uttered in order for a potential flood of imagery to coalesce around a discussion about function, fashion, style, or genre. These are shared experiences that are disseminated by mass marketing, event broadcasting, celebrity endorsement, and the flood of imagery and emotion invoked to imbue meaning. The appropriateness of garments in different settings and times (Hunt 1996) is easily a subject of conversation – moral and aesthetic boundaries are drawn, shared experiences are conveyed, and contentious pronouncements shape the way actors represent their knowledge and place within consumption hierarchies. Navigating the sea of symbols that make up the market of consumables becomes a mechanism by which people may come to know one another in a nightclub. This process fleetingly transcends the coagulated hierarchies of class, gender, and race but mostly reinforces them. In a nightclub, discussion is hardly necessary and in any case difficult, given the volume of the music.

The contemporary display of logos, of affiliation to a particular genre or style of aesthetic production, is obvious and instantaneous. This is necessary in an orgy of fractured meanings, a stunted canivalesque consumption of others as aesthetic objects of desire. Logos are emblazoned across T-shirts, stitched over the heart of long-sleeve button-ups, and tagged onto the backside of jeans. Parasuco competes with Polo, Vitton with Von Dutch. We constantly advertise, project meaning, smile, or scowl in our costumes, awash in furtive glances and hungry eyes – a buffet of visual disgust and delight. The more we are able to rely on the immediacy of symbolic meaning to know a nightclubber, the more wedded to a fetishistic and alienating understanding of the social world we become. We seem to become nothing more than walking and dancing advertisements and corporate logos. We aspire to connect to the feelings associated with that commodity – it is not enough to wear it or drink it; we must project it to signal our supposed place within the spectacle of consumption in the nightclub. It is a form of conspicuous consumption (Veblen 1902) that belies the craving for rarity or scarcity in the face of limited acceptable options. We try to transcend boredom, the mundane, but apparently find ourselves co-opted. Knowing the world of goods is a form of cultural capital and knowing a subset of a particular genre conveys subcultural capital (Thornton 1995). The final product is us. We consume each other through a prism of symbolic accoutrements in the nightclub – from soundtrack to striped shirt to sex appeal – another robust manifestation of commodity fetishism and consumer society.

This frenzy of nightclub consumption is supposedly freeing. Not only does it untether us from the everyday, mundane work world but it also literally unhooks itself from the rules of industrial society. It is thus ostensibly postmodern. But the quest for free expression, the need for transgressional experiences, the creation of leisure space for the purpose of escape is hardly new. The circus served its purpose even for the Romans.

It did not challenge the state, it merely anesthetized the masses. *Consumption in a nightclub is voracious and it is violent.* As Hannah Arendt (2000, 186–7) reminds us, the quest for freedom has as its pre-political act the necessity for violence. Total freedom necessitates violence. This is why the state has a supposed monopoly over its use. The Greeks demonstrated that we can access freedom only through the political realm and should access the political realm at our leisure after we have already used violence to escape from the necessities of life (i.e., through enslaving others). The supposed freeing act of consumption – of finding oneself, of labelling oneself – through an attachment to commodities is thus also inherently violent. It is destructive. To truly use things completely is to destroy them. Indeed, in the political realm, it has become a responsibility of citizenship today to consume. It is even a patriotic obligation to answer mass destruction and devastation with mass consumption, to become an unwavering, perfect consumer, in the process destroying again: "The perfect consumer leaves nothing of the product and is thus made ready for further destruction, emotionally as well as economically" (Presdee 2004, 280).

What happens, therefore, if we ourselves become the commodity, at least symbolically? How is our engagement with one another conditioned by this consumption principle in a nightclub? How are we devoured and therefore deconstructed? *Caveat emptor* now extends not only to the flow of commodities exchanged on the open market but also to the symbolic cluster of desires in a nightclub that make up others as objects of aesthetic consumption. This seems like a risky proposition, but it also holds the promise, no matter how ephemeral, of constant renewal and reconstruction in a playpen teeming with symbolic building blocks of identity, a playpen within which doormen actively participate in its production. This workplace milieu, its superficiality, its alienation wears on the psyche of the doorman. Its bounded transgressionalism belies its promise, producing a litany of risks that define nightclub and bouncer culture.

Risk

Risk is a ubiquitous and slippery concept that is as likely to come up in institutional deliberations and academic analyses as it is in everyday conversation. In some sense, risk has been with us as an evolutionary factor, a biological imperative in decision-making, rooted in the most rudimentary of "fight or flight" calculations (Cannon 1915). Thus, risk can be understood as merely an extension of humanity's natural survival strategy. But, of course, it is far more than this in the context of late capitalist society and in particular, the nightclub. This riskiness includes not only the possibility of violence, disrespect, and even public humiliation but also the wide gamut of legal and managerial risk to which the nightclub exposes itself when it opens its doors. Risks are thus potentialities that produce negative consequences such as harm or loss. They are real in their consequences and occur whether they are initially perceived or not. They may be cosmically occurring natural phenomenon or interpersonal conflicts. They are therefore the product of both transigent and intransigent elements of social life (Rigakos and Law, forthcoming). Risks are real, sometimes sought, experienced, meaningful, and often only partially known, and they significantly affect people along axes of race, class, and gender.

As a start, we must first concede that risk saturates the nightclub. From the manager's basement accounting log, to the bouncer's security office "album of the banned," to front entrance signage regulating attire and conduct, to the alcohol-fogged risk assessments made by partygoers on the dance floor, *risk in its various institutional and acute interpersonal forms is omnipresent in the nightclub*. But this rather suffusive notion of nightclub risk, while perhaps effective as an introductory theoretical declaration, is far too wobbly an account for building a cogent theoretical framework for analysis. The remainder of this section is aimed at reinforcing, in a more conceptually cogent manner, how risk can be usefully deployed as an analytic construct for understanding social contexts such as the nightclub.

Risk assessments and actuarial techniques designed to avoid harms, dangers, or "bads" have advanced so significantly through probability calculations that social theorists have begun to consider a conceptual distinction between *types* of risk calculation. In particular, everyday "precautionary" risks (Haggerty 2003) that seem somehow innate and/or irrational and that can affect decisions in a "blink of an eye" (Gladwell 2005) are counterposed to those associated with ponderous "institutional" and empirical assessments (e.g., Douglas 1986; Gordon 1991) aimed at the avoidance of negative consequences – often associated with insurance-thinking and economic, prudentialist, and cost-benefit analyses (Ewald 1991). The latter of these two areas of investigation (i.e., risk as institutional and empirical), as it is presented in the literature, can also be suitably understood within the framework of two meta-theoretical (Keat and Urry 1982; Wagner 1984) standpoints with associated ontological assumptions. In the first case we have *instrumental and economistic* risk thinking designed to construct practical risk-assessment tools and technologies through empirical analyses of potential harms. Here, the analyst is generally engaged in a positivist project, in making things known, be they natural or social, in the pursuit of progress. This is accomplished through the collection of data for the purpose of minimizing some future loss or harm.

At its best, this form of calculable foreknowledge can be progressive and emancipatory. For example, scientific "proof" of environmental contamination and the effect of this fallout can result in regulatory change and compensation for victims. Or, in the context of a nightclub, training programs for bartenders and waiters can be designed to prevent drunk driving. Failing that, associated judicial decision-making and provincial liquor regulations can make owners liable as a mechanism of deterrence. Indeed, there is a plethora of research on avoiding the risk of harm associated with drunkenness and the role nightclubs and pubs can (and should) play in reducing this societal risk. The pub and the nightclub have been objects of administrative regulation by the police since the seventeenth century (Emsley 1991), and today they are the increasing subject of municipal codes of conduct (Valverde 2003).

In any case, the policy implications of empirical risk research aimed at increasing overall public health and welfare tend to be in the general interest of the "public good," even if at times they have correlative benefits for capitalists. At its worst, however, this form of instrumental risk reasoning can become self-serving, empiricist, and prejudicial in its social implications. For example, the activity of police profiling that targets populations based on cultural or racial characteristics or the "red-lining" activities of banks that effectively segregate geographic tracts in the inner-city so that those residents are not eligible for business loans are, in both cases, probably technically defensible, but nonetheless morally questionable and politically stratifying. In either the best- or worst-case scenarios, however, risk is treated as real. Risk is accepted as a phenomenon in its own right, reified, and examined as a concrete object of analysis that must be understood in order to be controlled. Necessarily present in this form of inquiry, therefore, is an inherent realist ontological assumption about risk.

On the flip side of instrumental risk analysis is the study of *how instrumental risk thinking is constructed* and operationalized over time and its effect on the configuration of both governments and institutions and the subjects meant to be risk categorized (Foucault 1991; O'Malley 1996;

Pasquino 1991). This is the study of the study of risk, if you will. One of the most influential schools of thought on risk reflects the recent academic compulsion to stay away from any totalizing, generalizing, and especially politically prescriptive theoretical assertions. Governmentality scholars see risk as one important facet of how régimes of policy are rationalized and thought about over time and in different social contexts (Castel 1991; Defert 1991; O'Malley 1992). Risk is understood as an important social and political construct that may be employed in different ways throughout history to achieve certain ends that may be realized or frustrated (O'Malley 2004). This form of analysis can allow us to uncover the processes by which categories of risk are constructed in the first place and to study how these assumptions are politically mobilized to effect particular changes. For example, it is fascinating to see how risk-management techniques based on actuarial needs can come to discipline homeowners by co-opting the public police as security auditors at the behest of insurance companies (O'Malley 1991), or how the bureaucratization of risk, since the eighteenth century, has eroded the professional discretion of doctors (Castel 1991) and police officers (Ericson and Haggerty 1997). Clearly, this is a significant benefit to academic analysis.

Sometimes, however, either by effect or design (cf. Garland 1997), study of how administrators have controlled and conceptualized risk historically can result in a relativist and constructionist notion of risk, due in part to untenable pronouncements about political agnosticism and an overreaction to the realist understandings of risk they seek to interrogate (Rigakos and Law, forthcoming). In the study of these vicissitudes (O'Malley 2001; Rigakos and Hadden 2001), it would seem that on the one hand we have an instrumental and realist notion of risk while on the other we have a sceptical and constructionist perspective that understands risk as a rhetorical and political strategy for organizing populations.

There is, of course, ample room in the chasm I have excavated between these two approaches. Indeed, a wide gamut of sociological analyses already appreciate risks as negotiable, malleable, and open to political contestation, while at the same time treating them as real insofar as their effects on the social world are concrete. Perhaps the most obvious theoretical exemplar of this literature is the widely cited (and largely sociological) work of Anthony Giddens (1990; 1991) and Ulrich Beck (1992; 1999). Both accept that risk is clearly a contested social construct but that our era is one in which "reflexive modernity" has produced a citizenry that is more "risk conscious" of increasing cataclysmic, epidemic, and ecologically global risk. Beck argues that dichotomous analyses based on ontological declarations about risk are incomplete: "Risk science without the sociological imagination of constructed and contested risk is *blind*. Risk science that is not informed about the technologically manufactured 'second nature' of threats is *naïve*. The ontology of risk as such does not grant privilege to any specific form of knowledge. It forces everyone to combine different and often divergent rationality-claims." (1999, 4, his emphasis).

The "risk society" perspective, therefore, proposes the following: changes have been occurring since the Second World War that have produced a new set of social relations based on risk identity, and an increasing institutional demand for risk knowledge has produced new subjectivities. We are thus increasingly living in both a risky world and managing our own personal biographies within this "new modernity." Risks are bottomless and self-actualizing. As certain technological advancements attempt to resolve societal ills, science uncovers yet more risks that are produced by the very "solutions" we have deployed in the past. Beck has termed this process "a system imminent normal form of the revolutionizing of needs" (1992, 56), or "boomerang effect." Societal unease is exacerbated as the mass media comes to depend on fear as a mechanism by which to sell information (Furedi 1997), and security and expert organizations (both public and private) also "sell" their ability to satiate these desires for safety (Spitzer 1987) on the open market. As a result of all of this, new subjectivities emerge that seek their guidance in risk dispersal rather than class rule. "Risks have become a major force of political mobilization, often replacing references to ... class, race and gender" (Beck 1999, 4). The new risk society thus radically individualizes citizen-consumers; they must negotiate their own risk profiles, from credit to health to safety, in order to secure a future. Beck argues: "Poverty is hierarchic, smog is democratic" (1992, 36).

There is, in my opinion, an analytic problem with this form of analysis which is imparted by the theoretical supposition of an epochal change occurring in the distribution of risks over time. A series of contemporary social relations are then understood as "new" and somehow reflective of an emergent "risk society" rather than part of a rather consistent "olde modernity" rooted in the needs addressed by early projectors at the behest of an emergent bourgeoisie and seventeenth-century capitalist state planning (Linebaugh 1991; Rigakos and Hadden 2001). This claim about new risk inequalities ignores the very long history of policing the poor through insurance thinking and leads to assumptions about risk categorizations that somehow now subsume and/or overcome older class cleavages and other forms of stratification, including race and gender. Beck and Giddens thus give risk its

ontological due in a manner that could be considered a realist reading (Bhaskar 1975; Harre 2001), but arrive at political conclusions that
are, for Marxian analysts, counterproductive. They obfuscate the gendered, racialized, and class-based nature of risk (see Rigakos and Law,
forthcoming).

These are debates that have been brewing in other venues, and they
need not slow our discussion here (see the excellent review by Kemshall
2003, 28–34). Indeed, we must concede that in the final analysis competing notions of risk rely on seemingly unassailable, a priori metatheoreti-
cal choices in the form of both ontological assertion and political purpose.
The task of establishing a sociological problematic around risk, therefore,
rests on advancing conceptual decisions that are unavoidably influenced
by disciplinary, political, and philosophical assumptions.

The basis for employing a critical realist notion of risk, consisting of
both granting its contested nature while treating its effects and consequences as real, serves sociological analyses generally, and my analysis of
nightclubs more specifically, in the following three ways. First, sociology
must by necessity fix its objects of analysis in order to understand them.
As a social science it is required to treat its objects as real in order to conceptually manipulate or measure them – this is a disciplinary imperative,
a first step to understanding (Basu and Kenyon 1972; Liska 1974; Mc-
Kinney 1966). Not even the most cynical of social theorists would argue
that perceptions and analyses of riskiness, of the need to negotiate safety
on an institutional and interpersonal level, should be ignored in the context of a nightclub. This social context should not be set aside. Rather, it
must be embedded in the very nature of the analysis, within the very con-
structs employed to understand the setting to be researched.

Second, a constructionist (or relativist) notion of risk lends itself to
political paralysis. If social scientists cannot make truth claims about risk
because their understanding is based entirely on its slipperiness, then
there is no empirical consequence that can result in political mobilization. Political neutrality in criminological analyses has long been prob-
lematized (Becker 1967; Mills 1959, 177) and the power of realist advocacy
research praised for its potential (Maclean and Milovanovic 1997; Young
1997), albeit with mixed results (Menzies 1992). As others who have reflected on this problem in the context of governmentality studies have
already opined (e.g., Garland 1997; O'Malley, Weir, and Shearing 1997),
the researcher can and should want to do more by advocating policy re-
form or social action.

Third, on a basic philosophical level, we must ask the question: Is it
really even possible to do science, no matter how critical or reflexive, with-

out conceding ontological realism in the first instance? The natural extension of the social constructionist view of risk can lead to the denial of its occurrence – one can defensibly make the preposterous assertion that the volcano did not erupt despite the fact that hundreds were killed. Or more likely, to avoid any such pronouncements altogether, anti-realism would only wonder how risk as a construct may have been understood differently before and after the eruption. Obviously, we can miscalculate; we can be wrong about risk. But to concede this rather rudimentary truth is to concede an associated ontology: an epistemological falliblist must by necessity be an ontological realist (Manicas and Secord 1983; Palys 1992: ch. 1), so that to admit we can be wrong means we must be wrong about something. This is the kernel of the critical realist understanding I wish to invoke for a working notion of risk for the remainder of this book.

In a nightclub, risk is omnipresent and wide ranging. Our analytic lens must also reflect this. There is real risk to bouncers, patrons, servers, owners, entertainers, and shooter girls embedded in the very structure and the decision-making processes that are invoked in the nightclub setting. Typically these are associated with avoiding violence, although as I have already argued, violence is already part of the consumption spectacle of the nightclub, and its avoidance can only be understood in relative degrees. There is a string of risks associated with simply being in a nightclub that are impacted by one's gender, race, and class. Public humiliation, crises of respect and belonging, the frustration of unrelenting social hierarchies: these play on the observer-participant, producing effects that are real in their consequences.

Even before nightclub patrons enter the club, however, from the moment of initial contact, they are screened for their suitability on the basis of risk. The bouncer makes assessments of the character of individuals wishing to enter. He examines whether or not they pose a risk to the liquor licence if they are underaged but also the risk they might pose to compromising the ambience and experiential lustre of this site of consumption. The correct dress, deportment, skin colour, and overall aesthetic contribution that the nightclubbers offer may become part of this risk assessment. Undesirables are kept out through posted regulations, metal detectors, CCTV cameras, and even electronic identification card readers. Once inside, patrons are exposed to a wide gamut of risks associated with the type of nightclub and their negotiated place within it.

On an institutional level, the nightclub seeks to minimize risk by mobilizing a series of surveillance and security techniques aimed at reducing harms to the establishment. Standing operating procedures are rehearsed so that bouncers understand where to go in times of need and how to communicate with other doormen and staff. Signals are choreographed so that information may be passed from bartender to waitress to bouncer in order to remove problem patrons quickly and quietly. "Secret shoppers" are deployed by bar owners and managers in order to assess the service quality of their bouncers, servers, and bartenders. Both patrons and nightclub staff are under constant scrutiny and surveillance, through natural panoptics or surrogate surveillance cameras mounted over cash registers. This surveillance capacity is already an embedded extension of the voyeuristic compulsion of the nightclub. This is the seduction of risk in a nightclub: of being noticed, of standing out, of channelling desire in others, of being devoured – all part of a wider structural nexus of consumption and insecurity.

Risk in a nightclub is as brutal and atavistic as it is nuanced and sophisticated. Institutional protocols and paper realities exist in parallel with the chaotic spaces of the dance floor, the bar, and all the traffic in between. Nightclubs have increasingly become the subject of state scrutiny and self-regulation through tort law. Litigation in a risk society conditions the distribution of harms and transfers them onto corporate entities that then typically download them to corporate denizens (Doyle and Ericson 2004). Training programs for bouncers are geared towards nonviolent means of securing compliance. Bartenders and service staff are given instruction or required to take training courses on how to deal with inebriated patrons, lest the nightclub be the subject of litigation due to harm occurring to patrons or third parties as a result of excessive drinking. Law and risk (Law Commission of Canada 2005) thus conditions the very nature of doing security in a nightclub. The socio-legal context of risk is the umbrella under which pulsating dance-floor masses are illuminated by the panoptic eye and recorded by the clicking gears of the nightclub's institutional risk machinery. All of this is accomplished under the pretense of seduction. But here as elsewhere, there are limits. And these limits, which themselves become yet another source of transgression and seduction in the nighttime economy, need their police.

Security

The concept of security is as ubiquitous and far reaching in its implications as risk and consumption. Indeed, in a society increasingly sensitized to risk and the need to consume, security becomes imbued in all social relations, intimately connected to the mystification of commodities and policy (Neocleous 2000a). Often it is considered a condition of safety.

Under capitalism, however, it expands from the state (as in "state security interests") to the market. Security becomes the cornerstone of the bourgeois legal structure in that it comes to be identified with the freedom and liberty to pursue one's individual self-interest. It is thus an essential and decisive criterion for the peaceful enjoyment of property. In this way, it has become, in Marx's view, "the supreme concept of bourgeois society." Security mobilizes a series of policing initiatives that seek to condition and disguise the actual underlying *insecurity* of property relations and class cleavage.

The global nature of risk and consumption in international capital (Wallerstein 1979) spawns with it a global awareness of potential harm. These harms are manifold but are conditioned by the need to maintain the circulation of goods and persons, to allow capital to proliferate, to make the world open for exploitation, and to expand the markets. The domestic and international nomadism of labour is freeing but troublesome, necessary but potentially dangerous to capital (Hardt and Negri 2001). The control of "sturdy vagabonds" and "masterless men," has been a longstanding problem for "police" and has produced a myriad of projects aimed at making these populations "known" (McMullan 1996; McMullan 1998; Neoclcous 2000b). The flight from the countryside of dispossessed serfs and their transformation into a mobile industrial army produced a particular qualitative problem of order in the modern city. With the decline of mass industrialism in advanced western democracies (Bell 1973), its substantial relocation to developing economies (Callinicos 1989; Kellogg 1987), and its substitution with service-sector employment, order has been re-emphasized in qualitatively new ways. This produces an incessant problem for urbanization, and for police, the Greek derivative of the word, in fact, meaning "city" (see Knemeyer 1980).

The contemporary urban centre has been re-positioned as a twenty-four hour mall, a cornucopia of desires and consumables in late modern capitalism. This has been long described by social theorists of the urban experience (Lash and Urry 1994), but recently the intimate connection between consumption and the need for security has become more globally prescient (Jones and Newburn 2006). As Hayward (2004, 15) eloquently puts it, this is evidenced by "the growth of an entire industry of 'security as prestige,' with the 'feel-safe' factor constituting a new form of urban conspicuous consumption and lifestyle desire. In this ongoing mutation of urban experience, society's current fascination with security and auto-surveillance has become yet another incitement to consume."

To be sure, comparing urban centres to malls is more than a theoretical metaphor. Empirical research in Canada has already identified the privatization of mass outdoor spaces that were formerly the patrol districts of the public police (Huey, Ericson, and Haggerty 2005; Murphy and Clarke 2005). Where private security guards do not patrol on their own, they are coupled with local public police, or failing this, the police themselves are purchased on a paid-duty basis to do the work of security personnel, entering stores and arresting for trespass on private property at the behest of proliferating Business Improvement Areas BIAS (Gavendo 2006). The mall has been literally turned inside out, and this has been accomplished by the territorial reordering of security.

Throughout the day, flows of population are ordered by public police, but only in the gap between mass corporate sites of consumption. From the daytime to dusk, urban environments cater to a variety of experiential and material desires: from festivals to omnipresent retailing and souvenir shopping. Large tracts of "mass private property" (Shearing and Stenning 1983), these private fiefdoms of security ensure compliance through seduction, through vigilant risk monitoring, through seemingly innocuous regulations based on minimizing risk, and in particular through the risk of litigation. Security agents are required to enforce these codes of conduct (Shearing and Stenning 1987). Consumers, like corporate denizens, pass through bubbles of governance (Rigakos 2000) under the eye of private security. When the Downtown Yonge Business Improvement Area (DYBIA), representing Canada's busiest commercial zone, found that it was having difficulty securing the diligent patrol of the Toronto Police (TPS) officers they had contracted, it requested and received specialized shift reports, signed by the officers, which detailed the work of these extra-duty municipal public police officers. The DYBIA thus seems to have temporarily operationally privatized the TPS on public streets during retail shopping hours. Policing the circulation of goods and people is not simply a metaphysical quality imbued in all commodities but finds its structural form in the doing of security work – of unproductive labour in the service sector of policing.

Today, no discussion of urban renewal, of rebuilding the market centre, is possible without first examining security (Ruppert 2006). Indeed, the very notion of BIAS is founded on the premise that consumption must take place within well-ordered régimes of safety, security, and predictable patterns of homogenized international retail experiences. "The capitalist production system has unified space, breaking bondaries between one society and the next ... it was bound to dissipate the independence and quality of places. This power to homogenize is the heavy artillery that battered down all Chinese walls" (Debord 1995: 120). Mass insecurity, especially economic insecurity, is not conducive to mass consumption, although the security products and services sector may benefit in the short term. This is a cyclical pattern of capital to re-colonize space and smooth the surface of consumption, to make things nostalgically respectable, to Disneyfy (Bryman 2004). It is here that we begin to see the overlapping logics of consumption, risk, and security. The citizen is cast as consumer, and security is interchangeable with scrubbing sidewalks, stringing tree lights, and handing out leaflets announcing upcoming sales. The heavy hand, the iron fist, is held in abeyance. The city centre becomes softly bathed by CCTV and uniformed "ambassadors" (Mopas 2005). Security is nowhere but everywhere, imbedded in the very act of being out in the city. It is part of the spectacle because its means are simultaneously its ends. For Debord (1995, 15), it is "the sun which never sets over the empire of modern passivity."

Debord's metaphorical sun, however, is replaced day after day by a lunar spectacle. For all of the seduction of consumption in the daytime, the nighttime urban economy holds the promise of something sexier, transgressional, and risky. The proliferation of international capital has demanded the colonization of time through constant production and now produces the twenty-four hour city with round-the-clock consumption (Bianchini 1995; Hall and Hubbard 1998; Hobbs et al. 2003; Lovatt and O'Connor 1995; Malbon 1999). Urban centres are reordering themselves as international sites of consumption, acquiescing to a tourist gaze (Urry 2002) that demands excitement within well-ordered boundaries. This international urban consumption niche is only an image, one more ahistorical cityscape in a world of superficial heterogeneity that always belies its promise. Cities across the world are being paved over by the rationalities of neoliberalism (Eick 2003) and crime prevention through environmental design (Newman 1973) using the gambit of security.

The miraculous rehabilitation of New York City under Mayor Rudy Giuliani and Chief William Bratton, and in particular the re-making of its centrepiece, Times Square, was both a policing project and a representational "drama" (Manning 2001) of sweeping the city clean. In 1995, as the city's homeless were loaded into the back of NYPD paddy wagons, identified, disciplined, and relocated, Giuliani was actually invoking the ghost of early police intellectual Patrick Colquhoun (1800) as he peered out the window of his limousine to take account of the rabble-ridden twilight streets of New York City. Some two hundred years earlier, Colquhoun had also drawn back the curtains of his horse-drawn carriage to lament the state of disarray on London's streets. He catalogued vagrancy and detailed plans for the reclamation of the city through his new police. The project of police, therefore, has a very long history. I say "project of police" or "policing" rather than "police" in order to signal that I am speaking of something far more important and overarching than the local municipal law-enforcement officer we have come to understand as police. This latter group is only one recent manifestation of a long, broad, and significant intellectual history of ordering populations and rendering them known (Neocleous 2000b).

By the time Colquhoun began his analyses of crime and disorder in the very early nineteenth century, London's streets were being patrolled by a hodgepodge of public and private officials. The ancient feudal arrangements that had worked well in England's static society were no longer viable as dispossessed serfs flowed into the city (Thompson 1963). London was being policed by a wide assortment of characters ranging from constables housed in magistrates' offices, the legendary Bow Street Runners, night watchmen, and eventually Colquhoun's own Thames River Police, financed by private interests but created through legislation (Emsley 1991). Aside from these "official" organizations, private thief-takers worked both sides of the law, setting up rival criminals to take the fall and reclaiming property for a fee (Beattie 1986; Brewer 1989; Linebaugh 1991). In this early modern history of policing, often seen as chaotic and corrupt, the need for a uniformed, centralized, and professional service seemed inevitable but only because the economic conditions that produced such chaos in the first place necessitated their own brand of security. The new form of value in a capitalist society was no longer solely in property but rather in the mobility of goods and labourers.

The Metropolitan Police of London came into being in 1830. In the Anglo-American context, this is seen as the starting point for the new public police. What must be remembered, however, is that private policing arrangements never disappeared. In fact, they re-emerged quite spectacularly in the United States less than a century later. Private policing organizations such as the Pinkerton Detective Agency ("the eye that never sleeps") played a significant and often brutal role in strike suppression and the intimidation of workers during labour unrest in the early twentieth century (Weiss 1978). It is now common criminological knowledge on the part of police researchers that the configuration of public and private policing has dramatically changed in most advanced western democracies since the late 1960s and early 1970s. In the Canadian context, private security agents now outnumber public police by at least two to one (Campbell and Reingold 1994; Sanders 2003; Swol 1999). This resurgence of privatized forms of policing has, not coincidentally, occurred in tandem with rather fundamental changes in social relations of production and consumption since post–World War II and accelerated after the OPEC crisis (Mandel 1995).

This matters for our understanding of security in two ways. First, insofar as "policing" is a constituent definitional component of our notion of security, it should be understood in its broad historical and contemporary forms as a generic labour activity. Indeed, as I have argued elsewhere (Rigakos 2006), it is often conceptually unhelpful to think about policing as "public" or "private," given entanglements with respect to territory, duties, and sources of funding. Instead, policing should be broadly understood as "activities of any individual or organization acting legally on behalf of public or private organizations or persons to maintain security or social order while empowered by either public or private contract, regulations or policies, written or verbal" (Rigakos 2002a).

It is in this context that I analyze bouncers as policing agents. In fact, with respect to security, I argue, first, in the urban nighttime economy, bouncers are a central policing entity. For most criminologists and sociologists of policing, this will not come as a particularly provocative declaration. It is already largely accepted that policing is a very wide-ranging phenomenon of human activity, but it is important for the reader to understand that by invoking the notion of policing, I am intentionally triggering a connection to the broad historical project of ordering populations and the governance of the city. In the nighttime economy, the major iconographic regulators of population and especially their flow between public and private urban realms, is the bouncer.

Second, *security must also be understood as a feeling of negation* (Spitzer 1987), the absence of fear or risk. This feeling is ever present in the insecurity of late capitalist risk societies, imbuing aesthetics, persons, lifespans, and commodities. Security has become so fetishistically inscribed in social relations of the commodity that the doing of security labour comes into constant crisis and can no longer be understood outside an aesthetic appearance, statistical representation, or a projected imagery of labour in a concrete, material, and tangible form. This is the basis for the notion of "private security" – its oxymoronic impossibility is its own success, and its means are simultaneously its ends. In late capitalism (Jameson 1984; Mandel 1975), objects and interactions are infused with (in)security – from credit cards, babysitters, virus scans, and five-star vehicle safety ratings to colour-coded Homeland Security threat advisories. This crisis of appearance produces material manifestations of security in many forms: home alarms, CCTV, and even electronic check-point systems for security guards. Late capitalism must translate security into the concrete; it must make it productive. Security is rendered *representationally* material be-cause its materiality is vanishing. The patron, the citizen, always seems to have to ask: where is my proof of security? Capitalists, having shaped the question, now answer with the latest commodity.

These two aspects of security act interchangeably insofar as our fetishistic appreciation of security entangles itself with risk and con-sumption. The security commodity and the bouncer dialectically sup-port each other in relations of nightclub production. This becomes possible only when the patron is refashioned as the aesthetic object of consumption, labouring as both consumer and consumable. Buyers are the commodity; their optic labour is necessary, their consumption ex-pected. They become an integrated part of the risk market of the night-club. I will take up these connections in detail in the following section. Suffice it to say here that within the array of security activities engaged in by a variety of policing organizations, *the bouncer is an essential con-stitutor of identity for the nightclub as an aesthetic site of consumption.*

Elsewhere (Rigakos 2006) I have argued that policing activity (both public and private forms) may be divided into five essential types: (1) polemic; (2) sentry-dataveillant; (3) investigative; (4) patrol; and (5) civic-sumptuary. The second of these types of activities, sentry-dataveillance, is the primary locus of policing labour for the bouncer. The age-old custom of "keeping the watch" or sentry duty is a basic occupational role of policing. Of course, access and egress control is a job performed by a wide assortment of indi-viduals ranging from doormen to receptionists to military cadets. Sentry-dataveillance consists of keeping out those who do not have access or a right to be on the premises being guarded. Increasingly, like other forms of policing labour, sentry-dataveillance is becoming automated. Checkpoint systems and pass cards now do the work of the memory power of security personnel. Indeed, gatekeepers become attached to surrogate instruments of recognition: CCTV surveillance, pass-card readers, and biometric facial analysis. The immediacy of transmitting information produces a connec-tivity that is instantaneous or telematic (Bogard 1996). Databases link up to create surveillance capabilities heretofore unimaginable.

Dataveillance is the process by which people may be tracked through data trails. The post-industrial, masculine workforce (Connell 1995; Messerschmidt 1993) that often constitutes the corps of bouncers (Hobbs et al. 2003, 211–42; Winlow 2001, ch. 3) in the nighttime urban economy becomes increasingly connected with this apparatus. In Edmonton, the denial of entry or banishment from certain nightclubs results in blanket denial to other nightclubs on the same network. Card readers lift the information of patrons desiring entry directly from driver's licences. In Montreal, businessess store this personal information for later marketing: "Thank you for your visit. According to our records, it's your birthday. Please stop by for two complimentary drinks." The software vehicle used as a database of the nightime's damned or to assess riskiness at the door is at the same time a marketing technique.

Panoptic surveillance is a technology to make persons known, to discipline them through the presumption of perpetual observation. Jeremy Bentham's prison design sought to replace the eye of God with an earthly surrogate of deterrence. His prisoners never knew when they were being watched, only that they might be observed at any moment. Foucault (1977) tells us that this is the moment at which the few watched the many, the spectacle of ceremony was replaced by the routine of surveillance. Of course, as we shall discuss in much more detail later, the nightclub is just as panoptic, just as surveilled, but equally a spectacle of delight, a *synoptic frenzy* where the watcher is watched and the watched are watched by others. Security *is* consumption in the nightclub. These connections announce the nature of the nightclub as a risk market, delineate its role in the policing of populations in the nighttime economy and in making these populations transparent and available for consumption.

Risk Market

To understand the nightclub as a risk market is to do nothing more than analyze the ways in which the conceptual nexus of consumption-risk-security operates within it. A nightclub is only one particularly provocative and illustrative risk market. Elsewhere (Rigakos 2002b, 24–5) I have discussed what a risk-markets orientation entails for analyzing "the new parapolice" – a particular form of retributive private security. One important reason I use the term risk *markets* rather than risk *governance* or risk *society* is to differentiate my approach from the type of thinking in governmentality research that often unnecessarily eschews issues of class, race, and gender (cf. Chan and Rigakos 2002; Rigakos 1999b; Rigakos 2001) or general social theory that obfuscates these realist categories (Rigakos and Frauley 2007) relative to "new" relationships of risk (Beck 1992; O'Malley 2004). These produce political implications (Feeley and Simon 1994) that are counterintuitive to critical scholarship. To summarize for the purposes of moving forward, we can therefore (re)articulate the following theoretical premises:

1. The contemporary late capitalist urban landscape is dominated by the compulsion to consume. This has manifested itself in fetishistic desire and a detachment from production processes. Consumption is culturally regulated and market driven. Both the material production processes that directly affect the way patrons relate to one another through alienated communication in a nightclub, as well as the way in which we come to view others as a conglomeration of such symbolic cues as wardrobe, style, deportment, and body type, are inextricably linked.

2. The modern institutional response to risk relies heavily on the production of knowledge about "dangerous" populations. This knowledge is based on actuarial practices and seeks to make risky populations known through the disciplining practices of surveillance. Although these techniques seem to depoliticize the construction of suitable enemies by erecting rationalistic and economic decision-making templates, they nonetheless reproduce the same disparities and elicit similar and often violent forms of resistance in the nightclub.

3. In the contemporary city, security provision is not typically organized around the state. Multiple private arrangements operate under corporate and other local controls that defy artificial dichotomous formulations such as public-private. In the nighttime economy, the nightclub is one essential fiefdom of private policing, surveillance, risk management, and consumption. The bouncer is a central policing agent in the nighttime urban economy.

4. The nightclub must be understood in the context of late capitalist production and consumption processes. The nature of security provision in a nightclub is conditioned by the fetishistic translation of the aggregate symbolic capital of patrons into commodities. Within the synoptic frenzy of the nightclub, security, risk, and consumption are bound up with the contemporary spectacle of society that aims at nothing other than itself.

While the first three of these assertions will seem familiar to the reader, having been discussed in the three preceding sections, the fourth, rather ambiguous point is in dire need of clarification. I intend to expand on this last point throughout the book, but it is important to set up a theoretical scaffold in this regard as soon as possible. To argue that the nature of security provision in a nightclub is conditioned by the fetishistic translation of the aggregate symbolic capital of patrons into commodities means to accept that persons are treated as commodities, even though within the current mode of production they cannot be commodities. A basic maxim of Marxian thought is that the value produced in capitalist societies is extracted from labour activity. Generally speaking, nothing in the circulation of capital or its accumulation adds value outside human labour. While all may be at an economic equilibrium and things sold at their value, only labour adds more value than it needs for its own sustenance (Marx 1973; Marx 1977). Surplus value, therefore, can only be extracted on the backs of workers' unpaid labour-time. This means, from a strictly Marxian orientation, that people can never become commodities within our contemporary non-slave-owning mode of production. However, in a *society of the spectacle* (Debord 1995) we can take Marx's notion of commodity fetishism further so that "all that once was directly lived has become mere representation" (12), so that "an ever-growing mass of image-objects" becomes the "*chief production* of present-day society" (16, his emphasis). Debord's extension of Marxian thought to an analysis of the predominant role of imagery in late capitalist societies is based on the notion that the image of objects and their alienation from our own knowledge of their production reaches its height in the spectacle: "Here we have the principle of commodity fetishism, the domination of society by things whose qualities are 'at the same time perceptible and imperceptible by the senses.' This principle is absolutely fulfilled in the spectacle, where the perceptible world is replaced by a set of images that are superior to that world yet at the same time impose themselves as *eminently* perceptible" (Debord 1995: 26, his emphasis).

Not surprisingly, Baudrillard rejects Debord's notion of the spectacle, because it is based on concepts such as alienation and repression that presuppose the existence of something that is being alienated or repressed. To suggest a difference between real and imagined, true and false, is antithetical to Baudrillard's notion of simulation – such binaries are meaningless in the hyperreal. For Baudrillard, Debord has not grasped the fundamental flaw of Marxian thinking, erroneously assuming some intrinsic value bounded by materiality and use. Instead, it is "in the sphere of simulacra and the code" that contemporary "global processes of capital are founded" (Baudrillard 1983, 99).

Of course, we have already dispensed with Baudrillard's (unfounded) critique of Marxian political economy generally and may now, by extension, do so of his critique of Debord's notion of the spectacle, which is based on the same rationale. There is no foundation for the assumption that Marxian analyses of the commodity somehow affix a static notion of use that hampers our understanding of the circulation of images in late capitalist society. This is well captured in commodity fetishism, and the elasticity of use-value is a given in Marxian thought. What all three commentators overlook, however, and that Foucault renders central, is the important disciplining power of the panoptic impulse that seeks to make known those who come within its gaze.

Some twenty years after *Society of the Spectacle*, Debord revisited his thesis by examining its relevance to contemporary society and, in so doing, the role of surveillance. Not surprisingly, he finds the spectacle even more salient in 1987 than in 1967 but unfortunately misapprehends the magnitude and form of surveillance to the detriment of his own argument. While it is undoubtedly true that there are many secrets kept by those in power and that their organized surveillance groups mistrust even one another – creating "innumerable mysteries" (Debord 2002, 55) in a world of unverifiability – Debord's notion of surveillance is far too "political," strategic, targeted, statist, and conspiratorial. This actually undermines his own concept of an *integrated spectacle* based on the "diffuse" (8) and global nature of contemporary capital. Within the logic of the integrated spectacle, we would best be served by understanding surveillance not as "the secret of domination" (60) with its "indefinite number of police and counter-espionage services" (81) but rather as open, dispersed, transparent, and comprising a wide gamut of police entities with routinized and obvious intents such as security guards and bouncers. In this sense, Debord's perceived conundrum that surveillance has "encountered difficulties created by its own progress" (81) in the face of "the mass of information collected" is actually no problem at all. Rather than a "struggle," surveillance information becomes an endemic commodity within the spectacle, producing surplus and creating inventory. It is integrated by virtue of its visibility, not its secrecy. In a nightclub, visibility is the task, the game, the prize, the reward, and the risk.

This visibility matters insofar as displays and visibilities are circulations of symbolic capitals. Thus, when I refer to the nightclub being conditioned by the fetishistic translation of the aggregate *symbolic capital* of patrons, I am specifically utilizing the concept's use by Pierre Bourdieu (1984), and particularly the superordinate notion of social capital. For Bourdieu, "social capital" acts as an aggregate of the actual or potential resources of the network or group that provides its members with "the backing of the collectivity-owned capital, a 'credential' which entitles them to credit, in the various senses of the word" (1986, 248). Social capital is deployed by Bourdieu to facilitate a critical theory of society beyond material capital alone. It is aimed at explaining the way in which social stratification is preserved and legitimated, a way by which the bourgeoisie maintain their status.

In his rich empirical analysis of the French education system, Bourdieu (1984) offers insight into the role that cultural knowledge plays in determining access to elite institutions, occupations, and social circles. Unlike liberal theorists like Putnam (1993; 2000), who view social capital as some aggregate of interacting actors and their resources in which persons may "invest" for later consumption, Bourdieu's conception is not reducible to an economic relational network. The political consequences of Putnam's notion additionally leads him to make the obvious entreaty that we must use the concept of social capital "to learn how communities break out of ... vicious spirals" including Progressive Era developments "when people faced many problems [such as] income inequality, political corruption, degradation of cities, fear of immigration, and racial tensions" (Putnam 1988, vii). Such an argument suggests that "bowling leagues, neighborhood barbecues, church choirs [and] Girl Scouts ... will fundamentally affect the health or illness of society," regardless of increasing privatization, corporate de-responsibilization, the general decline of the welfare state, and the rise of neoliberal economics (cf. Somers 2005, 11–12). Social capital, in a non-Marxian sense (see Adam and Ronãeviç 2003; Lin 1999), therefore, becomes nothing more than some buttressing mechanism for economic development – an argument that prompts Somers (2005, 5) to mock, "Let them eat social capital." According to Bourdieu, we must instead understand capital as "accumulated labour" from which agents can "appropriate social energy" in the form of either "reified or living labour" as part of the "imminent regularities of the social world." And, moreover, this social world cannot be "reduced to a discontinuous series of instantaneous mechanical equilibria between agents who are treated as interchangeable particles" (Bourdieu 1986, 241). Capital, therefore, can present itself as an *economic (or material) capital* that converts immediately into money or property; as *cultural capital*, which can also convert into economic capital and is exemplified in body image, institutionalized education, and the acquisition of writings, paintings, and other arts; and finally, as *social capital* made up of social obligations and memberships in prestigious groups and familial lineage – also convertible into economic capital and institutionalized "par excellence" as nobility (243–53).

It is of particular importance for our analysis to recognize that Bourdieu's (257n17) "social capital is so totally governed by the logic of knowledge and acknowledgment that it always functions as symbolic capital." Symbolic capital, in turn, "presupposes the intervention of the habitus" (255n3) that comes to form the everyday lived experience of Bourdieu's

French citizens. There are thus multiple forms of capital beyond simple material wealth. The nouveau riche and the upwardly mobile must invest in cultural training and social adaptation to entrench themselves in established elite circles. While Bourdieu concerns himself with elite institutions, capital in its various forms is, of course, just as applicable to the other mileux. In a nightclub, material (or economic) capital can surely get one past the queue and a quick entrance into the VIP lounge. Being ensconced as a player within the *sub*-cultural genres that any given nightclub wishes to project will also garner significant social capital. For example, the celebrity of well-known DJs, band members, and artists helps make up the rich cultural ambience that many nightclubs shrewdly attempt to fabricate. In this way the nightclub through its ability to vet populations "at the door" becomes a reified bubble of governance, an architectural representation of inclusivity and exclusivity in the urban nighttime economy. Social capital takes many forms connected to axes of class, race, and gender. Attractive women, for example, have the capital of body image, of being desirable objects of aesthetic consumption in the heterosexed nightclub; in this regard, they can muster just as much capital through flirtation and mere bodily presence as the material-based capital necessary to jump the queue by greasing the palm of the doorman. Because the heterosexual nightclub is constituted and sold largely on its ability to attract desirable women, sex becomes an essential ingredient, indeed possibly the most important constituent aesthetic product of the nightclub.

The spectacle is self-reinforcing because its failure is its success. In the nightclub, commodification is bound up with spectacle and security. It is perhaps the ultimate manifestation of the commodification of social control that not only are its agents and their technologies for sale and rendered as a symbolic commodity in risk markets but moreover *the subjects of surveillance and policing are themselves commodified by virtue of the same process.* The bouncer (as agent of the owner) produces the nightclub through his ability to select and/or reject who will populate it. People attend nightclubs to be seen and see others, to consume others as aesthetic objects of desire and to elicit desire in others – the desire to be desired.

As patrons are risk-profiled at the door, they are simultaneously self-disciplining themselves for the purposes of entry; their appearance should ostensibly match the ambience and aesthetic of the nightclub. While they pay to enter, and this is dependent on social, cultural, and material capital, they also become objects of optic consumption. Others have paid to see them or see others see them. This is part of what I consider to be the *synoptic frenzy* of the nightclub as a risk market: where the nightclub is constituted by seductions of the night under the gaze of a vigilant panoptic eye; where the bouncer becomes an iconographic, masculine nighttime policing agent of inclusion and exclusion. Violence is routine because it is freeing; race, class, and gender become amplified; voyeurism is celebrated. In the nightclub, alienation is perfected because separation is complete, because it produces lonely crowds, because it fosters crises of respect, and because in the end "it is the opposite of dialogue" (Debord 1995, 17).

In this chapter I have argued that the nightclub can be best understood within the theoretical context of a "risk market": a spectacle of consumption, risk, and security. Bouncers are iconographic producers of the nightclub, central policing agents of the nighttime economy, and regulators of transgression. The remainder of this book is thus an empirical elucidation of the nightclub as a risk market and the bouncer's role within its production.

3

"Policing" and "Bouncing"

Who's pigging it tonight? (09: white male doorstaff)

Listen, buddy, I don't know if you've figured it out yet, but it's all about consuming. Consuming, man! You understand? They drink, they eat, they groove, they dance. The rest is all traffic, just traffic. Somebody has to move the traffic ... and I don't make any money off of traffic. That's why these guys [doormen] are here. (nightclub manager)

Bouncers are not only essential contributors but perhaps the *primary* policing agents of the nighttime economy. In downtown Halifax on a busy Saturday night they will (quite conservatively) outnumber the public police by at least ten to one. Nonetheless, there are fundamental differences between bouncers and police officers. These range from legal status to uniforming to training and even mission and mandate. It is important to keep in mind that while I am intentionally conflating "policing" as a generalized activity in this book, this does not negate the rather profound differences between organizations and persons who are ostensibly challenged with performing such activities. This generalized function of policing, however, is entrusted to multiple public, private, and quasi-public organizations in late capitalism, and it is a theoretically impoverished view to ignore this multiplicity and variability of security provision. In city centres, where nightlife is promoted as an attractive incentive for company relocation and tourism, it is often difficult to disentangle the private from the public interest (Eick 2006). Indeed, many business improvement areas are based on such public-private partnerships where, in contemporary Canadian indoor and outdoor retail centres, police officers are literally patrolling alongside private security guards.

It is common in Halifax for nightclubs to hire public police on a paid-duty basis to idle outside their entrances. Police officers are encouraged to enter the nightclub to "check things out" and are in constant communication with doorstaff. Both doormen and police officers pile onto the same troublemakers. Territorial boundaries between public and private policing are not only mottled theoretically but also physically in the brutality of bloodstained sidewalks. Routinely, bouncers crowd public spaces. By way of an innocuous example, I was amused by the sight of four bouncers chasing away pigeons one early evening outside of the Beacon. It was a ripe moment for some ribbing: "Hey guys, I think that one over there is getting mouthy. Why don't you put it in chokehold? That'll teach him!" However, I decided to let the opportunity pass. The bouncers were terrorizing the pigeons because their droppings were soiling the entrance-way and sidewalk.

While the banning of pigeons from a public sidewalk outside the nightclub may not be the most prescient of examples of public and private overlaps of interest, the sidewalk is nonetheless a focal point of interaction between state and private interests. Typically, bouncers are encouraged to "mind the business of the nightclub first," which supposes a rather solid territorial demarcation – but this is often only a guideline designed to absolve to nightclub of unnecessary liability, an often-ignored directive. Bouncers can do far more than shoo away pigeons on public sidewalks. A few hours later during the same evening two doormen were approached by a rather disconcerted rickshaw driver outside the nightclub entrance. Three young men who were in the queue to enter the Beacon had apparently not paid for their trip from another nightclub. The two doormen discussed the matter and decided to confront the patrons, who were standing in the VIP line. They told the three men that they would not be allowed entry unless they paid the rickshaw driver. These two doormen had, in effect, exercised their power of denying access in order to rectify what was ostensibly a harm against the public good. In the haze of early morning fisticuffs, the state is undoubtedly a present but habitually passive recipient of the night's "human refuse."

In this chapter I first examine the routine, nightly personal and occupational interactions between Halifax Regional police officers and doorstaff – how these policing bodies work together and how their tasks functionally overlap. Second, I consider risk and violence by making

direct comparisons between the Halifax police, area RCMP, and bouncers. These comparisons are based on quantitative measures. This survey
analysis is based on data gathered from fifty-two doorstaff and 189
Halifax-area public police. Table 3.1 clearly demonstrates the rather
marked differences between these comparison groups. Ninety-eight per
cent of doorstaff and 81 per cent of police officers are male. The average duration of occupational experience for bouncers is only two years,
for police officers 11.9 years. While 80 per cent of police officers are
married, only 14 per cent of doorstaff are in conjugal relationships. Not
surprisingly, given Halifax's five local universities, 72 per cent of doorstaff
are either in university or have completed a degree; this compares with
65 per cent for the public police. Thus, before moving on to a more detailed comparative analysis of these policing organizations based on
measures of workplace violence within the context of occupational risk,
it is important to point out these very basic demographic differences
between groups.

Having considered the occupational roles and functional connections
between public policing and bouncing as well as their comparative susceptibility to occupational risk, in the third part of this chapter I return

Table 3.1: Demographic information for doorstaff and police officers

	Doorstaff	All police	Halifax Police	All RCMP	Urban RCMP	Rural RCMP
GENDER						
Male	51 (98%)	153 (81%)	50 (83%)	103 (80%)	18 (78%)	82 (80%)
Female	1 (2%)	36 (19%)	10 (17%)	26 (20%)	5 (22%)	21 (20%)
Total	52	189	60	129	23	103
Years of service (mean)	2	11.9	11.3	12.2	10.8	12.5
MARITAL STATUS						
Married/common law	7 (14%)	152 (80%)	47 (78%)	105 (81%)	18 (78%)	84 (82%)
Single (never married)	41 (79%)	27 (14%)	12 (20%)	15 (12%)	3 (13%)	12 (12%)
Separated/divorced	2 (4%)	10 (5%)	1 (2%)	9 (7%)	2 (9%)	7 (6%)
EDUCATION						
High school graduate	15 (29%)	66 (35%)	17 (28%)	49 (38%)	7 (30%)	41 (40%)
At least one year of university	26 (50%)	61 (32%)	22 (37%)	39 (30%)	9 (39%)	29 (28%)
University degree	11 (21%)	62 (33%)	21 (35%)	41 (32%)	7 (30%)	33 (32%)

to the issue of the legal status of the bouncer. I do this mostly in the hopes of answering those recurrent questions from students that invariably begin: "Where do they get the right to…?" and "Are they allowed to…?" Thus, the final section of this chapter considers bouncers' use of force, arrest, detention, and potential vulnerability to criminal and civil sanctions.

The Police Machine: Public and Private

The public police have no monopoly over concerns with urban design and safety, even though at times they may appear to be the hub of security knowledge in a risk society (Ericson, Haggerty, and Carriere 1993). The need for security, for its manufacture and design into the layout of urban grids (cf. Hayward 2004), has been well documented in cities from Los Angeles (Davis 1990) to Manchester (Hobbs et al. 2003) and is now part of the depoliticized desire to create safe zones of consumption open to the tourist gaze. The police machine is a massive assemblage of security thinking and incorporates a labyrinth of embedded policing personalities within public and private institutions. Nightclub proprietors and doormen see themselves as part of this urban regeneration project: "We don't want to have that image. We want older folks to come in and watch jazz night and not worry about the neighbourhood and all this stuff. And they're tying to clean it up outside, and they're trying to make the place look better. And downtown's getting bigger and it's growing this way. You know, it can't go that way any more, it's got to go this way. So, that's the way they're looking at it as far as this bar and that sort of thing" (visible-minority male supervisor).

Doorstaff often understand their roles as connected to the improvement of the Halifax nighttime experience:

> There's never any reporting about the positive things that happen when people are downtown. There's a lot of nights when absolutely nothing goes wrong. But they never talk about any of those times. It's just the one time that something does happen to go wrong that they blow it way out of proportion. Then people are nervous to go downtown, and they shouldn't be. *Like there's enough of us around that if anybody feels insecure, or anything like that, they should come to us.* Like, a lot of the female patrons here, they'll make small talk every once in a while and my kind of help to them is "Look, you need anything, you see any of us in yellow shirts, if somebody is

talking to you and you don't want them talkin' to ya, they're buggin' ya, whatever it is, you come and tell one of us." (03: white female doorstaff, my emphasis)

The need for better and more security is frustrated in the ostensibly private realm of the nightclub, reflecting the same type of economic scarcity that impacts public policing: "They're saying it's cost prohibitive. I'm not sure whether that's the case or whether they're, you know, looking at a … at a profit, you know, profit margin or the bottom line or whatever. But I do know that it makes our job much, much easier" (06: white male supervisor).

It should come as little surprise, given what we have considered thus far, that the concerns and functions of bouncers and police officers overlap and often synchronize in the Halifax night. It would be a gross oversimplification to suggest that one policing organization simply augments the other. While nightclubs indirectly employ police officers, they cannot depend on them to be corporate lackeys. Police and nightclub interests and policies may just as easily come into conflict.

That relations between Halifax Police and nightclub security management can be stressed under the pull of competing interests is clearly evinced by a security supervisor's response when asked about the lack of police presence on a particular Saturday night at the Mansion. "Oh, you should have been here last week. A lot of shit went down!" The previous Thursday a group of five or six off-duty police officers were drinking at the Mansion. A couple of the officers had worked nights on a paid-duty basis for the nightclub. The officers noticed a group of Hell's Angels members sporting their jackets and gang colours in the bar. One of the off-duty officers approached the security supervisor, whom he knew, wanting to know why the notorious biker gang members were allowed to wear their colours. According to our respondent, the officer had a few drinks and became upset when the security manager refused to remove the men or request that they take off their jackets. He was reminded by the manager that the Mansion did not have a dress code. Despite repeated attempts by some of the other off-duty police officers to reprimand the doormen posted at the entrances, the Hell's Angels were not removed. Two of the off-duty officers then exited the nightclub and approached their fellow uniformed officers who were working for the Mansion on a paid-duty basis. One of the paid-duty officers then entered the nightclub, approached one of the Hell's Angels members, pointed his finger at him, and told him he could not wear his colours inside the nightclub. The exchange between the Hell's Angels member and the uniformed officer reportedly became heated, and the Hell's Angels member approached the nightclub's doorstaff supervisor to protest the fact he was being asked to leave. At this point, the head doormen regretted that there was little he could do, shrugged, and purportedly said, "Well, they are the police." The Hell's Angels left the bar in a foul mood.

The next day, a representative from the biker gang called the bar manager requesting permission to rent out a section. The Mansion had a policy against making group reservations, and the Hell's Angels representative did not protest. Later that evening, however, a group of Hell's Angels members showed up in force. Our respondent believed that there were approximately forty gang members in the nightclub wearing colours. On that same Friday night, there were also a handful of off-duty Halifax police officers drinking in the nightclub who again noted the bikers' presence. Not surprisingly, a violent altercation occurred later in the evening between a group of Hell's Angels and a drunken patron.

The following Monday, the Mansion's management received a letter from the Halifax Police informing them that they were refunding the nightclub's retainer for future paid-duty services and would no longer provide such services until they stopped allowing gang members into the club wearing their colours, logos, or paraphernalia. While our respondent initially boasted that these developments would have no effect on the nightclub's security, we later found his assertion to be misleading, and he conceded as much. Indeed, bouncers at the nightclub had threatened to quit, and he had issued an ultimatum to the nightclub's manager and owner that if the situation was not rectified he was also going to quit. Furthermore, we later learned that plans were already underway to install cameras, metal detectors, and recording equipment, as well as to equip doorstaff with radios and provide them with minimum training. All of this was to be implemented by the end of the month. In fact, the withdrawal of services by the public police resulted in significant security changes.

The conduct of the off-duty police officers in the nightclub, the role of their paid-duty colleagues, and the eventual issuance of a letter withdrawing services by the Halifax police raises a number of interesting questions about the conflation of public and private spaces and the role of paid-duty police officers working at the behest of private clients. From the perspective of the police, they could not in all good conscience service a client who allowed organized crime members to frequent the same establishment they were being paid to police and protect. We would do well to take note of the fact that controversy swirled around not just the

Hell's Angels but their ability to wear their colours in the nightclub. Working in such close proximity to a nightclub and frequenting the establishment while off-duty created a sense of entitlement among Halifax police officers to enforce their own code of conduct. When this was not supported by the nightclub's management, they simply withdrew their services. Of course, the symbolic importance of the "colours" the Hell's Angels were donning and how this represented an affront to the police in the Mansion is another matter of interest, given the close relationship between aesthetics and violence that the nightclub fosters. We shall leave this discussion, however, for later analysis (see chapter 7). For now, it is important to take note of the perception that the police played a significant deterrent effect at this nightclub and their withdrawal of services resulted in a security crisis. At other nightclubs, the police played a less significant role, but those same nightclubs also typically had extensive security systems and routinely deployed a host of technologies to augment sheer muscle.

As we discuss in more detail later (chapter 4), in the context of training and recruiting, many doormen harbour desires for employment with law enforcement or corrections. Unlike the parapolice (Rigakos 2002b), however, there is no generalized "wannabe" culture among doormen to become police or correctional officers. In any case, some police officers are actually former doormen and work on a paid-duty basis outside the same nightclubs that used to employ them as bouncers. In other cases doormen are former high-school friends or teammates with police officers:

> Several police officers have been door staff, you know, in the past.
> I can think of two or three that were doormen, or head doormen,
> that are police officers now. So you know, they're not bad, they
> understand the job and the situation and like I said, they're very
> helpful. (03: white male supervisor)

> A lot of the newer cops, I went to high school with, played football
> type of thing, the majority of guys are all right. You still have guys
> from the old school usually come in, and I mean they're ignorant
> or whatever, fight with everybody, black people, white people.
> (15: visible-minority male doorstaff)

Many bouncers are uninterested in public policing or law enforcement and see bouncing as a transitional or part-time job until they finish their studies or finish their certification for other vocations. Nonetheless, by virtue of sharing similar haunts, hours, and enemies, the police and doormen come into frequent social contact, which in many cases is quite amicable. Most doorstaff believe that "generally, the police are okay" (11: white male doorstaff) and attribute their camaraderie to the fact that they are doing similar work and dealing with the same "problem" populations. These episodes of camaraderie would poke through the constables' veneer of professional detachment. On one occasion outside of the Galaxy, I witnessed two police officers turn up their portable communication radios so that doormen could hear a high-speed pursuit in progress involving an ATV. Both doormen and police were trying to guess the identities of the officers involved in the chase. The ATV eventually flipped over. One officer turned to both the other and the bouncers, shaking his head: "He's crazy." The doormen joined in their disapproval, sharing a moralizing moment.

Functional cooperation between police and doorstaff can become so cozy that bouncers fill out paperwork to assist the police officers in their reporting:

> RESPONDENT: If I think there's going to be any repercussion, like anything, oh, we ripped his clothes, or somebody tore something or some little thing, I'll get my guys to write up a report, and then I'll just put it on police report paper in case they ask for it later on. And sometimes the police come to me and they'll say "I need reports from this such incident and that such incident."
>
> ME: Oh, so they're what, done on Halifax Police letterhead, is that right?
>
> RESPONDENT: Yeah, yeah. It's it's Halifax Police forms. I've got a few forms, from them, yeah.
>
> ME: So they're basically, you fill out the statements, you sign them?
>
> RESPONDENT: Yeah …
>
> ME: And you give them, you give them the [CCTV] tapes too?
>
> RESPONDENT: Yeah. If they need them, they'll request them and I have them saved. (03: white male supervisor)

Indeed, Canadian research indicates that security firms that share intelligence with their clients are less likely to share intelligence with police (Lippert and O'Connor 2006). Proprietary (or in-house) nightclub security, however, seems to have no such reservation. In many cases police officers will even elicit the security supervisor's opinion about how best to dispense with troublemakers: "They say, 'What do you want done with them?' I'll say: 'Nobody was assaulted on our side. Just send them on their way.' They shoot them into a cab" (03: white male supervisor).

Given their close working relationship, police officers are usually more likely to listen to the evidence presented to them by a doorman than by a drunken patron:

> They believe what we say and anybody ever had a problem that the police were called, there's no controversy between staff members and the police … [One of our patrons] got out of the back steps and then he fell down the back stairs … He was so drunk he fell down and banged his head. And when we did explain to the police, like he had another story – like he was pushed or what not, and we explained to the police what happened, and they totally understood and they listened. And they took [the bouncers'] side of the story and, there was nothing else the matter because they knew that that was what would happen, right? No, we get along good with them … They know somewhat what we put up with, every night, being in a bar and everything, as staff, but I don't think they'd stick their necks out for us, though. (18: white male doorstaff)

The police will even assist doorstaff in keeping out patrons who may not have proper identification. Bouncers will refer patrons to the police and advise them that if they can convince the officers that their identification card is legitimate, they will be allowed into the nightclub. One bouncer said he told patrons with suspect ID, "Tell ya what, you want your ID back, go call the police. They'll come down. You'll get your ID back.' A guy did that once. Police took the ID, looked at him, said, You're under arrest for fraud [*laughs*] … I have good relationship with them. If there's any problem, I say [unintelligible]. They just come down here like, 'What's going on? you know, like 'What's goin' on, [M]?' and I'll just shoot the shit with them for a minute and 'What happened here?' and I'll tell them" (09: white male doorstaff).

According to this same respondent, relations between the police and doorstaff were so amicable that one police officer even forgave a bouncer for mistakenly punching the constable in the face:

> The police were walking by, just out on the beat walking around, guy came up over the top, the police grabbed our guy, and one of our guys came over the cop and [*smacking sound*] hit the cop. Didn't realize it was a cop, eh? But he really didn't! The cop that got hit, he was cool, he was like "No no, it was a mistake, I know it was a

mistake, 'cause I only seen him from here up, and he could only see me from here up." You know, from the chin up? And one of the older cops, this guy was kind of younger, probably thirty, thirty-two, and the old guy, probably forty-eight, was going, "Charge him, charge him, charge him," and the guy's like, "No, I'm not going to," ya know what I mean? "Don't get that way." (09: white male doorstaff)

Inevitably, close working relationships in the face of potential violence and legal repercussions necessitates the development of trust and respect:

RESPONDENT: If we ever need their assistance and we make a call, they're here really quick, and most of the time on the busy nights, Fridays and Saturdays, they're standing there with us so we have almost an instant reaction from them.

ME: So you do feel like they're an ally?

RESPONDENT: Oh, definitely. They're on our side big time … They usually just take them away and ask questions later, it seems … I think probably more than anybody they give us respect, because half the time they're the ones rolling around on the sidewalk with us … They seem to trust our judgment more than I no-ticed four years ago. And I think we work really well with them, we just seem to interact really well with them, they listen to what we have to say, they don't just shut us out. (01: white male doorstaff)

Indeed, bouncers perceive themselves as doing work similar to police officers because of their close occupational relationship and the fact that they routinely use force against the same subjects:

If you've got the guy in a simple arm bar, he's on the ground, he's up against the wall, then they're pretty responsive. Say, they come up, and you need to give them a hand, hold an arm while they cuff him, that type of thing. (15: visible-minority male doorstaff)

We're doing almost the same thing, in a way … Every time we're outside and they drive by like, from out the back door, they'll wave to you, and we'll wave back. So it seems like a pretty good relation-ship we have with them. (13: white male doorstaff)

So they have a good understanding of what we have to go through and, you know, likewise we understand what they have to go through. The only thing they have is a whole team with radios and clubs and guns and you know, [unintelligible], things like that. We have no weapons. (03: white male supervisor)

It's like you're a cop, bad cop, always doing these kind of things. One guy, you know, you may get somebody outside who'll say, "Ah that guy's an asshole," don't worry about it. (15: visible-minority male doorstaff)

Yeah, you know, we've gone home, let's say I'm trying to get home at the end of the night and I'm speeding, or I go through a red light, or you know, there's nobody around, we've been pulled over, and it's "Ah, you work at the [Galaxy] slow down, drive careful next time," or whatever. Stuff like that. I just walk into work, the cops will pull over and give me a ride to work. (04: white male doorstaff)

In one case a patron ended up with a black eye, but the police: "took her away and told us they weren't able to press charges ... as far as assault because it's part of our job." The respondent continued, "It's nice to see that there's a police officer standing and talking to one of our doorstaff. It's comforting, almost. Our bar has a really good reputation with the police, I would think anyways. We have police on staff Fridays and Saturday nights. We have former employees who're now police officers ... One of them used to be our head doorman" (03: white female doorstaff).

Of course, as in all cases of social interaction, much depends on preconceived notions. In those cases where police officers have a negative image of bouncers, it is likely that a doorman's actions will come under greater scrutiny: "Some of the things they hear around here, you know, 'You're trying to be heroes,' and other ones realize you're just tryin' like, anyone, cops who've actually ever worked in this field, know you do shit, and [you're] trying to get paid. And other cops try and, they act like they think that you're tryin' to be a big hero, tryin' to, you know, beat people up all the time. It's kind of frustrating" (19: white male doorstaff).

Despite largely amicable relations, bouncers can harbour resentment against police when they do not receive adequate and timely assistance or, as previously discussed, when police officers *cause* difficulties in the nightclub while off-duty.

RESPONDENT: [A woman] had passed out ... and we were trying to help 'cause there was a hundred, two hundred people inside of the dance floor, so we started moving people out of the way. This guy started arguing with one of the doormen ... He was an RCMP officer. Started arguing with one of the doormen and I went over, and I said, "Could you please move?" And he said, "No, I'm not getting the fuck out of the way here."

ME: Was he on duty?

RESPONDENT: No, he wasn't. He was here with his girlfriend. We ended up throwing him out. Ah, he tried to charge us with assault, but then we told the police what he had done. And what we were trying to do, then that was dropped ... it was actually kind of funny. We were throwing him out ... two of us grabbed him and he was only a little guy. Probably 150, 160 pounds, and we didn't realize how light he actually was ... and actually ended up hitting his head off the top of the door frame. And then just kind of dropped him and went, "Oh my god, what'd we do!?" We just kind of scooped him out the door and left him for the shore patrol. 'Cause it was totally unexpected, we didn't even mean to do it, that was the worst thing. We just kind of looked at each other: "Oh my god! We dropped him!" (04: white male doorstaff)

Response time has always been a particularly salient measurement of trustworthiness in both public and private policing. As a barometer of commitment, mutual assistance has tremendous cultural relevance to officers. The ability to muster support quickly is paramount. If a fellow bouncer doesn't "have your back," then one's ability to act effectively is compromised. For bouncers, this thinking sometimes extends to their reliance on the police:

If you call them and say, "We might need you in ten minutes," they'll like call us in ten minutes, and that's what they do, right? And it ticks me off, sometimes you call them and like, you don't often get to an operator, and she's like, "What's happening?" and it's like "I'm calling because I need the police, I'm not calling to have a conversation. Come deal with the situation." (10: white male doorstaff)

They don't respond well. They definitely don't respond well. And now, like when I was at [Nightclub #4], um, their demeanor was entirely different as to how it is here. At [Nightclub #4] they came down, almost with the attitude that we had started the fight. And it was, yeah, that type of point. And that had something to do with why they would take so long, obviously. You know, and the police station's right across the corner … Oftentimes on the phone, we would be told if we had a fight, it was our problem. And they wouldn't come … [One time] this guy had thrown beer bottles at several people in the crowd. And they held him for half an hour on the ground, and finally they just let him go cause the police never showed. And they were called, right? (05: white male doorstaff)

They take forever to arrive. (05: white male supervisor)

The following respondent relates a series of incidents in which he believes the Halifax police acted slowly or did not act at all. This included police failure to apprehend a suspected murder and a man who had tried to stab someone with a screwdriver.

When the police came, they basically witnessed the guy, who was actually a suspect in a murder case, throw bricks through the front window. And I said to the officer, I'm like "Sir, that's the guy who just threw those bricks through the window, do you maybe want to do something about that"? He's like "Oh yeah, we're gonna do something about that." The [suspect] starts walking away. I'm like "He just threw bricks through the window. He just smashed bottles on people's heads. You wanna do something?" And the cop was just glaring, "Blah blah blah," and things like, "Yeah yeah, we're gonna do something about that." The guy just basically walked away and the cop just watched it … It was like he didn't want to even bother dealing with this person. I don't know if he was scared or whatever, but it was kind of frustrating … [We had] guys [who] just got on the news … in here and out back, tried to stab someone with a screwdriver. And, basically the cops didn't do anything until he spit at a police officer. And then the other guy was [unintelligible] and we have situations where, you know, someone's been doing something in the bar, and we end up like having to hold them down, and you're sitting there looking at the police station, you see cop cars going up Connaught Street, and you're holding this person. You know you called the cops fifteen minutes ago, and this person is trying to bite you, trying to scratch you, and you're trying to hold him for the police and, I mean it's kind of a pain in the ass. You should be inside dealing with the customers, instead of outside holding this person who's trying to bite you and all kinds of other stuff. (19: white male doorstaff)

In another case, the police were purportedly unhelpful because they allowed suspects to pass counterfeit fifty-dollar bills and then leave the scene without incident. The head doorman contemplated whether it would have been better to take matters into his own hands:

In the end we lost all the money because they never did go get the guys and give our money back. They just put it into this investigation thing, right? So I ended up going over to the police station and went through all that crap for absolutely nothing. And you think to yourself, "Well, what if I had just got all the boys out there"? I mean is it worth it, it's two hundred bucks and change, whatever, right? To go out there, you get all the boys out there, to muscle these guys down and get our money back. I'm like, who's right and who's wrong, eh? Like we would have been charged with assault and every other thing, right? That's, like, I don't know the end result there. (14: visible minority supervisor)

Another doorman seemed to verify the story, but whether the incident actually unfolded this way or not, the point here is that bouncers expect a certain level of police involvement when they call them. Failure to do so may result in the worst of masculine subcultural epithets: cowardice: "Right about five minutes to two, [we assisted in] a takedown, take-out, the week before … for counterfeit money, or something like that. And [the accused persons] came back, probably with weapons; we called the cops, probably five or six cars. They didn't really do much. Just kept them, everybody, separated, just kept them away from us. I think they acted cowardly" (07: white male doorstaff).

Bouncers are more aware than most that the reputation of the doorstaff at a nightclub dramatically affects how the police will handle an incident. The Halifax bar scene caters to a variety of crowds, and certain establishments have reputations for rougher handling of troublesome patrons. Police officers are far more likely to trust the judgment of certain bouncers and their managers than others:

I hear that we're the least-respected doormen in the city, down here at [Nightclub #4] anyways. But, the police think that we're like the worst, I guess … [Our doormen] were like coming onto thirty years old and juiced up on steroids and just punching nineteen year olds out for no reason. So that's, they don't work here anymore but definitely they rode some of them [out of] here in the past. (06: white male doorstaff)

We have a good rapport with the police 'cause we treat them good, really well. I don't know about what the other bars are like, but here, they don't see us, like I said, as that general perception of doorstaff. They don't see us make, we don't make bad decisions, we don't assault people. We don't use force, like excessive force, you know? So they see that. They respect us for that. And they respect us 'cause we let them have the ultimate decision in arresting somebody. (05: white male supervisor)

One explanation of differences in rapport between certain Halifax police officers and doormen at various nightclubs may be proximity and ongoing working relationships such as extra-duty contract policing. One night outside the Galaxy, one doorman told me that many of the police officers who work outside the nightclub used to be doormen themselves. When I suggested that knowing this must come in handy, he laughed. "They generally don't ask too many questions ... like, 'What happened?' Or, 'Why is he bleeding?' ... We had a meeting and we were told that uh, there would be a police officer standing outside. And on nights like that, if there's anything that goes wrong in the bar, they're around usually around thirty seconds or a minute" (11: white male doorstaff).

Indeed, the position of the bouncer in policing the night can be a precarious one, and most doormen acknowledge as much. Their ability to avoid arrest and their discretion in using force is often contingent on their own and the nightclub's reputation. It makes sense, therefore, that so far as they can, doormen cultivate relationships with police officers: "[We] hire them twice, two nights a week, so they're here a lot. And that means when they're working their regular shift, and something happens here, they'll come, and they'll usually listen to our side, and if [there was] not [an] offence, lean towards us, I'd like to think most of the times. Just because they know we have good judgement. Especially the supervisors" (01: white male supervisor). Said another, "We don't have to worry about them taking our word for it, 'cause they know, like we all know each other, to a certain point, right?" (visible minority male supervisor).

While the constant presence of police outside some nightclubs can put over-zealous bouncers at risk of detection and sanctioning, most doormen welcome the general deterrent effect of armed municipal police.

The presence of public policing was perceived to be invaluable by both door staff and nightclub management. At the Mansion, two police officers are stationed at the front door from 12 A.M. until closing time on Wednesdays, Fridays, and Saturdays on a paid-duty basis. Throughout the night police officers walk the perimeter of the building and intermittently enter the bar "to check things out."

> You're less likely to have someone try to run you over with a car, or pull out a weapon, you've got two uniformed officers standing there. (06: white male supervisor)

> Police on the door – it makes a huge difference. We've had, uh, incidents, we'd thrown out large groups of people and they've been, would have been certain brawls, and with lots of bar staff, except for the fact that, two policemen walked around the corner at that time, and they left. And, you know, uh, some of people have weapons in their cars. (05: white male supervisor)

> [T]he police are definitely an asset. Or if you have problems inside with three groups of twenty or thirty guys, and you have football and rugby teams, or baseball teams, if you're going to approach somebody like that, you'd be an idiot to say, "You gotta go," because I guarantee you got thirty guys fighting and there's only twenty-two of us working on a Saturday or something. Or if it's a Tuesday, there's only five or six of us. And we got twenty guys, we'd be stupid to go out and say to a guy, "Yeah, you gotta leave." Again, you're gonna be in a huge fight you're not gonna win. I mean, people are gonna get hurt. And I mean, you've got the cops at your disposal, call them up. Have them wait outside. Tell them there maybe a call for later. So the relationship with this bar and the police is pretty good. (visible-minority male doorstaff)

In terms of public accountability, even more salient to a manager's everyday business operations than a Halifax police officer is the provincial liquor inspector. Indeed, no other guest with the exception of gang members and celebrities caused as much anxiety and radio chatter among doormen: "Liquor inspector on site!" I would listen as his whereabouts and activities were incessantly relayed to other doormen and supervisors. I learned from the inspector that he was the only alcohol and gaming enforcement officer who visited bars and cabarets in Halifax. He returned to the front entrance with a very young-looking woman in tow. She was asked to produce her identification, and the coat-check girl located her jacket. The young woman had legitimate identification, and the inspector took up a position next to the doorman and began to look over the identification cards of the other prospective patrons in the queue. As others have observed (Kneal 1999; Levy and Valverde 2001), the penetration of the state into the affairs of pubs and nightclubs is a rather spotty affair, typically marked by the very local politics of imbibing and potential violence.

Occupational Risk

Having considered risk as malleable, socially constructed, and politically charged, yet nonetheless palpably real and sometimes manifested brutally, we are in a better position to critically assess comparative workplace violence data on public police and doormen. In keeping with the theme of this chapter and by way of empirical introduction to nightclub violence and bouncer subculture, this section details results of what I will refer to as a "Workplace Violence Survey" (wvs) consisting of a fifteen-item questionnaire administered to fifty-one doorstaff, sixty Halifax Regional Police, and 129 Halifax area RCMP officers. These items are part of the larger survey, "Interpersonal Conflict at Work Scale" (ICW) (Spector and Jex 1998). The wvs focuses on physical and emotional violence perpetrated by patrons or citizens on bouncers or police officers, and the ICW scale focuses on physical and emotional violence perpetrated by fellow workers/officers and supervisors. I deal only with the wvs here and leave a discussion of the ICW results for the following chapter on bouncer culture.

There is a long-standing, self-deprecating aphorism among sociologists that social scientific research often seems only to empirically validate the blatantly obvious. That both police officers and doorstaff are the routine subjects of workplace violence, both physical and non-physical, will surely come as little surprise to the reader. Indeed, table 3.2 shows that in the year prior to the survey, three-quarters of doorstaff and 80 per cent of Halifax police officers responding to the survey were hit while at work, and over two-thirds of both groups were kicked; 88 per cent of doorstaff and 84.3 per cent of Halifax police officers were grabbed. Workplace physical violence among RCMP officers was less than that of bouncers and Halifax municipal police. However, 90 per cent of bouncers, Halifax police, and RCMP officers were shouted at, sworn at, or glared at in the previous year. More doorstaff than Halifax police or RCMP officers were assaulted

Table 3.2: Number of occurrences of physical violence and non-physical violence committed against doorstaff and police officers in the last year (in percentages)

Number of occurrences	Doorstaff				RCMP				Halifax Police			
	1	2-3	4+	Total	1	2-3	4+	Total	1	2-3	4+	Total
Physical Violence												
Hit	21.6	25.5	27.5	74.6	20.2	16.9	12.1	49.2	19.0	29.3	32.8	81.1
Kicked	20.0	30.0	16.0	66.0	15.9	14.3	7.9	38.1	29.3	12.1	27.6	69.0
Grabbed	6.0	34.0	48.0	88.0	15.9	25.4	22.2	63.5	24.6	28.1	31.6	84.3
Shoved	12.2	20.4	53.1	85.7	18.3	22.2	23.0	63.5	24.1	24.1	32.8	81.0
Pushed	17.6	15.7	49.0	82.3	18.9	20.5	23.6	63.0	25.9	20.7	31.0	77.6
Bitten	22.0	16.0	6.0	44.0	7.1	0.8	0.0	7.9	24.6	3.5	1.8	29.9
Object thrown	17.6	31.4	9.8	58.8	14.3	21.4	11.1	46.8	19.0	25.9	15.5	60.4
Assaulted with weapon	17.6	5.9	3.9	27.4	9.4	4.7	3.1	17.2	13.8	8.6	3.4	25.8
Injured with a weapon	9.8	3.9	0.0	13.7	7.1	0.8	0.0	7.9	8.6	1.7	0.0	10.3
Non-Physical Violence												
Spat on	19.6	19.6	15.7	54.9	23.8	6.3	4.8	34.9	27.6	15.5	19.0	62.1
Yelled at	7.8	15.7	68.6	92.1	5.5	21.3	61.4	88.2	5.3	12.3	77.2	94.8
Shouted at	4.1	18.4	67.3	89.8	5.5	22.8	59.1	87.4	5.3	14.0	73.7	93.0
Sworn at	7.8	11.8	74.5	94.1	4.0	19.0	68.3	91.3	3.4	3.4	87.9	94.7
Glared at	3.9	7.8	84.3	96.0	4.0	15.1	73.0	92.1	1.7	6.9	86.2	94.8
Door slammed in face	10.0	24.0	16.0	50.0	13.6	26.4	16.8	56.8	26.3	19.3	42.1	87.7

with a weapon or injured with a weapon in the previous year. All three groups experienced similarly high levels of non-physical violence. A direct statistical comparison (shown in table 3.3) based on the frequency of experiences with violence demonstrates that when bouncers are compared to Halifax-area police officers (including RCMP), they are statistically significantly more likely to experience both physical violence in the workplace (t= -3.3, df=234, p<.001) and overall violence (t= -2.3, df=234, p<.05).

Collapsing RCMP officers with Halifax police, however, may be problematic, insofar as many RCMP officers working around the greater Halifax area have almost nothing to do with urban policing. Given that part of the mission of this book is understanding the context of policing in the urban nighttime economy, rural RCMP and Halifax Regional police officers were hived off from the comparison (see table 3.4), although even a passing glance at average violence frequencies demonstrates marked general differences between RCMP and Halifax police. Thus, when RCMP officers and rural Halifax police are removed from the sample and urban Halifax police are directly compared to downtown Halifax doorstaff, any significant differences in physical (t= -0.88, df=107, p=ns), non-physical (t= 1.83, df=107, p=ns), and overall (t= 0.17, df=107, p=ns) workplace violence disappear. Nonetheless, urban RCMP officers are less likely to suffer from both physical (t= -2.62, df=79, p<.01; t=-3.39, df=72, p<.001) and overall (t= -2.44, df=107, p<.02; t=-2.27, df=72, p<.05) workplace violence than both urban Halifax police and Halifax doorstaff. This may be as a result of the RCMP's deployment criteria (often federal investigations), area of patrol, the populations they are charged with policing, or even their status and standing in the community.

On the issue of occupational risk, therefore, we may say that Halifax doorstaff are empirically just as likely as Halifax-area urban police officers to experience physical, non-physical, and overall violence in the workplace, and are statistically significantly more likely to experience physical and overall violence compared to Halifax-area police officers as a whole. These findings, at least superficially, are rather predictable but nonetheless alarming insofar as we recognize that there are currently no minimum training standards, methods of certification, or background screening measures for doorstaff in Nova Scotia.[1] Moreover, what these statistical comparisons unfortunately do not reveal is the *use* of violence by bouncers and police against patrons and citizens,[2] for which, in the case of doorstaff, we instead must rely on interview an ethnographic analysis.

Empirical findings from the WVS seemed everywhere reinforced by both "war stories," or "door lore" (Hobbs et al. 2002) and the altercations I personally observed in the field. Indeed, the routine violence I had sus-

Table 3.3: Comparison of means (t-test) between all police officers and doorstaff on measures of violence

	n	Mean	SD	*df*	t
Physical violence					
Police	185	7.9	6.6	234	-3.3***
Doorstaff	51	11.3	6.4		
Non-physical violence					
Police	185	11.9	4.4	234	-.281
Doorstaff	51	12.2	4.2		
Physical and non-physical violence					
Police	185	19.9	10.1	234	-2.3*
Doorstaff	51	23.5	9.8		

***p<.001
*p<.05

Table 3.4: Scores for measures of physical, non-physical, and overall violence

	Doorstaff	All police	Halifax police	All RCMP	Urban RCMP	Rural RCMP	Police (urban)
Physical violence	11.3	7.9	10.2	6.9	6.0	6.9	9.0
Non-physical violence	12.2	12.0	13.6	11.2	12.0	11.0	13.1
Overall violence	23.5	19.9	23.8	18.1	18.0	17.8	22.2

Table 3.5: Comparison of means (t-test) between all police officers in an urban setting and doorstaff on measures of violence

	n	Mean	SD	*df*	t
Physical violence					
Police	81	9.0	6.7	130	-1.95*
Doorstaff	51	11.3	6.4		
Non-physical violence					
Police	81	13.1	4.1	130	1.32
Doorstaff	51	12.2	4.2		
Overall violence					
Police	81	22.2	9.9	130	-.75
Doorstaff	51	23.5	9.8		

* p<.05

pected took place in Halifax nightclubs was almost immediately supported through observational research. On only my second visit to the first nightclub in the Halifax study, I asked a doorman about the whereabouts of his co-worker I had spoken to on the telephone, only to find out that he was visiting a fellow staff member who was hospitalized after getting involved in a violent confrontantion when he punched a patron for spitting on him. He was seriously injured in the altercation that ensued. One doorman who had been in the business for over a decade recalled three incidents in which a gun had been pointed at him: "Well, two of the times it was outside and he was at a distance, and there's nothing you can do. There's no way I could get to him before he could shoot me, so you just stand there and hope that the guy doesn't feel like shooting you. And he didn't, and the third time was inside the bar, and I was lucky enough to wrestle the gun away from him before he had a chance to shoot me." (01: white male doorstaff).

Routine violence and threats become part of the accepted occupational risk of bouncing, increasing over time, given the number of removals and experience with Halifax's more riskier characters.

> I've been threatened to be killed like five, six times. I've had guys pull guns, I've been smacked in the head with beer bottles. Cut, punched, spit on. And for what? (05: white male supervisor).

> The longer you've been here, the more enemies you make, basically. (06: white male supervisor)

> But this guy, about a month ago, stabbed a guy. And I dunno the whole story, in connection with a birthday, that's okay. Pretty good off. And I guess me and that guy almost got in a fight earlier that night, before they kicked him out. And supposedly he was going to use the gun on me. When I found out the next day, when I was down here, it's not a good feeling. (07: white male doorstaff)

> And any time, you never know, like, how that guy's going to turn when you're driving home with him, or what he's doing to do, and so how much further you might have to go. (07: white male doorstaff)

Threats compound to a point where doormen believe it is simply a matter of time before an area bouncer is shot merely for doing his job:

> He was really good friends with some drug dealers, who were

known to be carrying guns. And our problem was with giving our names out, so maybe give me your name and I'll try hard enough, like, I could probably find you. So that was a problem that night. Like, he was deathly upset with us. (11: white male doorstaff)

You hear about doormen getting shot in Toronto and stuff, and I mean it's only a matter of time before it happens out here really. Just, people are like, you know what people say, "Oh yeah, I'm gonna come back and shoot you." And we had one guy in here, "I'm gonna get my MAC-10 dog and spread blood like ketchup." (19: white male doorstaff)

It is perhaps unavoidable that the "police mentality" so endemic to those who are asked to resolve safety concerns produces a litany of suggested improvements to the security system. Deficiencies are immediately detected by doorstaff who concern themselves with what is needed to increase surveillance, foolproof identification procedures, and safeguard staff. This is perhaps a common attribute of all security labourers and those interested in policing broadly defined. In Bogard's (1992) terms, it amounts to a "social science fiction" of surveillance: what is possible is always being imagined. This often translates into the demand for gadgets such as ID card readers, databases, CCTV, and metal detectors, but in other cases these demands are actually rather more mundane and immediately apparent to doormen. I often heard complaints about management "cutting corners" and "understaffing," which was not only said to compromise nightclub security but also the safety of doorstaff. "What are we doing here, really?" asked one rather annoyed supervisor. "They're taking away my guy upstairs, they're taking away one tickets guy, they're cutting the emergency lights guy, and a floater. This is NOT acceptable!"

They could just have more guys. They could have better guys, they could have metal detectors. They could have, you know what I mean, just stuff like that. Jesus Christ, I'd wear a bulletproof vest under my shirt, I wouldn't care. You know what I mean? If I get shot, what's gonna save my life? If I look dumb, I don't care how I look, I'm still working. Compared to [unintelligible], you know? I'm not in a fashion show for anybody. (09: white male doorstaff)

I think they should bring in, um, Polaroid cameras for, I mean major incidents outside the [unintelligible]. The other thing is, most of the guys go to school that work here. They may only work two or three days a week. So you're not going to see these people from say maybe on a Tuesday or a Friday night or something, so you're not gonna know. (15: visible minority doorstaff)

That doormen understandably spend a considerable amount of time worrying about their susceptibility to violence was made clear through both my discussions with respondents and simply overhearing general conversations. One evening in the entranceway to the Beacon, three doormen surveyed the street outside. As T. emerged wiping the beads of sweat from his shaved head, he casually offered: "We're a pretty good target for a drive-by." D. responded, "Yup, I know." I queried whether anything had happened recently that would make the doormen believe a drive-by was possible or even imminent, but T. responded, "No, not really. Just the usual, you know?" At first, I would dismiss such conversations as bravado, melodrama, or simply posturing for the researcher. As time went on, however, and the novelty of my presence passed, I began to record such discussions more carefully, both because they persisted, despite my continued presence and lack of reaction, and because the number of violent episodes and threats to doorstaff I had witnessed made such pronouncements all the more plausible. From my fieldnotes:

It is after 3 A.M. and the crowds are beginning to move from nearby nightclubs to the Beacon. Groups of two to ten begin to queue up. They are all in varying states of inebriation. One young woman is propping her friend up as she bumps off the outside wall of the nightclub. As I scrutinize the line-up, my concentration is broken by N. who pats P. on the shoulder and points down the street. "What's this?" he asks through squinting eyes, "a convention of banned people?" Our attention is turned to a group of black men in their early twenties who have mustered down the street on a corner curb. As we look in their direction, they glare back at us with hostility. They are talking amongst themselves, gesturing and pointing toward us. Two of them pause to lean into two idling cars that have pulled up next to the group. Before I have an opportunity to ask about the obvious tension, P. points to one of the men and explains that the Beacon's management has a peace bond on him. P. tells me that after the patron had been thrown out one evening, he returned with eight friends and his father to beat up the doormen. An earlier discussion about our susceptibility to drive-by shootings pops into my head. I retreat into the entranceway. Eventually, the group piles into their friends' cars and drives away.

The threat of retaliation for being banned seems all the more real when issued by known gang members whose sense of self-worth is tied to intimidation and self-righteous rage at the prospect of losing face or being publicly humiliated. On another night I observe:

It's after 2:35 A.M. on a very humid Halifax night. Outside, the fog hovers eerily yet peacefully over the nightclub. Inside the Mansion, I struggle with my earplugs under clouds of cigarette smoke, attempting to dull the percussive thud of yet another annoying dance tune. I save my eardrums but my organs still warble with the beat. My attention is drawn to what appears to be a potentially violent situation. Three doormen are checking identification as patrons enter the bar when a group of males in their mid-twenties dressed in hip-hop attire begin a rather heated exchange of words with the doormen. One man in particular, taller than the rest with slicked back brown hair and a full-length black leather jacket, is red faced with anger. He also appears to have been drinking. A tattoo of barbed wire or some thorny plant circles his neck and creeps up both sides of his sallow face.

One of the doormen (P.) motions to his supervisor, who comes over to assist. I follow. We all learn that the tattooed man has been previously banned. Overhearing P.'s version of events, the man and his posse get more wound up. They are all incredulous and repeatedly ask, "Why?" and "What the hell for?" I find it curious that none of the other doorstaff have moved to assist but am later to discover that P., who is handling the tattooed man, is actually an acquaintance. The tattooed man begins pacing in the doorway. The supervisor is trying to quiet him down by speaking in a calm voice, well aware of the fact that he is now encircled by the tattooed man's FUBU-clad friends. The other bouncers watch intently but do not move from their posts. The tattooed man continues his verbal assault while pacing and finally exhorts, "Take off your shirt, man, take your shirt off!" I assume by this that he is asking P. to put his job aside and defend his friend's case. Finally, the man begins to leave but he suddenly stops, turns, points directly at P. and says "I want to talk to YOU!"

P. agrees and leaves with the man and his friends, who are now joined by their girlfriends as they scurry out of the nightclub after them. I watch from the stoop of the bar entrance as the two interlocutors break off from the rest of the group and cross the street through the foggy night air to have a private discussion. P. stands in a defensive posture, left foot in front of right, as he watches the tattooed man yell and aggressively gesture. Across the street, the occasional curse manages to echo through the dense air and the queue's incessant chatter. As the two finish their exchange, the angry tattooed man looks over at a nearby duo of police constables who have also been observing his tirade intently. He shakes his head at them in disgust and disappears with his entourage into the foggy night.

When P. returns, he reports on his "conversation." The man was apparently a gang member, who "was expressing himself." In his anger, he had also made threats. According to P., the most significant was "Man, I'm so pissed I feel like coming back and spraying the place [with bullets]." Knowing the man's history, P. could only respond to him by saying, "Now, why would you come out and say something like that?" P. throws up his hands: "Why do I have to put up with this?" Exasperated, he marches back into the heart of the smoky nightclub and disappears into the gyrating crowd.

Worry, exasperation, and fear are part of the work environment of doormen. While occupational risk seemed to be reluctantly accepted by most bouncers as "coming with the job," there was far less acceptance of the possibility of revenge attacks while not at work. Although Halifax is a large enough city for a vibrant nightlife, it is small enough that most Haligonians are likely to run into someone familiar at some point in the week. Nightclub patrons tend to also attend other nightclubs, raves, and concerts, and frequent downtown shopping malls and restaurants. The fear of being threatened or attacked while away from work weighed on the minds of many doormen – especially those who had their own families.

In what after a certain time seemed to me like a rather innocuous ejection of a drunk patron from the Mansion for refusing to vacate the entranceway, an exasperated doorman turned to me, slapped his own thigh and protested: "For all the trouble in here, working for $12 an hour, it's just not worth it!" His reaction seemed disproportionate to the uneventful removal of the inebriated patron, so I surmised his complaints were probably cumulative. He asked rhetorically: "What if I'm walking with my eight-year-old son in the mall? What am I supposed to do if four of these guys that I deal with here decide they're going to even the score with me? I mean, what am I supposed to do then?" I realized that oftentimes workplace violence for doormen was not about the workplace per se –

where assistance from co-workers was readily available – but rather away from the nightclub where this collective protection was absent, potentially exposing family members to risk while off-duty.

These fears are likely warranted. One doorman related a story to me about an incident in which he was accosted at a nearby Subway sandwich shop while out one afternoon with his girlfriend. A man who had been banned from the nightclub where he worked approached him, demanding an explanation for his removal from the bar. The doorman said he asked the young man to return to the nightclub any night and take the issue up with management, but that he was currently off-duty. The man persisted, pushed the doorman, and tried to punch him. A scuffle ensued and both ended up on the floor in front of the counter. The man then brandished a knife and tried to stab the doorman, who wrestled it from him and punched him repeatedly in the face. When they separated, the attacker fled but was eventually tracked down by the doorman and a few of his friends. The man was arrested by police and is facing assault charges. The Subway employees had called the police and were to act as witnesses. As it turned out, the man who attacked the doorman and was later charged was also to begin working at the same sandwich shop the following week. His employment offer was rescinded.

Occupational risk can produce a state of constant anxiety that permeates the personality and choices of doorstaff. In some cases, doormen avoided public places with crowds or worried about being accosted:

I rarely go out in the malls, I rarely go to movies. I rarely do anything in public places. I've been cornered in malls by people I've thrown out, somebody I've thrown out and had barred for some reason. And you're shopping with your girlfriend at Christmastime at Mic Mac and all of a sudden you've got seven guys standing around you saying, "You barred me from such and such a place so we're going to beat the crap out of you." And you've gotta deal with it … You feel like going, "I didn't do it because I don't like you personally, it's not my fault you puked all over the bar and smashed somebody in the head with a beer bottle. You brought it on yourself." But they don't understand that.

I don't like crowds anymore either. Like, I just don't like them, 'cause I work with crowds. Like, a lot of people ask, "Are you gonna go to the concert?" "Uh, no frigging way!" If I don't have to be surrounded by a lot of people, I don't want to. This is my job, and I like my job – still, that doesn't mean I like hanging out in bars.

I always joke around and say, "You won't get me in a bar unless you pay me an hourly wage, and you won't!" … Somebody asked me to go to the mall with them one night, like, I cannot stand, and really I can't stand to be around that many people. It's aggravating. It's annoying. And I can't really pinpoint what it is. For some reason people seem to bump into me on purpose. And I know that's obviously not the case, but when I walk through the mall, I'll get bumped into by passersby. I'll question, like, "Can you not see me coming? I'm a fairly large person." Oh, I'm antisocial. I won't go out to parties. I won't go to a bar. I'll stay home (01: white male doorstaff)

I'm a little nervous, that I might run into someone that I've had to bar or throw out … Sunday night a couple of us went out for a while and we went to the [Beacon], and I just couldn't stay there. There were too many people that we've thrown out ourselves. I just didn't feel good about it. (02: white female doorstaff)

I can't go out, like, walk down Spring Garden, constantly see people who've I've thrown out of bars before. And I don't really, the only thing you can do is, they look at you, look back at them and sort of try and intimidate them so they don't try and mess with you … Like, they're down at Rainbow Haven beach, and I'm there with my girlfriends and this guy basically calls me on, tells me, you know, "We should go out in the ocean and see who comes back" kind of thing, right? It's like, "Whatever." Sort of brush it off and you're like, "Yeah, okay, whatever, buddy." Just hope they go away, for the most part. (19: white male doorstaff)

Once in a while you get the odd death threat. You know, I don't like those, but you get to learn not to take them too serious. I had a few guys turn around in vans, pointing their finger out the window at me and stuff. I wave at them and smile. That don't bother me any more. I guess, I get threats. I don't like that. (03: white male supervisor)

Nonetheless, doorstaff frequently venture out to public places regardless of the risk of being recognized: "If I'm out in public at the mall I'll be aware of my surroundings, 'cause I know, if I'm in Mic Mac Mall, I know there's some Dartmouth people who don't like me, maybe … And they mall-crawl too … but it never stopped me from going anywhere.

You know, I never said, 'Oooh, I can't go over there.' You know, I'll go out to Spryfield just as quick as I'll go to anywhere else, it don't matter to me" (03: white male supervisor).

The most palpable and immediate post-shift fear is of being followed home by an angry patron who has been ejected. One bouncer had been followed home. "I remember one night I had to drive around for, um, I lived in Bedford, I had to drive around for half an hour because I was followed home" (20: visible minority doorstaff). Another spoke of feeling unsafe: "A lot of people in Halifax don't know where I live. 'Cause I live on the other side of the Harbour, I have a dog, I'm not really worried about it. But yeah, sometimes I'll lock my door if someone threatened me, you know, 'I'll be back to get you,' you know, I might lock my door that night (18: white male doorstaff).

One of the telling signs of occupational risk to bouncers is the generally accepted practice of removing "security shirts" when going home after work in the early morning. This is clearly designed to discourage unwanted attention at a time when disgruntled and unfulfilled former patrons are still prowling the urban core. What is also interesting here is the complete shutdown of the nightclub as its own employees, indeed its uniformed co-producers, also vanish into the early dawn air. Violence is always more acute at closing time, and doormen more than others know this all too well. As one bouncer put it, "Anyone with a brain won't wear their staff shirt home" (13: white male doorstaff).

As for the staff, you know, basically they don't walk from the bar, when they're leaving after work, with their shirts on to a car that's parked far away. (06: white male supervisor)

There's one night I never covered up my shirt and almost got in a fight when I [was] leaving the building: "You fellow just beat up my brother, kicked out my brother last week" or something. Three or four guys trying to pick a fight with me. (07: white male doorstaff)

Every night somebody wants to fight, they get thrown, like, they go outside, guys get thrown out from inside, they don't care, they just see a security shirt. They go like, "I'm gonna kill you." (09: white male doorstaff)

Walking to and from my vehicle. I don't wear my shirt. I have a sweatshirt I put over, or I don't wear it at all. (03: white female Doorstaff)

I wouldn't walk around with you know, a jacket on. A guy this summer … had the shit scared out of him … people [are] stupid some times. It's just best not to be worn out. (11: white male doorstaff)

With every threat and potential attack, doormen who are contemplating careers in public law enforcement risk the possibility of getting charged with a criminal offence. This would not only jeopardize their employment with the nightclub but largely end their prospects of a career in public policing or corrections:

If you ever got charges laid against you, you'd be screwed. (04: white male doorstaff)

I guess my biggest fear is criminal charges. Whether they're bogus or not, that's the last thing I want … It affects any kind of chance getting a job, or anything like that, in law enforcement. (01: white male supervisor)

I'm like, I'm trying to join the police force. If I'm charged, I'm screwed. Like, they run my name through computer courses, and … my name came up seven times. But everything was being a witness. (09: white male doorstaff)

I've had charges laid against me about four or five times probably … I mean everyone always thinks they're in the right. I mean, if someone takes a swing at me, I go after them and throw them out, of course not unless they take a swing at me. It's my word against theirs. We do have a good reputation with the cops. (04: white male doorstaff)

Given their reduced powers compared to the police and their inability to acquire the best legal counsel, bouncers were concerned about potential lawsuits:

[There's] the lack of proper representation, when it comes to defending our rights, over the person. The doormen are very much underpaid. (05: white male doorstaff)

[It's hard] avoiding lawsuits, 'cause no matter what you do, somebody's going to have something in a particular bar allowed, sexual harassment, kicking a guy out where you had to be a little rough to him, you jumped him, you have to hold somebody till the cops get here, on occasion. (07: white male doorstaff)

I mean if we even touch someone, they'll cry, "Call a lawyer, I'm gonna do this, I'm gonna do that." But we all have been trained in the law as well, knowing what we can and cannot do. (02: white female doorstaff)

Doorstaff also become concerned when nightclubs appeared disorganized and unable to construct the "paper reality" necessary for an adequate legal defence: "I mean, here we don't really have incident reports. Other clubs I've worked, incident reports, everyone sits down and gets their story straight. I mean because, sure there's times I've worked, and I mean, I've gone too far, and I know other people have gone too far. And it's just a whole matter of being like stressed out, dealing with idiots, and then someone does something like stupid and you do something stupid, and then nobody wants to do, like, go to jail" (19: white male doorstaff). Indeed, the particular legal sanctions that threaten bouncers are such that they are discouraged from getting involved in any altercation above and beyond that needed and prescribed by their employment. Doormen self-police themselves so that they are not "left hanging" by nightclub management for engaging in security activities or violence off-property. As one doorman put it, "We aren't the police ... just get them out" (04: white male supervisor). Another describes how the boundary between legitimate and illegitimate intervention is reinforced by the police: "If I beat buddy's head off in the bar, yeah, there's not gonna [be repercussions], you know [they will] support me, and if I go outside off the step and start fighting with him, they're not gonna support me. But if I tell him to leave, he says no, and I drag him out – not, you know, do anything stupid, just force him out of the bar and don't throw him off the steps, but get him off the steps and leave him be – they'll support that" (09: white male doorstaff).

There is thus a general unease about doing anything more than removing patrons:

I have taught handcuffing as one of the courses. And my two supervisors were gonna carry them. But it's a legal aspect of it I don't like. Because once I put cuffs on you, I physically placed you under arrest so I am responsible for your well-being, and if I'm in the middle of things and I cuff you and I gotta go over there and somebody punches you, I'm responsible if they punched you. The whole Section 26 of the Criminal Code, right? And so I don't carry them. I might carry them in the new year, as an extra set, 'cause the police do run out once in a while. You know, if they got three guys to go and only two pairs of cuffs. Give them them and let them use them that way. But I would never, I would never want to use them. (03: white male supervisor)

Well, I don't call it an arrest. We hold the guy till the cops get there and they deal with it. You know, I'm not arresting anybody ... I have to get up early one day while I'm working the night before, so I can go to court and testify, "I seen this guy frigging rolling a joint." You know, what the hell is that? I mean that's not worth my time, his time, and God knows if he's a career student and he's gonna be a lawyer. (04: white male supervisor)

Concerns about bouncers' ability to use force, affect arrests, and remove patrons, and their susceptibility to lawsuits and criminal charges as a result of use of force are indeed salient issues that deserve closer scrutiny.

The Legal Status of Bouncers

The short answer to the question "Where do bouncers get the right to remove people?" is: common law. The core of a bouncer's powers lie with the common-law doctrine that an invitee becomes a trespasser when asked to leave private property. In fact, the Criminal Code also allows bouncers the right to use reasonable force necessary to remove from the premises a person who refuses to leave. In this section I outline the legal context of bouncing and case law concerning criminal sanctions and civil redress against doormen and nightclubs and finally overview doormen's source of power for using force.

One of the earliest and precedent-setting Canadian cases on the issue of use of force by doormen is the 1939 Brien[3] case. Brien set the precedent for removal from private property under the "trespass doctrine," and allowed for a degree of "reasonable force" to be used in these instances.[4] Bouncers are thus required to first ask the patron to peaceably leave the property before he or she becomes a trespasser. Salmond on Torts explains that "Even a person who has lawfully entered on land in the possession of another commits a trespass if he remains there after his right of entry has ceased," because "to refuse or omit to leave the plaintiff's land or vehicle is as much a trespass as to enter originally without right" (Salmond 1977, at 71, from *Cullen v. Rice*, [1981]).

In the context of a commercial enterprise, including tracts of mass private property like malls or nightclubs, the nature of the business is such that all persons are initially invitees, unless prohibited entry by staff. In instances where one is prohibited entry initially, the person is immediately a trespasser. The *Brien* decision has been held up and expounded in many subsequent decisions, including the *Franke*[5] decision of 2002. In this case, in circumstances similar to *Brien*, the bouncers directly told a patron "that he was trespassing and that he had to leave." The court supported this property doctrine that a patron, when asked to leave, becomes a trespasser.[6]

Of course, the question of how trespassers are to be treated has been subject to several court decisions, and almost invariably the test of "reasonableness" is utilized to ascertain the amount of force that can be used to eject a subject. Essentially, "No duty is owed to a trespasser other than to not injure him willfully or by reckless conduct."[7] The *Cullen* decision referred to two other decisions, CPR v. *Anderson*[8] and *Lathan v. Johnson*,[9] that reached essentially the same conclusion: only a "reasonable amount" of force could be justified in the protection of property;[10] murder, for example, could not be justified under this framework. The courts have specifically ruled that a "doorman or 'bouncer' in a tavern must ensure that order is kept within the establishment,"[11] indicating a judicial privileging of property rights over personal freedoms and rights of the patron who, usually up until a point of high intoxication or dangerous and unruly behaviour, has been an invitee of the nightclub.

This property law regime, in relation to ejection of "trespassers" from private businesses, has also been enshrined in Section 41 of the Criminal Code.[12] Section 41(1) is thus an explicit source of the power that the bouncers have in their toolbox. As an employee of the establishment, working "under the authority" of the property owner, bouncers have the right to use the same force that property owners hold. Recourse to Section 41 is thus more common for doorstaff because, unlike provincial trespass acts (Rigakos 2000), use of force does not depend on arrest for its legitimacy (as in the case of security guards in Ontario and recently reinforced by the Supreme Court in *Asante-Mensah*[13]). Unlike provincial trespass acts, section 41(2) of the Criminal Code is unique in declaring that any failure to comply with the removal order is an assault. Should any disturbance created by the removal or resistance of a patron come to a criminal or civil court in the future, that patron is by legal definition a trespasser who has assaulted the staff of the establishment. There is no requirement that nightclub staff show any justification for removal in the first instance. The law here, as elsewhere, is heavily biased in favour of the property owner.

Nonetheless, in *R. v. Swenson*, a Saskatchewan case where a bouncer was accused of going beyond a reasonable amount of force, the judge reinforced the notion of reasonableness, stating that bouncers "do not have an open licence to assault patrons."[14] Any force deemed reasonable must be applied in a fair and consistent manner, apart from external factors such as provocation of the bouncers by patrons. Doormen, as employees of the establishment, are expected to engage in professional decorum and not overreact based on personal feelings and emotion. Indeed, the question of whether or not a bouncer's actions were excessive is often the first question to be addressed. As early as *O'Tierney v. Concord Tavern*,[15] the burden of proof rests with the defendants to show that the bouncer's actions were not excessive. Thus, it is the responsibility of the bouncer, or the employer with respect to the bouncer's actions, to show that the force applied was reasonable and within the scope of the duties and responsibilities of maintaining order in an establishment. For the most part this is not problematic, so long as it can be demonstrated that the patron refused to leave the property and a certain amount of force was necessary for removal.[16] Generally speaking, the courts have scrutinized defence of property and defence of person (self-defence) in the same context for nightclub bouncers. Self-defence is a justification for violence based upon imminent bodily harm and the desire to protect oneself from such injuries.[17]

Today, Section 34(1) of the Criminal Code provides for a forceful statutory self-defence if one is unlawfully assaulted without having provoked the assault. The force used to defend oneself must be intended only to defend oneself and not be meant to cause death or grievous bodily harm.[18] Of course, the key word here is *intent*; whether or not the force applied actually causes death is not at issue. Section 34(2) also limits the justification of Section 34(1) by stating that the assault is justified if (a) it is caused under reasonable apprehension of death or grievous bodily harm, and (b) it is believed that there is no other way to prevent death or grievous bodily harm.[19]

Particularly salient to nightclub settings, the case of *R. v. Reilly*[20] has shown that Section 34(2) cannot take into consideration either the level of intoxication or whether or not one was intoxicated at all when using this defence. The definition of reasonably apprehending harm is determined using the objective mindset of one who is not intoxicated.[21] However, this does not mean that an intoxicated person cannot have a valid claim to using this defence. Section 37 further allows for a general defence of self-defence where one believes that one will be harmed. Unlike Sections 34 and 35, no reasonable apprehension of death or grievous bodily harm is necessary.[22]

In the *Thompson*[23] decision, self-defence is linked with the defence of property, where the judge ruled that justification based on defence of property was not established. There were no circumstances of self-defence or defence of another patron of the establishment; however, the bouncers were acting within their scope of employment, working towards a common goal and purpose: defending the club from a trespasser. The judge ruled that the injuries inflicted on Thompson could not be justified by defence of property as there were no elements of self-defence present in the case. Instead, the *Thompson* decision highlights the bouncer's power: when an invitee becomes a trespasser and refuses to leave the establishment, that person is considered to have assaulted the staff of the establishment. At this point, a rather fascinating legal redefinition takes place. The mere act of a patron refusing to leave switches the construction of the incident from a property issue to personal injury, even though no inherently violent or threatening act has transpired. The importance of the common-law notion of defence of property, now enshrined under Section 41(2) to define as assault resistance to reasonable force during removal, is the central enabling legal mechanism for the bouncer. Thus, the legal principles of self-defence, and not defence of property, are those that empower the doorstaff to use "reasonable" force to eject the trespasser from the establishment.

It is important to distinguish the powers of bouncers that are enshrined through the property-rights system and the defence of self-defence. In *R. v. Swenson*,[24] the judge reaffirmed that Section 41 gives bouncers the right to use reasonable force in the purpose of their employment. Despite the fact that the bouncer had gone beyond "reasonable" force, the force that was applied was not a random assault on an innocent person but within his scope of employment. The ruling cemented the notion that although Section 41 cannot be used as a defence to a crime, it does allow bouncers to use force in the first instance.

In a risk society, the fear of litigation against corporate entities is a driving force towards increased security measures (Priest 1990). Judicial decision-making has increasingly placed a burden on institutions to safeguard those persons who fall within their purview. More and more, nightclubs have been forced to prepare standard operating procedures and train their doorstaff on acceptable uses of force to protect themselves from vicarious liability. This issue is particularly relevant when it is not clear whether or not a bouncer is acting within his or her scope of employment when applying excessive force to a patron. In the case of *Cole v. California*,[25] the question was whether or not California Enterprises was vicariously liable for the acts of the bouncer, Wolf, who went well beyond reasonable force, inflicting severe injuries on Cole, the patron, who was suing for damages. California Entertainment strenuously denied that Wolf was acting within the parameters of his position and that the corporate defendant should not be held accountable for the rogue actions of an employee. In this instance, Wolf had left the property of the club before attacking Cole. The judge found that the physical location of the specific incident was inconsequential to the determination of whether or not Wolf was acting within the scope of his employment.[26]

It is little wonder that nightclub doormen, through whatever second-hand knowledge, have incorporated this judicial decision in lay terms to mean they should stay on the premises and not interfere in incidents that do not directly affect the establishment. In any case, the *Cole* decision effectively created a positive duty on the part of management to specifically instruct their employees on how to handle situations requiring force; otherwise the corporate defendants can be held civilly liable for the actions of bouncers where they believe they are acting within their capacity as doormen.

Similarly in the *Downey*[27] case, the failure of management to set strict guidelines and procedures detailing the proper use of force, in addition to a wilful blindness to past assaults committed by the doormen, opened the door to vicarious liability of the corporate defendant. In this case, again, a patron was suing the business for damages inflicted by the bouncer. The judge stated: "One of the bar managers had been aware of two of the four previous assaults and the owners were fixed with that knowledge."[28] The ownership and management of bars, clubs, taverns, and other establishments that employ bouncers thus have a court-created obligation to set clear guidelines and parameters that must be followed by their staff. Should such guidelines be exceeded, the corporate defendant would not be held liable for the actions of rogue employees who were clearly acting outside the course of their direct orders from their employer.

Canadian courts have increasingly professionalized nightclub security provision with the risk of susceptibility to civil litigation. Liability thus flows to the owners of these establishments because they would be considered negligent if they failed to set out proper procedures for doorstaff. In the *Downey* decision, the judge noted: "The numbered company and the two owners were personally negligent in: failing to properly train and supervise bouncers in the proper methods of dealing with patrons; and hiring bouncers whom they knew or ought to have known were violent and who would pose a threat of danger to patrons, without having properly checked their references or made inquiries as to their criminal background."[29]

Training in minimum corporate standards and policies is now prescribed to safeguard against lawsuits. Nightclub owners who hire doormen with criminal records and do not require criminal background checks are playing with fire. In *Renaissance Leisure Group*,[30] the judge stated that the corporation "took inadequate measures to provide for the safety of persons on its premises. At least two or more bouncers should have been present at the lounge."[31] This duty of due diligence is now enshrined as part of the risk of operating a nightclub.

Among the numerous court-imposed duties on businesses that employ bouncers is due diligence. This duty to protect patrons stems from the legislation of the occupiers' liability acts of the respective provinces, which outline that the person or business entity leasing a space has a duty to care for persons within that establishment.[32] Jurisprudence has been consistent in applying this duty. In *Pereira*, the judge determined that in the instance of a drawn-out bar fight, "the bar owner failed in the exercise of its duty ... to take such care as to see that persons who entered its premises were reasonably safe. The bouncer knew or ought to have known that the plaintiff was in danger and needed protection from any further conflict but instead of intervening urged the defendant on to continue the fight."[33] The court ruled that such outcomes were reasonably foreseeable and that it was the bar owner who had a legal duty to the plaintiff; as such, damages were not assessed against the bouncer but 75 per cent on the bar owner and 25 per cent on the plaintiff.[34] The precedent, however, was set that the employer must take responsibility for the safety of patrons when inside the premises.

This duty to care does not outweigh the reasonable level of force that may be used to eject a trespasser. Even where injuries have been inflicted on a patron, the courts have not always followed through with judgments in favour of the plaintiff. Excessive force considerations should not be confused with those imposed on police, because the damage award under duties requires a breach of the obligation of the occupier. When, for example, a bar fight occurs and the bouncers do little or nothing to attempt to decrease tensions in the first instance and to stop the fight once it begins, the nightclub will be held at least partially liable for ensuing injuries. The breach of duty under the Occupiers' Liability Act was most clearly illustrated in *Dombowsky v. Argyll*, where events transpired over a long period of time and clearly the bar staff had ample opportunity to prevent the incident from escalating beyond a trivial altercation.[35] These judgments, when taken together, place an onus on nightclubs to ensure the safety of their patrons and intervene in a reasonable amount of time to prevent injuries from occurring. In this regard, bouncers have been given latitude to use reasonable force pursuant to defence of property and person to fulfill this role. In order for a nightclub to be successfully sued for the conduct of its bouncers, it must also be established that the conduct was "closely connected" to the business.

In the case of *Sweet*,[36] it was ruled that the bouncer was hired "to physically dominate its customers" and as such found the tavern owner responsible for damages because the bouncer was acting within the scope of his employment. The *Evaniuk*[37] case clarified this test, so that the links between bouncers and management have to be authorized either directly or vis-à-vis failures to act on the part of the employer. Thus, it is the employer who is held accountable due to actions authorized. When bouncers fail to act when they should have reasonably foreseen harm to a third party, they may also be held liable.

Foreseeability, duties, and due diligence are deeply overlapping in judicial decision making in cases concerning nightclub liability. In *Pupus*,[38] there was a primary forseeability gap when the bouncers failed to intervene in a situation that would most likely become violent or dangerous. The attacker in this case wore and displayed brass knuckles. The doormen failed to intervene and had ample opportunity to stop the attack.

Due diligence in the nightclub setting is perhaps best demonstrated in the precedent-setting *Tonic*[39] decision. The case concerned whether the holder of a liquor licence was duly diligent in preventing disorderly conduct from occurring on its premises. The license holder was charged with permitting disorderly conduct but argued that despite the fact that its employees assaulted a patron on its premises, it did everything possible to prevent such occurrences from happening. Thus, for the judge, "If the corporate defendant can prove that it had had a proper system or plan in place that would have reasonably prevented any offences under the Liquor License Act, R.S.O. 1990, c. L. 19 or its related regulations from occurring, and that it had taken all reasonable steps to ensure the effective operation of that system, then the defence of due diligence would be made out."[40]

In this case the court clearly articulated the necessary threshold for due diligence to be achieved by nightclub owner. This included the requirement to train staff so that they would be able to handle dangerous situations: "Specifically, for the category of licensed drinking establishments, the defendant would be required to prove as part of its reasonable care defence, that it had properly trained and instructed its employees to reasonably deal with patrons, to avoid or not engage in disorderly conduct themselves, and that there were supervisors present at all times."[41]

The court raised several other questions: "Was there a proper system or plan set up by the defendant in preventing disorderly conduct from happening on its licensed premises?[42] Did the corporate defendant take reasonable steps to ensure the system or plan, if any, was effective in ensuring that disorderly conduct did not occur on its licensed premises?"[43] (See also *R. v. Sault Ste. Marie*.[44]) The defence of due diligence means that information, procedures, and policies need to be disseminated throughout the organization and employed in the everyday operations of the business. The defence requires "adequate information and instructions from the company right down to the man on the job."[45]

The nightclub as a risk market is saturated with the potential for violence. Training, surveillance systems, modes of deployment, and even background screening and vigilant access are circumscribed by the threat of litigation. The nightclub and the bouncer must exercise due diligence and foresee the potential for violence. Force must be applied in a reasonable manner. The nightclub appears at first as a chaotic, nocturnal, private space, slipping the bonds of the reluctant nine-to-five state. In its regulation (Joh 2004; O'Connor et al. 2004), however, the state has been historically insistent, and today the nightclub continues to be scrutinized juridically.

4

Bouncer Culture

Since the 1970s and the seminal work of police researchers such as Skolnick (1966), Westley (1970), and Manning (1997; Manning and Van Maanen 1978), the occupational culture of police officers has been a widely recognized determinant of police discretion and mobilization. With a few exceptions (Chan 1996) the 1990s saw not only a decline in empirical scholarship on police culture but also its theoretical marginalization in deference to institutional examinations focusing on organizational planning, policy, and management (e.g., Dandeker 1990; Ericson and Haggerty 1997). Scholarly analyses of private-policing occupational culture has been spotty (Button 2003; Micucci 1994; Rigakos 2002b; Wakefield 2006), but increasing academic attention has now focused on this emergent area, especially given the private sector's rapid expansion and increased likelihood of tackling tough "law-enforcement" priorities (Rigakos 2002b). While subcultural analyses of private policing have been rare, bouncers have received almost no attention. Hobbs et al. (2003) have produced the only comprehensive study of doorstaff culture in their multisite British examination but make no direct comparisons between bouncers and police officers.

This chapter examines bouncer culture both quantitatively, by way of direct comparisons to RCMP and Halifax police personality traits, and qualitatively, through interviews and an ethnography of doormen in action. Thus, while it begins largely as a comparative analysis, bouncer culture is the object of study and receives its own analytic treatment. The second section considers the roles of masculinity and violence, paranoia and risky situations, and the toll that bouncing takes on doorstaff's everyday life. A sense of social isolation runs parallel with the social inclusion produced by being at the centre of the nighttime leisure economy. The next section analyzes how doormen form bonds of solidarity with co-workers and develop reciprocal privileges and camaraderie with bouncers from other nightclubs. These connections are importantly conditioned by a sense that they share the common experience of dealing with "drunkards," "ruffians," "idiots," and "assholes" – the subject of the final section of this chapter and a convenient analytic and substantive reconnection with the public police, who, of course, share a similar cultural more.

Police vs. Bouncer Culture

Up to this point in this book there has been limited discussion of personality scales used as comparison measures for doorstaff and police officers. The general discussion in this chapter focuses on bouncer culture, comparing many of its central attributes to aspects of the occupational culture of public and private policing. This particular section also makes specific use of comparative standardized measures that allow for quantitative comparisons between police and bouncers.

The Interpersonal Conflict at Work Scale (or ICWS) measures interpersonal conflict in the workplace, which has been shown to be one of the most frequently reported job stressors (Newton and Keenan 1985). The ICWS is a four-item summated rating scale designed to assess the prevalence of workplace conflict. Items query how well the respondent gets along with others at work, including getting into arguments with others, and how often others act spitefully toward the respondent. In this chapter, we are particularly concerned with interpersonal conflict *amongst* bouncers and police officers rather than with third parties such as patrons and citizens. Five response choices are given, ranging from less than one incident per month or never, coded 1, to several times per day, coded 5. High scores represent frequent conflicts with others, with a possible range from 4 to 20.[1] The Job-Related Affective Well-Being Scale or JAWS (Van Katwyk et al. 2000) is a thirty-item scale designed to assess employees' emotional reactions to their job. Each item reflects an emotion, and respondents are asked how often they have experienced it at work over the past thirty days. Responses are made with a five-point scale with anchors: never, rarely, sometimes, quite often, extremely often, or always. JAWS includes a wide variety of emotional experiences, both negative and positive. The emotions can be placed into four categories (sub-scales) that fall along two dimensions: pleasurableness and arousal (intensity). The scale can be scored in three ways: 1) an overall score of all thirty items with the negative emotions reverse scored; 2) separate scores of all fifteen negative items and all fifteen positive items combined separately without reverse scoring; and 3) four scores matching the above four categories containing five items each. In this study we used the first scoring method.

The Job Satisfaction Survey or JSS (e.g., Spector 1985) is a thirty-six item, nine facet scale to assess employee attitudes about the job and aspects of the job. Each facet is assessed with four items, and a total score is computed from all items. A summated rating scale format is used, with six choices per item ranging from "strongly disagree" to "strongly agree." Items are written in both directions, so about half must be reverse scored. The nine facets are: pay, promotion, supervision, fringe benefits, contingent rewards (performance-based rewards), operating procedures (required rules and procedures), co-workers, nature of work, and communication. Although the JSS was originally developed for use in human service organizations, it is ostensibly applicable to all organizations.

The Work Locus of Control Scale (WLCS) is a sixteen-item instrument designed to assess control beliefs in the workplace.[2] The format is a summated rating with six response choices: disagree very much, disagree moderately, disagree slightly, agree slightly, agree moderately, agree very much. These choices are scored from 1 to 6, respectively. The total score is the sum of all items and ranges from 16 to 96. The scale is scored so that externals receive high scores. The infamous Right Wing Authoritarianism scale (RWA) was developed by Altemeyer (1988) to measure the three reliable facets of authoritarianism: 1) conventionalism (i.e., rigid conformity to group norms); 2) submission to higher status individuals; and 3) aggression towards out-groups and unconventional group members. Research indicates that the emergence of an authoritarian personality appears to be unrelated to intellectual ability or socioeconomic status (Altmeyer 1996). Originally identified by Lerner (1980) as the "just world hypothesis," the tenet asserts that "individuals have a need to believe that they live in a world where people generally get what they deserve and deserve what they get" (Lerner and Miller 1978, 1030). The just world theory has implications in how it may help people maintain the belief that their world is stable and orderly. Measuring belief in a just world was originally operationalized by Rubin and Peplau (1975). The scale measures an individual's belief in a just world in all domains of life (e.g., for both the self and for others).[3]

Finally, while *alienation* has a specific meaning for Marxian analysts relating to both the production process and its effect on labour's relationship to and mystification of commodities (see Mandel and Novack 1970), the alienation scale included herein is produced by Perrott (1991) and specifically relates to the measurement of in-group and out-group solidarity in the original context of police constables. Questions relating to police were simply reworded and recontextualized for doorstaff. For example, items included: "Sometimes I feel like it's we (cops/bouncers) against the rest of the world" or "The only person that can really understand a (police officer/doorman) is another (police officer/doorman)."

Table 4.1 illustrates that six of seven workplace and personality measures were statistically significantly different for police officers and doorstaff. These differences persisted when controlling for urban or rural deployment, age, or respective policing organization (i.e., RCMP versus Halifax Regional).[4] Comparison of mean scores on the instruments highlights interesting discrepancies between police officer and doorstaff occupational personality traits. Halifax-area police officers were statistically significantly more likely to report a higher degree of job autonomy (t= 2.25, df= 239, p<.05) and job satisfaction (t= 4.49, df= 235, p<.001). This may be largely explained through the statutory and common-law discretion bestowed upon the office of peace officer. Of course, no such standing is afforded bouncers who, as we shall see, are under scrutiny not only by internal policy directives, managerial oversight, and surveillance practices but also by the very police officers to whom they are being compared. Table 4.1 shows that police officers were statistically significantly less likely to report feeling alienated (t= -3.17, df= 236, p<.01) than bouncers. Thus, in-group insularity and an "us versus them" mentality were statistically significantly stronger among doormen. This is perhaps the most salient and telling finding in our comparison, because it indicates a much more powerful (quantitative) empirical basis for asserting that bouncer culture may be more marked and entrenched than police culture – the latter having received considerable scholarly and popular consideration for its dramaturgic, symbolic significance, and the former only now garnering attention from sociologists and documentarians. Thus, by virtue of our convenient empirical fixity on what is otherwise a fluid social form, there is increased cogency to the general argument that bouncer culture is an important aspect of understanding the policing of the nightclub and, by extension, the urban nighttime economy – a core assertion of this book.

Somewhat surprisingly, police officers were also statistically significantly more likely than doorstaff to harbour right-wing authoritarian values (t= 2.07, df= 234, p< .05). Popular depictions of the bouncer as unintelligent, prone to violence, and seeing the world through binaries of black and white, right or wrong, would suggest a general proclivity toward right-wing authoritarian values.

Table 4.1: Comparison of means (t-test) between all police officers and doorstaff on measures of personality, affect, and job satisfaction (reporting only significant differences)

	n	Mean	SD	df	t
JOB AUTONOMY					
Police	189	5.1	1.3	239	2.25*
Doorstaff	52	4.6	1.5		
RIGHT WING QUTHORITARIANISM					
Police	186	47.1	10.2	234	2.07*
Doorstaff	50	43.7	10.2		
BELIEF IN JUST WORLD					
Police	189	25.9	5.5	237	-2.06*
Doorstaff	50	27.7	6.0		
ALIENATION					
Police	188	4.1	1.1	236	-3.17**
Doorstaff	50	4.6	1.1		
JOB SATISFACTION					
Police	186	37.4	9.3	235	4.49***
Doorstaff	51	31.2	8.6		
INTERPERSONAL CONFLICT					
Police	189	7.3	2.02	239	-2.77***
Doorstaff	52	8.7	3.5		

***$p<.001$ (Equal variances not assumed, Levene's test for equality of variances significant)
**$p<.01$
*$p<.05$

Of course, on the other hand, the nightclub is ostensibly a transgressional space, and morality in that milieu tends to be more liberal, valuing openness and new experiences. In some cases, bouncers themselves were involved in illicit activities by dealing drugs or providing protection for dealers. Moreover, doormen were more closely linked to a university and youth party culture in which a right-wing authoritarian value system is often anathema. Police officers were also statistically significantly less likely to believe in a just world ($t= -2.06$, $df= 237$, $p< .05$) which, despite empirical evidence in support of a more entrenched bouncer culture, reinforces the observation that police officers' worldview becomes increasingly darkened by bearing witness to the human costs of victimization

Table 4.2: Correlations between measures of violence and personality, affect, and job satisfaction for doorstaff (reporting only significant differences)

	Work locus of control	Job affective well-being	Alienation	Interpersonal conflict at work
Physical violence				
r	.299* [.36]*	-.296*	.501*** [.40]**	.327*
n	51 [42]	51	50 [42]	51
Non-physical violence				
r		-.296* [-.34]*	.427** [.37]**	
n		51 [42]	50 [42]	
Overall violence				
r		-.320* [-.33]*	.509*** [.43]**	.291*
n		51 [42]	50 [42]	51

***p<.001
**p<.01
*p<.05
Pearson r
[n=controlling for months of service]

and crime (Crank 1998). Bouncers may see deviance and its occasional effects but perhaps not nearly the extent and gamut as do city police officers. Finally, bouncers on average experience statistically significantly more interpersonal conflict at work than police officers (t= -2.77, df= 239, p <.001), which suggests that the physical and non-physical violence they endure from patrons is generalizable to the work environment among fellow doormen to a much greater extent than among police officers. This is an important finding we return to later in this section.

For the moment, the relative effect of these personality traits on the experiences of physical, non-physical, and overall violence for bouncers is what interests us most. A subsequent analysis of the co-linearity of these attributes to experience of violence (see table 4.2) reveals that work locus of control (r= .29, n=51, p< .05) and interpersonal conflict at work (r= .327, n= 51, p <.05) are statistically significantly correlated to physical violence and overall violence (r= .291, n=51, p< .05), while job affective well-being is statistically significantly inversely correlated to physical violence (r= -.296, n=51, p< .05) and overall violence (r= -.320, n= 51, p< .05). Alienation was statistically significantly positively correlated to physical violence (r= .50, n= 50, p< .001), non-physical violence (r= .427, n= 50, p< .01), and overall violence (r= .509, n= 50, p< .001). Thus, the findings indicate that a sense of alienation, the trait we have most strongly associated with subcultural formation, is not only stronger among Halifax doormen than among police officers but, most significantly, is positively correlated to experiences of workplace violence compared to all other measures.

I controlled for the affect of experience for all four of these correlated measures to workplace violence.[5] One might surmise that doorstaff with more workplace experience would have more experiences with workplace violence, especially if they had been working for over twelve months (the study frame for this retrospective survey), or, relatedly, that newer doorstaff had not yet internalized feelings of alienation. The statistically significant positive correlations between alienation and physical violence (r= .40, n=42, p< .01), non-physical violence (r= .37, n= 42, p< .01) and overall workplace violence (r= .43, n= 42, p< .01) nonetheless persisted when controlling for work experience, providing further evidence that bouncer culture was relatively universal and consistent. Feelings of insularism, misunderstanding by others, and relative dependence on fellow bouncers (what makes up a higher score of alienation) alone are thus empirically linked to violence.

It is important to remember here that workplace violence is violence *experienced* and not *committed* by respondents. I do not believe, however, based on observational and interview data, that it would be any stretch at all to suggest that bouncers reciprocate violence with violence. Indeed, a cliché all too familiar and well worn by police sociologists and TV police drama writers is that a violent act against one cop is a harm against all others that cannot go unpunished. So too, it would seem, with doormen.

I have not attempted thus far to explain the meaning of the other correlations (see also table 4.2) as, unlike alienation, they are weaker and disappear when controlling for workplace experience. Generally speaking, however, it should not be particularly surprising that interpersonal conflict at work would be positively correlated to violence. The longer the length of a bouncer's employment, the more opportunity to experience conflict both from patrons and fellow employees in the thirty days prior to the survey. Longer lengths of service means increased knowledge of and connections with fellow doorstaff, which may allow for routinized interpersonal conflict. Job affective well-being would expectedly be inversely correlated as a co-indicator of workplace violence. A cynic might be apt to argue that we might also assume the worst in our subjects and expect positive job affective well-being to be associated with violence. This notion would purport that bouncers are violence-prone thrill-seekers far more happy when "mixing it up"; fortunately, the data seems to contradict this unflattering presumption. Curiously, work locus of control is positively correlated to physical violence (albeit weakly), hinting that if there is a reciprocal exchange of violence between doorman and attacker, violence is a form of regaining control.

In any case, this section cannot conclude without my re-emphasizing that doorstaff alienation is rampant and that this condition is empirically linked to workplace violence. As a measure highly suggestive of occupational culture, alienation is a pervasive trait among bouncers, providing a quantitative barometer of the pervasiveness and entrenchment of in-group solidarity, insularism, mistrust of outsiders, and a general sense of being misunderstood. This sense of alienation and in-group solidarity and the link to violence statistically supports the qualitative and theoretical work at the base of police (Manning and Van Maanen 1978; Skolnick and Fyfe 1993) and private police (Button 2007; Rigakos 2002b) culture. Such feelings of a "siege mentality" (Reiner 1992) are given strength by the consistent physical reminder of *danger* and *authority* which together "combine to produce ... a distinctive world view that affects the values and understandings of cops on and off the job" (Skolnick and Fyfe 1993, 90).

To be sure, private policing organizations and bouncers simply do not have the same confluence of interests that could ever lead to identical cultural attributes (Button 2003). Their milieux, level of authority, potential use of force, and weaponry differ in important ways. These differences are born out of the structure of the work performed. By the same logic, many other jobs have associated cultures that are born out of the circulation of situationally applied rules. For police cultural theorists, these "recipe rules" (Ericson 1982), "accepted practices" (Manning and Van Maanen 1978), or "habitus" of existing probabilities (Chan 1996) shape the worldview of officers. It is thus important that we are careful not to overstate the generalizability and causal power of occupational culture. Skolnick and Fyfe (1993, 92), for example, have argued that "the fundamental culture of policing is everywhere similar ... since everywhere the same features of the police role – danger, authority, and the mandate to use coercive force – are everywhere present." Most police culture theorists have been more careful, offering examples of a multiplicity of cultures based on rank structure, race, and tenure, and even questioning the very idea of "police culture" wherever it leads towards a monolithic codification of practices (Chan 1996; Chan 1997; Manning 1997; Manning and Van Maanen 1978; Shearing and Ericson 1991). Interestingly enough, the lack of a meaningful doorstaff managerial group creates conditions under which bouncer culture may not only be more (statistically) powerful than police culture but perhaps more generalizable across the workforce.

Doorstaff experience status frustration and reaction formation like other police and parapolice (Rigakos 2002b) organizations. While bouncing can be fun and interesting, the nightclub is awash in potential risks. Bouncers work in teams, they spend hours standing about talking to one another, and when they finish work, they tend to hang out together too. Their night-shift schedules, their fear of being swarmed while off duty, their heavy reliance on co-workers for protection, their tendency to eye people with suspicion, and their desire to avoid situations that might lead to public affronts about their jobs conspire to create conditions in which being a successful bouncer includes immersion within a sea of narratives that together constitute an occupational culture. They quite literally have their backs up against a wall. This strong solidarity and its attendant feelings of perceived public misunderstanding foster a siege mentality that, as in the case of police culture, produces hostility towards persons who challenge or criticize doorstaff authority.

The specific mechanics of bouncer culture I describe in this chapter are presented in six thematic parts: (1) making doormen; (2) getting paid to party; (3) masculinity and violence; (4) experience, trust, and safety in numbers; (5) solidarity and "door wars"; and finally (6) "meatheads" and "assholes." To penetrate this culture in a substantial way, however, requires immersion within the bouncers' habitus: the nightclub milieu. The remainder of this chapter seeks to understand bouncer culture through critical ethnography and interviews.

Making Doormen

A key aspect of forming subcultural identity for an organization or occupational group is its recruitment and indoctrination of candidates. While recruiting varies from nightclub to nightclub, and training varies from negligible to cursory to regularly scheduled exercises, trust and pugilistic potential remain at the centre of bouncer inclusion. If doorstaff do not trust that a new or potential bouncer is capable of using violence when needed without cowering in the face of potential harm and intimidation, the candidate simply will not be hired or last long on the job.

You don't select them, most of the times, for their brains. You know, you're looking people that, you want people to be intimidating.

You want them to be friendly, of course. But they look at people, and say to them, "They're not gonna mess with him," or "Not in this bar." (04: white male doorstaff)

If you're over six feet and over two hundred pounds, you can get a job bouncing and, you know, some places demand you have experience and stuff like that, but the majority, if you walk in, you're a big, tall, intimidating looking guy, they'll hire you. And you don't find out until too late that the guy's an idiot. That he loses it with everybody who walks through the door and calls him a name and, uh, you gotta have tough skin to do this job. (01: white male doorstaff)

At the Beacon a supervisor informed me that his doorstaff must take a five-day self-defence course; the majority enrol in his own program. The only training he would not accept utilizes pressure points, which he believes are "not that useful" and "just piss people off." Unlike other nightclubs, the Beacon's management does not rotate doorstaff between stations but leaves them in the same place throughout the night, "according to their strengths."

Well after closing time at the Beacon that evening, I was taken aback when, as soon as the last of the stragglers had been removed from the nightclub, the doormen began to roll out wrestling mats for an after-work martial arts training seminar. I could not believe these doormen had enough energy for martial arts training at 3 A.M. Wilting with exhaustion, I excused myself. The next day, we were eagerly introduced to a Croatian war veteran whose training and experience came from the military. His ability to acquit himself well in violent confrontations and his reputation for "having seen it all" made him respected as a top doorman at the club. He had previously worked in European nightclubs where he says it was not uncommon for doormen to be armed. His security supervisor informed me that this employee was so accustomed to violence that he had been thrown out of two Halifax dojos. Indeed, his reputation was supported by incidents in which he "cleaned up" against notorious Halifax gang members. Military experience is rare among doormen, but another doorstaff member told me he was a retired member of the U.S. Marines, claiming that many of the tactics and ways that he "does things" come from the work he did in the military.

Each nightclub, of course, can differ considerably in its relative attention to the training of doormen, their initial screening, and the degree to which they are subsequently managed. These factors weigh considerably on security managers when deciding on hiring doormen wishing to transfer from another nightclub. Hiring discretion is heavily influenced by the reputation of bouncers at competing nightclubs:

> I know the mentality of the bar itself. And I know if they worked there for a long time. Now I can't say I definitely 100 per cent won't hire you out of that bar, but the general rule, I wouldn't hire somebody from blank blank, because I know how they are. They've been there a couple years, and they run the show down there, I pretty much know what they're all about. (03: white male supervisor)

> The guys here are older, for the most part more mature. In better shape. And at the other place I worked, there was a really high turnover, so no one really got to know anyone else. And there was no rapport so therefore there was no team effort type of thing, it was an individual thing. And I find that the [Beacon], it's a totally different crowd. Younger crowd, more rough. So I just didn't really feel safe. Very aggressive, way more aggressive. (02: white female doorstaff)

Nightclubs vary wildly in checking the background of potential bouncers, even though the threat of a civil action is always possible where there is a lack of diligence in this regard (see chapter 3):

> We do background checks before we hire people here, and call references, make sure they're bondable, that type of thing. (06: white male supervisor)

> Everybody's made mistakes, you know what I mean. Maybe for violent oriented stuff, but you know what I mean, as long as it's nothing that would conflict with being a bouncer. My own opinion of course is some people make mistakes in life and it shouldn't be held against them. (05: white male supervisor)

Once on the job, there was no standardized training regimen for doormen in Halifax. In certain cases doormen were just told to get to it:

> They were just kind of like, "Here's the rules, don't beat anybody up, uh, good luck." (06: white male doorstaff)

> No. No we don't have to do no training or nothing. (08: white male doorstaff)

They just said "Go [out there]. Pretty much it. It's pretty much about it. Like they just kind of said, "Just don't kill anybody. Take another guy with you. Use your radio." You know, "Don't be a hero. Don't try to hurt anybody." The job's ... "don't drink on the job." Things like that. We had a "non-violent crisis intervention" thing upstairs for all the doormen, busboys, waiters, management. (09: white male doorstaff)

Doormen are expected to have already acquired fighting and restraining skills before their employment at Halifax nightclubs:

My training to them is sort of hands on. I point out what their responsibilities are and give them response, like they're responsible for their own actions. I'm not going to sit there and babysit them. (05: white male supervisor)

I was at [Nightclub 4] and I was there I think about a year, year and a half. Um, they did have us do a doorman course. A doorman's self-defence course. Which lasted for, it was like a Sunday afternoon. We went in and one guy, one guy was brought in and he showed us some things we could do. But, as far as the training goes, we were pretty much on our own type of thing. You kind of, a lot of guys, most guys, come off the street into these jobs not having any previous experience. (05: white male doorstaff)

Even doormen who have undergone training by nightclubs almost invariably have their own martial arts or boxing background:

I think I have a great deal of training, because I've been in the industry for eight years and I've done three or four different security jobs on top of that, so I've taken courses since I was a teenager ... The entire doorman staff here took, it was ten classes, ten weeks long, and we learned all kinds of things ... instructed by Independent Armed Transport ... I thought it was really good 'cause all the newer guys were bouncing for a year less. I didn't have this opportunity when I was bouncing for a year less and I learned all that stuff the hard way. When the new guys start, I'll say, "Do this and do this but don't this," and they'll go, "Well, why not?" And I'll say, "Well, I know because this can happen and it has." But I think that was probably the best thing I've ever seen that the management ordered ... a training course. It's good to learn all that stuff, but it's one thing for me to fake a punch at your head and you know how to block it, take it down, and stay calm – but somebody you don't know now turns around and smacks you in the face, are you going to freak out and lose it and start beating the crap out of them? You can't do that. You have to have some self-control, and that's one of my big things. (01: white male doorstaff)

For one doorman, recruitment was a matter of convenience and training non-existent: "I actually started as a bus boy, and the way it works at [Nightclub 4], they kind of take anyone, if they need a spot filled, they'll take ya. So I was working one night, and they were short a doorman, so they asked me to do it. And it just went from there" (05: white male doorstaff). Not all nightclubs have standard operating procedures or manuals: "This job was different. I actually, we have a manual, which, uh, it's pretty thick." (11: white male doorstaff). In other clubs, the manual *was* the initial training program: "A lot of guys here have some sort of martial arts training, some stuff like that. Me, I basically [have] Strong Man competition, second or third a couple of times" (07: white male doorstaff).

An impediment to the development of a generalized level of training and a constant source of unease among veteran bouncers is the high level of turnover among junior doormen, largely resulting from seasonal fluctuations in the university student population. Varsity team members from Saint Mary's University or Dalhousie are common among rank-and-file bouncers.

We have probably, out of [x] guys on staff, might have ten that are, have been here for, you know, an extensive period of time, a year plus? Most the other guys turn over pretty quickly. Students here for eight months, then they go home for the summer. Vice versa, students come home for the summer, work here for just the summer, for four months. But there's probably around ten or twelve guys that are here, full time students, that work, live in Halifax, for the duration of their university studies will work four years maybe. (01: white male supervisor)

Working Saint Mary's, or going to school at Saint Mary's, I was in athletics, and for my schedule I preferred it to be the best time to work here. I started back in 1993 and it was just a part-time schedule, it was just part time work time. (20: white male doorstaff)

Of course, not unlike with private security (Rigakos 2002b, 126–34), there are many doormen who are interested in careers in law enforcement. I often had longer discussions with respondents who, after learning I was a criminologist, wanted to discuss options for career advancement in policing. In many cases they viewed bouncing as a stepping-stone towards a career in public law enforcement or corrections. Often these discussions would centre around the criminology program offered at Saint Mary's University:

> I want be in the police. That's where I want to use my life.
> (09: white male doorstaff)

> My older brother's a police officer. He's been one for three years. I had a chance to go to RCMP depot in Regina, ah, witness some of the things there, which kind of impressed a lot. (01: white male supervisor)

> I wanted to be an RCMP officer. I like the idea, you know, the possibility of helping people. The possibility of, or the opportunity to, to stop criminals. (11: white male doorstaff)

> I did building security, which sucked, minimum wage, it's like one of them rent-a-cop looking guys. And then I worked for these guys. I had handcuffs and the whole nine yards. I looked like a cop. People used to think I was a cop sometimes. And then, and now I got this. That's what helped me get this job … [My career choices are] first, fire department, second, bodyguard. (13: white male doorstaff)

> I was trying to get in the correctional centre. I just went in on the list, so that's originally why I did it and I thought it'd be good for some background experience … I'm the next one in for the correctional centre. I can't wait. Working here may help me with the first few years, being just a guard. I've run into a few inmates, I did a placement there, and I've run into a few inmates here, and I haven't had a problem. (02: white female doorstaff)

Doorstaff interested in careers in law enforcement are especially concerned about the risk of litigation and are seen as more attractive candidates by security supervisors who are looking for good communicators who do not take excessive risks:

> I go through resumés. I'll go through the resumé and I'll see what kind of qualifications they have, like if they have a c.p.r. course,

that's a plus. Their age is a plus. I find the younger students, the younger kids, a little more high strung, more out to prove themselves. I don't need that here. I don't want the, as I call it, the cowboy attitude. I want the, you know, I like guys twenty-four, twenty-five years old. I'm not looking for big muscular body-building type guys. I hire a guy for good talking ability, good mind. If he got some martial arts background, that's always a help 'cause he's less apt to hurt a person if he has to get forceful. 'Cause if he's just a brute, and you take somebody to the ground, that you have to, you're, you're not trained. A trained person is always better, better control, mind control, too. And I'll look over the resumé and if I see they've got some good qualifications, I got a lot of guys that are, have the prison course, the prison-guard course. (03: white male doorstaff)

The following account is a typical example of many Halifax doormen, where varsity sports is intermingled with correctional training, night life, and a stint as a bouncer:

I worked with the sheriff's department for two years, before I came here. I was with the Department of Corrections, under the solicitor general, so I got all my training through them. And I also kick-boxed for three years before that. But I had to get out of that 'cause I got a bad eye, from getting hit in the face too much. So … I had to get out of kick-boxing; And then, when I was home, after I left, I went to school for a year at Bishop's. Played football. And then after I finished that season, I came home at Christmas and I started working with the sheriff's department and trained with them for two years. So I got all my correctional training through them. (14: visible minority male doorstaff)

Some doorstaff had other occupations beside nightclub bouncing and were using the additional pay from weekend and night-shift work that nightclub security provides as a stopgap measure until other career or business opportunities developed. One doorman had been a drug counsellor with drug dependence services in a high school: "So I'm just basically waiting to see what's going to transpire over there to get back over there, right? In the [meantime I also do] restoration work. And this is proxy maintenance, right? It consists of drywall, painting, roofing, building up that hope, you know, just, ah, maintenance" (16: white male doorstaff).

In two of the nightclubs we examined, security supervisors also selected from their employee rosters members for their martial-arts businesses, which they ran alongside their nightclub jobs. They used their position as supervisors to enlist students and were, in effect, their direct workplace supervisors and dojo masters. This sometimes peculiar relationship produced a fierce tribal loyalty not otherwise to be expected in a manager-employee relations:

> The head doorman here, [P.], he teaches jiu jitsu and we can go take his classes if we want. And do, what jiu jitsu basically is, like, it's like holds, arm locks, shoulder locks, ankle locks, things that'll help you basically restrain somebody, without having to use more force than necessary. 'Cause once they're in one of those holds, you can feel it, that if you're gonna keep fighting, your arm's gonna get broken. Or your shoulder's gonna get broken. So it's just a lot of holds like that, that you can put somebody in that'll cause them to stop struggling. So that's basically the only training that they offered here, I think. Through that, through the jiu jitsu. (14: visible minority doorstaff) '

> I train a lot of them in martial arts, outside of work. And I knew a lot of them before I started working here so we, I get along quite well with them. (06: white male supervisor)

As might be imagined, the lack of standardized practices for recruiting, the high rate of turnover, the need to create solidarity and trust among doormen, and a tendency towards fierce fraternal allegiances has, as one bouncer aptly put it, created a "clan"-based system of recruitment:

> You know a lot of these positions are given as clans. In buddies and that type of thing so. Where the interview process [...is] not all that stringent. Where you come in, you may be a friend of mine, and I say, "Yeah, he's a good guy." You may be a good guy but you may have a bad temper. I mean there's probably guys that I know when I played football with, and he asked me, "I need a summer job," or whatever, "give me a reference." And I'm like, "No. I'm not giving you a reference 'cause I know what kind of guy you are on a football field. I mean you get in a bar and people are spitting in your face, I know the first thing you'll do is you'll punch somebody in the chops. And I'm not going make a referral and it's gonna look bad on me, and they say, 'What're you doing, bringing this kind of guy in here?'" So, like I said, the interview process I think, for most of these positions, it's basically they come in, "You want a job?"

"Sure." And, I mean, it's kind of match [if you can] meet the physical requirements. You have to be huge, but I mean they want you to be, I mean, a guy your size, a guy his size, I mean, there'd be a variance on the amount of problems you would get, I would get, and he would get. I mean again, skin colour may help me out at times, people may be intimidated because of a colour thing, or it may be a bad thing where, I mean he's coming in being white and they may say, "I'm not gonna give this guy a problem." (15: visible minority male doorstaff)

This loose network of recruiting revolves around masculine venues such as sports teams, gyms, and even high-school cliques:

Three of my good buddies [got] jobs here, I grew up, went to high school with [them]. Like, I got two of those guys jobs here. Other guys I've made good friends with, [R.M.], he's my good buddy now. (09: white male doorstaff)

I was working out in the gym and someone just came up to me, asked me if I was looking for work and it went from there. I came down and spoke to the guy, and three nights later I started here. (02: white male supervisor)

I don't take resumés. I hire through friends and sort of, if you vouch for someone, you know what I mean, I'll take your word for it. And I pretty much go through friends and people I have on staff. I get them to look through their friends. (05: white male supervisor)

In the following case, a doorman was discovered when he decided to pounce on a patron, thereby giving his friend a hand at a nightclub:

We were sitting there having a drink, waiting for my brother to play, and there was a fight in the pool room. And I seen L. running by, and so I just jumped over the rail and ran in to help L., helped him break up the fight, and then I just jumped back and grabbed my beer and Larry came over and bought me a beer for helping him out and then he said "the manager wants to talk to ya." And I said, "Well what's up?" you know. The manager comes over, he says, "You want a job?" and I turned her down. I said, "Well, no thanks," but "I'm busy enough as it is," right? And then I thought about it and I said, "Well, I don't have a social life" so why not get out and meet people and get paid for it. And so that's how I got into it and that's how I met G. and that's how I ended up here. (04: white male supervisor)

As this previous respondent indicates, the decision to become a bouncer is influenced by the fact that the job is far more exciting and socially rewarding than other low-paying service sector positions. As Hobbs et al. (2002) and others (Lister 2002; Thomsen 2005; Winlow 2001) have observed, bouncing is an edgy but legitimate masculine occupation for men who would otherwise have been employed in respectable blue-collar jobs before the loss of industrial manufacturing. Limited blue-collar employment opportunities in Halifax may mirror conditions in Manchester. The longshoremen are dwindling in numbers, and shipbuilding has all but vanished. Conditions once favourable to working-class Nova Scotian men in the shipyard, mine, fishery, cannery, or factory are becoming a rarity, and have for some time created a characteristic gender-affective economic angst among proletarian men (Faludi 1999, part 2.2). Bouncing is a respectable and enticing alternative, opening up encounters with economic, media, cultural, and even subcultural elites in the nighttime economy.

Getting Paid to Party

While the implications of a nightclub – its reinforcement of hegemonic masculinity, its blatant racial and class exclusivity, the ever-present potential for violence – can depress any analyst, it is also important to concede that in hanging around with bouncers, the atmosphere can often be amusing, jovial, and light. It was not uncommon for doormen to conduct a scathing running commentary about patrons and fellow staff. Indeed, it was not uncommon for these supposedly dimwitted ruffians to have me laughing aloud at their pranks and ribbing. Tests of strength, courage, or masculinity, for example, are commonplace in male-dominated occupations. These may be self-destructive when they take such forms as alcohol abuse and/or other unnecessarily risky behaviours (Gough and Edwards 1998), but in other instances these "feats of courage" can be harmless. I recorded in my fieldnotes:

The night is only now beginning and it is already 11 P.M. My internal clock has not adjusted to this work cycle and probably never will. Four doorstaff at the Beacon are alleviating their boredom with a "fireball match." The object of the contest is to stuff as many of the hot and spicy candies as possible into your mouth and eat them without spitting them out. The bag of fireballs was brought in by one of the coat-check girls. For the next hour and a half, E. worked on 13 fireballs. I sat next to him and watched other doorstaff stop by and inquire, "How are you doing now?," "Is your mouth burning?," "You didn't spit any out out, did you?" The doorstaff had apparently started to wager on the outcome. I must admit I found this puerile behavior quite amusing, particularly after several of the staff throughout the night complained that the fireballs were making their mouths burn, had given them intestinal cramps, or had left them with a "pasty mouth." We were all amazed at the sight of E.'s cheeks as they bulged like a chipmunk's.

Horseplay could involve doorstaff alone, doorstaff and other night-club staff, or even doorstaff and patrons. Flirtation was commonplace. For example, doormen working the entranceway enjoyed play-fighting with a petite female club-goer who challenged them by saying, "Come on, I could kick your ass!" They taught her how to throw a punch, plant her feet, and kick. On another occasion, a head bouncer from a rival nightclub sneaked up on one of the doormen I was chatting with and placed him in a chokehold. Both of us were stunned and relieved when the monstrous attacker (he had to be over three hundred pounds) turned out to be "just joking around." The doorman I had been talking to told me, "I knew it was a bouncer because no drunk ever puts people in a chokehold." Horseplay between doormen is to be expected in a largely youth-oriented, pugilistic, and male-dominated culture. Bravado, tests of strength, and hierarchies based on use of violence and skill with one's fists were understandably reinforced through intermittent scuffles between bouncers. This may also explain the rather high scores for interpersonal conflict at work if doormen were reporting these innocuous behaviours. Horseplay, and play in general, is a key attraction among those men who choose bouncing as an occupation. The nightclub places them at the centre of what's happening.

"It's a good-paying job, it's a social job," one respondent said. "Like, I don't have to go downtown because I AM downtown, you know, it's accomplished. I don't spend any money on alcohol, period. I don't drink at all, actually, anymore. Why would I want to go to a bar when I'm here five nights a week? (01: white male doorstaff). "Pretty good times," said another (17: white female doorstaff).

For some, bouncing is not even work. It's getting paid to hang out with like-minded friends and having fun:

It's pretty easy way to make money, really. Like, I mean, it's fun, this product, it's, it's in a club. Like basically you're hanging out in a bar. People come to bars to have fun. You're just hanging out. (19: white male doorstaff)

You get paid to come hang out downtown. It's usually a pretty relaxed atmosphere. Usually you're just hanging out with your friends … if you have to work somewhere, after midnight on a Saturday night, it might as well be a bar. That's where everybody's at. (07: white male doorstaff)

The biggest thing is the fact that I get paid for it. Right. I have a lot of the people that I know in the process of being a body-builder come here, right. Just to hang out. You know what I mean? And at the same time, I'm working. (16: white male doorstaff)

Indeed, so attractive is the environment of the nightclub that some bouncers have to remind themselves that they are actually working in order to stay sharp:

You're basically going out, but you know what I mean, every night, just enjoying yourself yeah, and you get paid for it … I just always try to remind myself that I'm working, and like, not to have too good a time … to keep on top of yourself and everything else. You know what I mean? If you start going out partying and coming here hung over, coming here not sleeping, enough stuff like this. (12: white male doorstaff)

It's the best for getting paid to interact with people all night, and just basically have fun. Like tonight all's I'm going to end up doing is standing around. People come up and talk to me, I'll talk to them, but I'll keep my eyes peeled on my guys, and on the crowd and, that's all tonight'll be like. So, getting paid to basically [do] nothing sometimes isn't too bad. But you still have to keep your eyes open all the time. Even if there's five people in here, they can start fighting with each other, you know. (13: white male doorstaff)

Getting paid to do something you have fun doing is certainly appealing, as is partying without having to spend any money. Rather than going out and squandering their income on weekend socializing, doorstaff are in the thick of nightclub excitement without spending a dime.

Some guys think it's a great big [waste], no prestige, there's no money in this. We get paid nine bucks an hour to stand there. I dunno. I get paid pretty good for standing, doin' nothing. I work four nights a week, so I don't go out. Like instead of going out, Saturday nights I'll be going out to a bar. So at the same time I'm part of the herd, I'm making money, I'm saving probably hundreds of bucks I'd be spending if I went out that night. I'm probably saving money pretty good. (09: white male doorstaff)

I like working at night. I'm not really a morning person, so. And it's relatively stress free. You just hang out at the bar. If I wasn't working here, I'd probably be out spending my money on booze ... it's kind of a fun atmosphere to work here. And like I said, there's not really all that much trouble that goes on ... A good way to meet girls, I guess too. (06: white male doorstaff)

Part of the excitement of securing a nightclub and being ensconced in the urban nightlife is the opportunity to meet celebrities and other notables. The Mansion, for example, originally became well known as a result of cinema and music stars visiting the bar while they were in Halifax filming or performing concert tours. One security supervisor was proud of the fact that he had met Kevin Spacey, Elizabeth Hurley, Harrison Ford, and many other stars: "A wide variety of people, you know, influential people, celebrities ... [You] get to go out [and do] cool things, you know, 'cause you're kind of on the inside with all the bars, so you get tickets and working backstage at concerts and just, yeah, just kind of inside of a Halifax bar scene" (05: white male supervisor).

The excitement of the nightclub is often augmented (indeed, even created) by the availability of licit and illicit drugs (Measham 2004). Rave nights were awash with Ecstasy (E), marijuana smoke was detectable nightly in the parking lot, and toilet-roll dispensers bore the residue of white powder left behind by sloppy cocaine users. It was difficult to get any general sense of bouncer culture in relation to drug use. Doormen varied considerably in their attitudes towards drug use and availability. On one end of the spectrum I was sometimes told that there was "zero tolerance" inside the nightclub or that certain doorstaff "don't put up with that bullshit." While attitudes towards drug use varied from individual to individual, they also varied from nightclub to nightclub. Indeed, at one nightclub it was common to see groups of patrons smoking marijuana immediately outside the entrance.

The temptation for involvement in the drug trade among doorstaff is significant. The sale of marijuana, cocaine, or Ecstasy during concerts, raves, or dance parties is an important aspect of nightclub culture. There were many rumours about doorstaff being involved in "protection" for drug dealers in the nightclub. Ostensibly, they were being compensated for allowing dealers to ply their trade unencumbered and without competition. Rival drug dealers would be thrown out of the nightclub. While I would get hints of this activity on an ongoing basis, I never actually saw a drug deal take place or witnessed patrons ingesting or injecting heavy drugs. It was not uncommon, however, for doorstaff to have had a drink before the bar opened, although nightclub policies prohibited them from drinking while on duty. In any case, patrons or dealers who openly dealt or smoked up in plain view were quickly hustled out of the nightclub. Many bouncers viewed this as a "sign of disrespect" rather than a violation of policy or moral conduct.

When I questioned doorstaff about the circulation of drugs in their nightclub, there were flat denials of personal involvement about heavy drug use. One person did, however, confide that in one particular case a nightclub doorman routinely "dealt coke." This nightclub was part of the ethnographic study and was indeed notorious for rampant drug availability. While the doorstaff admitted that one of their co-workers was dealing cocaine, they refused to name him and joked that the researchers "failed to put that tidbit on the survey." A doorman overhearing our conversation added, "Perhaps they did, just under 'Other income!'" The group laughed at the comment, but additional questions later yielded fewer specifics. They would simply confirm that "there were quite a few shady characters" who worked as doorstaff.

The widespread use of marijuana at one nightclub was viewed as innocuous. I recorded in my fieldnotes:

> After meeting with the bar manager and the assistant security manager, I am escorted by one of the doormen, who remembers me from the previous week's visit. "So, hopefully tonight will be less violent, eh?" chides the manager as he passes me off. "Of course!" responds K. I try to ask questions, but it appears that my tour guide looks a bit disoriented and distracted. His responses are either monosyllabic or indifferent: "Yeah," "I guess," or "Whatever" seem to be his favourites tonight. Annoyed, I finally notice K. has glassy, red eyes and is moving sluggishly through the nightclub. I surmise my tour guide is stoned. K. opens the door to the "band room" past the stairs leading to the stage area. On the other side of the room

two other staff members, a man and a woman, are sprawled on the old couch across from us. The smell of marijuana smoke is strong. I nod politely in their direction as we ascend the stairs behind the bar. I am wondering whether the five-hour second-hand smoke bath that I will be exposed to this evening will sufficiently overpower this scent of pot.

I even overheard the owner of this nightclub ask for "some weed" to make the task of snow-blowing the parking lot more bearable. A passing patron added, "Did someone say weed? Yeah, that would be nice."

Aside from either dealing directly in illicit substances or acting as a protection racket for dealers, doormen benefited financially in other ways from the drug trade – a rather dubious financial perk in at least one nightclub. Undoubtedly, this was facilitated by a strong ethic of mutual support among doormen (a topic discussed in more detail later). There was little condemnation of other doorstaff who engaged in questionable activities. Indeed, complicity was common when it came to making an extra buck, no matter how insignificant. I observed:

By about 2:40 A.M. we retreat to the warmth just inside the club's entrance. It is far too cold to continue checking identification outside. On these frosty Halifax nights, my breath hardens into ice crystals, sticking to my moustache and goatee like little stalactites. As they now melt, my facial hair is turning into a soggy mess. We continue to thaw, waiting for a third doorman to deliver us milk. As blood starts to circulate back into my ears and nose I watch as the two doormen continue checking IDs and motion patrons towards the ticket counter. One patron, a man in his early twenties wearing a long leather jacket, enters with a group of friends. He has had a few drinks. As he reaches to pay for his cover charge, a folded $20 bill accidentally flutters out of his pocket and towards the floor. With remarkable dexterity T. reaches down and snatches the bill out of mid-air, just as quickly tucking it into his own pocket. He looks over at C. and says, "You miss that one! "How much?" T. responds with a smile of self-satisfaction, "Twenty!" The patron, of course, is completely oblivious, and no one informs him otherwise. This was not the first time I had observed such conduct. Throughout the night and at other nightclubs I had witnessed bouncers, like scavengers, checking ATM receipts or other debris such as cigarette cartons and gum wrappers for hidden cash in nightclub entranceways … unintended tributes paid by foggy-headed pub crawlers. "It's a 'stupid' tax," said one doorman.

The sight of bored doorstaff scrounging for lost bills somehow seems to belie their status in the nightclub. Bouncers have the power of inclusion and exclusion in the nighttime economy. This provides them with a social capital that can be very beneficial. In their own circle of nighttime leisure activity and in the context of exchange with the daytime world, they are able to trade on this authority. They are bribed and offered perks of every sort, sometimes by influential people but mostly by those who want to be placed on a VIP list or simply remembered when they once again reappear at the door:

> We get a lot of free movies. They come down here, like ya know, they let us in free, we let them in free. Ah, other deals. I was at the studio the other day, ha. I got a deal … like I was debating buying a shirt. Guy's like, "If you let me in, I'll give ya a deal on this." I didn't know what he was talking about. "You get me in free Wednesday night, I'll give ya a deal if I get in as a VIP." And there's stuff like, [by knowing me] you don't have to wait in line or anything. You know, it's stuff like that … We go in other bars [and they say], "Where you wanna sit?" (09: white male doorstaff)

> I mean, you get the odd perk from a liquor rep, like a jacket or something, but I mean, just a jacket. It's just a jacket, right? But I mean, just, I mean me and Jeff Healey and Colin James and all these stars and stuff. I mean it's not, they'd never remember me from Adam you know, but it's just something I can take with me when I'm done with this place, right? (04: white male supervisor)

> [We] get a little bit of perks, if you go down to pick up some coffee, for example, and someone sees you working at the bar, then they may give you a deal on the coffee. The next time they come up, you let them in for free. Just little things. You'll go to another bar, they know you work in another bar, you get service a little quicker. Just different things like that. (20: white male doorstaff)

> You know, the beer reps and stuff give you the odd … I just built a home so I built a bar downstairs, I got a few things. Some glasses and some signage, some stuff like that. You get that once in a while. You get, um, you're recognized. My nickname is [omitted] and everybody knows [it]. "Oh you're [so and so] from the [omitted]" … I eat at Burger King, and as bar staff, they give me like 20 per cent on food or whatever. And sometimes just slide me a free burger or something, you know? I don't ask for it, they just give it to me.

But things like that. Guys at Joe Mac golf, they take care of us pretty good and we honour them, 'cause they're all forty, thirty-five, forty years old, and they're good guys. Let them in once in a while and they appreciate it, throw you a glove once in a while for golfing, or a few balls or something. You know, give you a couple of lenders of the good Calloway Big Bertha clubs or something. The $600 clubs that I can't afford, they'll lend me. You know, little perks like that are good. (03: white male supervisor)

The power of inclusion in the nighttime economy and its central iconographic connection to the doorman cannot be overstated, but it would also serve us well to remember that this power of inclusion rests entirely on a masculine archetype and the ability to use violence.

Masculinity and Violence

Discussions about violence often revolved around tricks of the trade. These included martial-arts techniques, chokeholds, and general tips for staying clear of legal consequences. While it was not necessarily company policy, at least three doormen told me that they removed jewellery such as necklaces to avoid strangulation and cuts during fights, as well as rings to avoid breaking the skin of patrons or leaving imprints that would "look bad in front of the judge." Martial-arts techniques were compared, and sometimes heated discussions would ensue about the best manipulation holds, Tae-kwon-do was compared to jiu-jitsu, wrestling to boxing. Doorstaff compared equipment such as leather gloves lined with lead to gel-packed speed bag gloves. Were heavy police boots better, or lightweight Nike sneakers? The use of legitimate violence in difficult situations is contingent on many factors, including nightclub policy, and doorstaff disposition and experience. "Nobody does anything violent unless I do," one supervisor told me. "That's the general rule" (06: white male supervisor).

Doormen with poor communication skills who must resort to violence are seen as liabilities, even though bouncer culture values the use of force when necessary:

A lot of doorstaff have heads with hair triggers. They work in this job because they get to fight legally. They can bounce people around ... I know guys, I've worked with guys, you know, I work with guys right now that have hair triggers. Who, like, somebody will look at them just crooked. Something stupid ... they do have a hair trigger, it probably ends up protecting me, so I'm not that worried. But at the same time their hair trigger could start a huge fight, and I could end up dragged into it. (11: white male doorstaff)

I get respect, because I proved myself many times in situations. That's often the case. New guys get total disrespect by even other bar staff, until they get to know them, or even learn to respect them, through experience. (06: white male supervisor)

Well, I know, there's some doormen, who I know, who work here, who people don't like 'cause they have a bad attitude. (06: white male doorstaff)

New doormen who resort to violence too quickly endanger the safety of fellow bouncers, a trait that, when discovered, places them into immediate disfavour among co-workers. Nonetheless, the masculine culture of bouncing necessitates that doormen are intimidating simply by their appearance, as one respondent explained: "One guy's standing over you that big, you look and you say to yourself, 'I hit this guy he's probably not going to go down anyhow, and then I'm just gonna get my ass kicked.' Where a guy that's smaller, they may say to themselves, 'Maybe I'll challenge this guy, see what he's got,' type of thing" (15: visible minority male doorstaff).

Appearance, as we will discuss further in upcoming chapters, is a crucial component of the production of the nightclub. In this sense, hegemonic masculine archetypes are an aesthetic necessity for hyper-heterosexed spaces.

A recent addition to at least one Halifax nightclub that has surely had an effect on hegemonic masculinity and violence is the presence of female doorstaff. One of their primary responsibilities is to check the women's washrooms. As I followed one woman on her patrols, she told me that she checked under the stalls for two sets of feet. She also watched women as they touched up their makeup in order to discern whether they'd had too much to drink. Each time she entered the women's washroom, she retrieved a handful of glasses and bottles. "I like clearing out the bathroom in case people use them as weapons," she said. That night, she also found a $20 bill on the bathroom floor and decided to keep it.

The gendered nature of violence in a nightclub and its attendant attributes and narratives, including the "damsel in distress" and "deserving versus undeserving" victims, must be reckoned within our understanding of bouncer culture and the role of violence. One doorman I spoke to, whose girlfriend was also a member of the security staff, said that since the hiring of female doorstaff, doormen have refused to get involved in removing female patrons: "Since they've hired women, a lot of other guys have become lazy. They won't take any women out because now there are girls to do that."

Female doorstaff are not issued radios because they are not assigned permanent posts. On the other hand, another doorman complained that female doorstaff suck up resources because they cannot do removals alone. Indeed, in potentially violent situations, one female doorstaff conceded, "Everybody comes running because they're overprotective of the females." When I asked her if this bothered her, she replied, "No, because I know they are there. And if a girl is getting into his face, I'm right in there too. I am overprotective of them too!" A predictable division of labour has developed wherein female bouncers handle female patrons and male bouncers male patrons. Of course, in the final analysis it is typical male physical violence that is the final resolution in either case. "If a fight breaks out," one woman said, "we usually let the males go in there and handle it" (02: white female doorstaff).

The dominant narrative of a strong protective male rescuing a chaste woman from the clutches of an unscrupulous man is dramatically played out in nightclubs on a routine basis. It is a generic reamplification of the general feminist wisdom that "paternalism is merely the benevolent face of patriarchy." For many bouncers, however, a nightclub setting itself predetermines that the women present are unchaste, unreliable, and generally unfit for rescuing. This is reinforced by stories of ungrateful or "crazed" women who have turned on doormen, a narrative not uncommon among some police officers (Rigakos 1995) who respond to domestic violence calls.

The worst thing that I've seen was a husband knocked his wife out of the doors. How often [unintelligible]? Not very often. Held them on the ground. She woke up, jumped on my back, to try and let her, uh, husband go. I didn't know, of course, right away that it was her husband or whatever, but that came out a few moments later. And I think that's the worst thing, I mean emotionally, to see someone get slapped by their husband, and then two minutes later, for her to come to me and say, I mean, "Let him go, it's all right." I mean, that's domestic abuse kind of thing. It pisses me off. And I've seen people stabbed, and people see me takin' knives that I don't equate that as being as bad as a husband punchin' his wife in the face. And knocking her out. (15: visible minority doorstaff)

Bickering or violent couples are a great source of consternation because there is a general belief that iatrogenic violence results when the bouncer intervenes:

There was a couple who were in here in [our nightclub], a guy and girl. The guy was, had apparently hit his girlfriend, and doorstaff saw it and came over and tried to separate the two. They were gonna kick him out, and she turned on the doorstaff ... they didn't see the woman. There was two or three doormen who had had scratch marks all over their necks, the bruises, from her trying to choke them. The doorman that went to the hospital had his nose set, and he had to have it rebuilt then later on. And, um, doorstaff that were limping for a long time because they'd taken kicks to the groin, just from her. I mean, the guy was still punching, you know, the doorstaff, and cut one of the guys. (11: white male doorstaff)

Then the fight started with a couple [in the] bar ... this girl punched one of our doormen, and really hurt him bad actually. His nose. Then this fellow was about three hundred pounds, he was a large guy ... [and it took] a lot to get him out, he got injured pretty bad ... so, um, the police were called. (20: white male doorstaff)

There is a general rhetorical stance among bouncers that women are more dangerous because of their unpredictability:

They're crazy. Like they are, they're more dangerous. They've been more flippy. Like they'll turn around and punch ya in the face a lot quicker than a guy would. Probably jump on your back and choke ya, or dig your eye out or something. Women are nuts. (13: white male doorstaff)

Girls are, often you have to watch for girls. Coming out of the crowd and attacking, if we had to put her boyfriend out or something. That type of thing. (05: white male doorstaff)

My brother's working at the [Galaxy], a couple of guys being put out one night by a doorman, and the girlfriend's, somehow cracked this guy, and he kind of fell down. And she kicked him in the face with her high heels. And he needed over a hundred stitches to clean himself up. That was the end of him. The end of him. He never worked in a bar again, and he was very scared by this episode. It's potentially very dangerous. (05: white male doorstaff)

Women are a problem for the masculine culture of bouncing because to hit a woman is clearly unchivalrous, but to be physically injured by a woman in an altercation is humiliating because "nobody wants to be beat up by a girl":

I dunno, girls. You don't want to be as rough with a girl, but you have to be rough. Like a lot of girls, you want to take them and just drive them through a wall. But you never do. (09: white male doorstaff)

If I just had her arm, she could still turn around and hit me. And I can't, morally I wouldn't hit her back … Certainly some people will jump on an opportunity to grab a woman and later on say that, you know, "I had to take her out, and somewhere down the road I walked out the door where I grabbed her, you know. I could really think about it that time, there was a fight going on." I wouldn't put that past some people. (11: white male doorstaff)

Drunken female pub-goers are seen as dirty fighters who claw and bite and therefore must be handled with force swiftly:

Like, girls start a fight, girls get in a fight, whatever, right? They claw, they kick, they scratch … she kicked me in the leg. When she kicks, she's like, "You're a fucking asshole, you're this or that." (09: white male doorstaff)

Sitting there, we heard this commotion. And I looked up here, I'm like "What's goin on?" You know? I couldn't see anything. And then I see a chair. Going over the crowd. Well, we went running up, eh, and we get into it, with one girl. One girl is like three hundred pounds and crazy. She can't get up, eh? She's sitting there. And usually chicks are well behaved, they don't, okay, they don't, like, punch the guy like a man would punch somebody, but a chair … And we grab her fast, and we get her out here. (09: white male doorstaff)

As a result of taking precautions against the risk of physical injury and psychological emasculation, some bouncers wear protective cups, while others turn belligerent women over to the police as quickly as possible:

> Some of the guys wear cups, they wear cups all the time, just 'cause they've got kicked from girls and stuff. (03: white male supervisor)

> Sometimes with women, women become violent or physical with us, they won't leave. Easier just to bring the police in, ask her to leave, and nine times out of ten she'll leave. (01: white male supervisor)

This masculine presumption about the volatility of women is apparently amplified rather than allayed by the presence of more female doorstaff. As Hobbs et al. (2003, 132–36) have observed, women doorstaff report more difficulty dealing with women than men. One female doorstaff (02) told me, "If I have to talk to a female it would usually turn into, the female would usually escalate the situation just because it's a female-female thing, women are catty? I don't know. Whereas a male, most times they'll just leave." When I asked whether males were more apt to respect her requests to leave than females, she agreed. "Yeah, females, I find, they're the ones who would give the snide remarks or dirty looks or what have you, more so than what males would."

Women doorstaff report a particular brand of woman-to-woman status degradation when a female patron is asked to leave. On the other hand, the presence of the female bouncer can have the opposite effect on a male patron who does not see them as a threat.

> FEMALE RESPONDENT: It's huge, huge. Different men that have come up, and of course they're "Uh uh, you're a bouncer?" Actually, "Yes." "Oh … well, you ask me to leave, I'll leave, but one of those great big guys comes at me, I'm fightin' my way out." And as soon like this was said, I immediately go to Joe, like, you know, "Guess what this guy said to me?" But I mean, it has, I've seen the difference. Because I've gone up to men before and said, "Look buddy, you know it's time for you to …" "Oh okay." But on the other side, the females are more defensive. A guy goes up to a female, it's not so violent, but when a female goes up to a female, they get a little … yeah. We actually had an incident this past weekend … "I'm really sorry, but it's time for

you to go." So she started up... and I said okay, told the guy to follow me kind of thing. She wanted to go find a friend. I allowed her to go do that. She then threw some profanity at me. I said, "Well, you've got two options now. You can either go out nice and quiet, or I can take you out." So I proceed to take her out because she started to go again.

ME: How did you do that?

FEMALE RESPONDENT: Joint manipulation. And she got ahold of me on this arm. And when he saw that she got me here she then started telling me, "Let me go" and I'm like "You let ME go and I'll let YOU go." And there was no way she was gonna let go, so he tried to grab on to her and then there was a great big kaffuffle and he had to carry her away and she was kickin' and punchin' and she head-butted him. (03: white female doorstaff)

The sexualized nature of the presence of women in a nightclub is something we consider in far more detail later, but it is illustrative here of the relational and gendered nature of violence.

Experience, Trust, and Safety in Numbers

Earlier in this chapter I quantitatively compared police officers to bouncers on a range of personality and group trait measures, controlling for job experience, in order to illustrate the relative power of bouncer alienation in subcultural formation. I now wish to revisit the data in the context of experience and workplace violence, but in this case to indicate the difference between police officers and bouncers in relation to the pugilistic trials of new doormen.

Table 4.3 illustrates that months of service for police officers resulted in statistically significant inverse correlations to non-physical ($r = -.21$, $n = 185$, $p < .001$) and overall violence ($r = -.16$, $n = 182$, $p < .05$), while table 4.4 shows that for doorstaff, more experience means statistically significantly more physical ($r = .40$, $n = 47$, $p < .01$), non-physical ($r = .40$, $n = 47$, $p < .01$), and overall violence ($r = .40$, $n = 47$, $p < .01$). Thus, experience meant more workplace violence for doorstaff and less workplace violence for Halifax-area police. Months of experience varied considerably between doorstaff at different nightclubs (from 47.2 to 15.5 months). Overall, however, the mean level of experience was less than two years for doorstaff in Halifax, and almost a dozen years for police officers. The mean age of Halifax

Table 4.3: Correlations between years of service and violence, personality, affect, and job satisfaction for police officers (reporting only significant differences)

Pearson r	Non-physical violence	Overall violence	Work locus of control	Job affective well-being	Alienation	Interpersonal conflict at work	Right-wing authoritarianism
Years of service	-21***	-.16*	.24***	-.17*	-.21*	.25***	.19**
n	185	182	185	185	185	186	183

***p<.001
**p<.01
*p<.05

Table 4.4: Correlations between months of service and violence, personality, affect, and job satisfaction for doorstaff (reporting only significant differences)

	Physical violence	Non-physical violence	Overall violence
Years of Service	.40**	.40**	.40**
n	47	47	47

**p<.01

doorstaff was only twenty-four; however, age was not correlated with violence for either doorstaff or police.

Length of service was positively correlated to work locus of control (r= .24, n= 185, p< .001), interpersonal conflict at work (r= .25, n= 186, p< .001), and right-wing authoritarianism (r= .19, n= 183, p< .01) among police officers. Occupational experience also had an inverse relationship to job affective well-being (r= .17, n= 185, p< .05) and alienation (r= .21, n= 185, p< .01) for police officers. None of these relationships was present among doorstaff, who, as we have already seen, report statistically significantly lower levels of right-wing authoritarianism and statistically significantly higher levels of interpersonal conflict at work and alienation compared to police officers in the first place (see table 4.2).

An explanation for increased experiences of workplace of violence among doorstaff versus police officers based on months of service (notwithstanding the intervening effects of alienation already considered) may be the higher sub-cultural significance of use of force among nightclub security staff. While both occupational groups, at least rhetorically, value the ability to de-escalate and use compliance in lieu of coercion, the typical neophyte doorman is compelled to prove himself on the basis of the routine use of physical violence. Based on the assumption that violence typically begets violence, especially in the nightclub, it would appear that nightclub security staff who do not exercise force (both verbal and physical) and do not involve themselves in physical confrontations are likely to be pushed out of the job. This cultural imperative was repeatedly reinforced by respondents during the interviews.

> We joke around with the new guy, and it's "You haven't proven
> yourself yet." It's kind of a joke, like "You haven't been in a big
> brawl"… like the new guys that we have, and the new guys I've
> worked with over, for almost ten years, every time a new guy comes
> in, they can't wait to get into a fight. They can't wait to prove themselves, or, you know, they want to roll around on the ground. And
> I'd be lying if I didn't say I wasn't like that when I was nineteen or
> twenty. (01: white male doorstaff)

> You have that "little man syndrome," where you wanna try and
> prove stuff, and you'll find it, probably with age too, you'll have
> guys that are nineteen, they're still eager … Like there's a guy that
> works now and he says it every once in a while, and I'm like "That's
> the last thing you want to do, is have to club someone. Every time
> you club someone, there's an assault charge right there." Right?
> And as a guy that's older, I don't want to touch people. I mean,
> say you're thinking future and career and stuff like that, you don't
> want a criminal record. (15: visible minority male doorstaff)

New doormen are not trusted until they can prove their mettle in any
violence situation. Bouncers reserve judgment until they have seen the newbie in action. "It takes a long time for you to develop trust for somebody,"
one respondent said. "You don't know how certain people are going to react
in certain situations unless they've been there." (04: white male doorstaff).
Another agreed it was impossible to know how someone would act in a situation before it actually happened: "You can't simulate something like that.
So until that happens in the environment of work, I can't really judge them
on their abilities, or capabilities" (01: white male supervisor).

It is perhaps a universal trait among policing organizations that newbies, outsiders, civilians, and patrons are viewed with a degree of suspicion. In public policing research, this has been accepted in subcultural
analyses as a constituent identifier of the working personality of a police
officer, a side-effect of job requirements to collect information, expect deception, and arrive at a foundation from which to reasonably exercise discretion (Crank 1998). Similar attitudes can be found in the context of
private law enforcement companies (Rigakos 2002b), who also come into
contact with "suspicious persons." Moreover, the ever-present occupational
risk of attack by a suspect produces heightened vigilance bordering on

paranoia. Bouncers are lied to at the moment of first contact with prospective patrons through fake IDs and other fictions to gain entry. Throughout the night they will be lied to further by patrons who are breaching nightclub policy or are heavily inebriated. Bouncers, like police officers and security guards, become cynical and suspicious of pub-goers. When the potential risk of being blindsided or "sucker punched" by an angry, drunken patron is considered, risk-aversive behaviour and generalized suspicion do not seem far fetched, since both physically and emotionally, bouncers often have with their "backs up against a wall":

Generally, I try to keep my back to a wall. For the most part, I mean as best as I can. Man, when you're fooling around, like, if you got a job, and then we have floating – there's one to a crowd. (19: white male doorstaff)

Personally I like having my back to a wall ... so nobody can sneak up behind me. But like I said, when you really talk to somebody, [unintelligible], other than that I just keep my eyes open, watch my back. (17: white female doorstaff)

Fortunately, I've learned to keep my back to the wall, I've learned not to underestimate anybody. Just cause the guy is only five foot four and weighs ninety-eight pounds soaking wet doesn't mean he doesn't have a knife in his pocket or he's not some kind of ninja or something like that. Or he's got a gun in his glove compartment and he's gonna come back, you know ... The few times my friends dragged me downtown somewhere, I'll stand with my back to a wall 'cause I don't trust anybody that's in there, unless I'm in this bar, and even then I'm usually not that far away from the doorman, and we're always working. When I'm in a bar, no matter where it is, I can go out to Vancouver, walk into a bar, and I will find a place against the wall, instinctively without even thinking about it, and scan the crowd. But my friends with come up and say "Will you stop working!" (01: white male doorstaff)

The doorstaff's vigilant posture requires constant awareness, constant optical surveillance, and the search for cues relating to potential danger:

I'll just like always have my eyes open for moves ... Just that I put like two pairs of socks on. Tie my shoes really tight, for extra support. (12: white male doorstaff)

Generally the best thing to do when you're talking to someone is to look at their face. You know, you can tell if someone starts going like this and looking away from you, you can ... it's a lot of experience. You can tell when someone is going to take a swing at you. You know, if they're making fists, or they're turning the bottle in their hand, they're shifting their stance into a stance with a ready position. Things like that. How they work in pairs – you have one guy stand off to watch around the confrontation to see if there's any friends getting ready, you know, to jump in. And just things like don't stand square face on to them, so you can't be head-butted or kneed in the groin or, you know, when you're talking, just keep your hand up above your chin so if you're gonna get a swing taken at you, you can block it and, just you know, common-sense things. (06: white male supervisor)

I'm always looking over my shoulder and, yeah, just pretty much keeping my eyes open for what might be going on. Or if I see someone that is just pounding back the alcohol and I know that maybe later on they're going to be a problem, I might keep an eye on that person. (01: white female doorstaff)

Female doorstaff tend to take even more precautionary measures. One woman told me, "Like at the end of the night, like I said, I'm dating one of the guys that works here, if he doesn't happen to be working that night, I always get one of the guys to either walk me to my car, or they drive me, or they watch me walk." I asked if she knew if the men took those kinds of precautions. "No. It's different," she said. "It's different for them. It's for me, it's to make me feel, okay, like, I don't know if 'Jane' that I kicked out, escorted out two weeks prior or whatever, is waiting." (03: white female doorstaff)

Another cultural characteristic shared among bouncers and the parapolice (Rigakos 2002b, 138–46) is the anxiety created by being outnumbered. Large gangs or groups of patrons can overpower doormen in violent situations. Of course, the key is to keep these groups out of the nightclub in the first place, especially if they arrive en masse, but this is not always possible:

[I'm] afraid of ... if we're outnumbered, if we're outnumbered, it's been like, you know, this is gonna be kind of crazy if things buck loose and people start swinging. But you know you have to do it because you just have to get them outside and get them out of the bar. (18: white male doorstaff)

When I first started working, fifty or sixty people came down together, just because we kicked somebody out the week before that. (07: white male doorstaff)

Yeah. You get a big group of friends, some rowdy, and one of them has to leave. You generally will approach one their friends and say, "Your friend's gonna have to go." Nine times out of ten they'll comply. The other time, "He's gotta go" – "Oh no, he's okay. He doesn't have to go." Well, he does have to go, and it leads to this and then. "What's going on"? And they come over and, "Well, no, no, he's not leaving." And then you look around and there's six of them and two of you. So you call for more backup and then just cover your butt. And then they show up so [the patrons] think that, "Well, look, all these doormen around, I guess it's time to go." And they'll, maybe they'll want to fight. (01: white male doorstaff)

The biggest one I've ever been involved in down here was the night we had a bunch of American sailors here. It was a year ago, I think, a year and a half. And one of them threw a beer bottle at one of the waitresses that was working. And then made a, made a racial comment towards one of the doormen who approached him about it. And we ended up, all seven or eight of us, fighting with about nine, ten, eleven, navy guys. That night, that was the biggest thing … one of the other navy guys, we never even found out who he was, pitched a beer bottle, [unintelligible] one of the doormen. Cut his eye open. But beyond that, I don't think there were any injuries to those people. (05: white male doorstaff)

The fear of permanent and/or life-threatening injury produces a state of anxiety so that bouncers believe that in certain situations they are fighting simply for their own survival. "Like a lot of times guys get scared," one respondent admitted. "If you're, like, two doormen in a bar, and all of a sudden ten guys come in, you're just, it's almost like you're just defending yourself. You don't care if it's a job anymore, you're just defending yourself. A lot of people don't realize that. But like, you're in a position sometimes where it gets down to that" (10: white male doorstaff).

Even after a large party has been removed, there is always a possible threat of the same gang attacking staff as they make their way home that night or even days later. In the following incident, bouncers relied on the police: "A few months ago, we're at the end of the night, [unintelligible] kicked out a few people – it was on a Wednesday night – and then on the following Saturday at about ten to two (we close at two) about twenty of them showed up outside, waiting for us to come out. When we got off … So we just stayed inside and called the police. And the police came and they all took off. We don't really like when that happens 'cause you don't know what they're gonna have with them. They could have knives or bottles or anything" (06: white male doorstaff).

Added to the fear of being outnumbered is the fear of being out-gunned. Possible hidden weapons are just as threatening to doormen – perhaps more so. Stories abound about persons drawing guns or knives on bouncers. Pat-downs and metal detectors are designed to radically reduce such incidents inside the nightclub, but doorstaff still feel vulnerable at the entrance, after work, and even still inside if the metal detectors are not working or something was missed.

> Anything with a weapon is always a dangerous situation. But anything basically where you're outnumbered, being outnumbered is never good. Especially if you know that they're going to cause a problem … drunk people, crowds, the loud music. Threatened with death, I'm blind from the light. Um, what else could we do? The hours. The danger now. (04: white male doorstaff)

> People … pulling weapons on us, people striking out at bouncers, or staff … We've been maced. I've had beer bottles, broken beer bottles, thrown at my head. That would be dangerous. The macing was deadly because it completely blinded me … nowadays people are so crazy out there, you never know. Like you just push out the littlest kid or whatever, he's smallest and he could be whatever. It's just, yeah, the weapons. I'd say weapons and dealing with gangsters would be the dangerous part about this job because you still make personal. (05: white male supervisor)

> The bat I have in my car I took off of a guy swinging it outside on the front sidewalk. Taking guns off people – I tackled a local guy, I'm not gonna mention his name, he's a very dangerous guy, I took a nine-millimetre hand gun off him. I took a revolver off a nineteen-year-old Spryfield kid, out trying to make a name for himself. I've had knives, pepper spray. But you know, anything like that is

always dangerous. Anytime there's a weapon involved, you know, things can go drastically wrong. But, I'm with the habit. Anytime you're involved in a situation where you're outnumbered ... There're the rough and tumble kind of guys, who don't mind going to jail for a night for fighting or, you know, don't mind, wouldn't think about hitting you with a bottle. You can get in situations like that, dangerous. You're outside, you've only got three guys outside, there might be six or eight of them. And you've gotta watch the time, you know, they're standing there talking to ya. You know, threatening ya, and any minute one of them's gonna hit ya, and then it's on and you're outnumbered. So those situations can be dangerous, you know, and it's a shitty job. (06: white male supervisor)

I'm not afraid here. There's too many – I got so much backup, and [if] I call in all my backup, I don't care how big you are, you're gonna just have to leave and [even if] you don't wanna leave, you're gonna leave. When weapons get involved, that's when it gets kind of scary. Weapons, you know, people are a little unstable. (01: white male supervisor)

It should come as no surprise that those individuals most likely to be perceived as a threat for swarming a bouncer or carying weapons are gangsters or members of organized crime who frequent nightclubs. They can be destabilizing presences because of their volatility, previous experience with violence, and need to maintain a public face of intimidation. To the local "hood," removal from a nightclub is a serious affront and humiliation. The volatility is even more elevated in cases of young hoodlums trying to make a name for themselves:

Like the criminals that come in here, like, they come in packs of wolves, right? They don't just, you know, stray in, they come in a group, and they grab a corner of the bar, and they just disrupt that whole corner, you know. Anybody walking by is a victim for whatever joke is the minute, you know what I mean? Throwing something, whatever. That's just stuff we gotta deal with and and it's weird, it's almost like, I dunno how to say this properly – some of the biggest gangsters, who've been, who are around long enough, and survived all their wars, right? They're at the point now where they've matured, and when they go out they don't want to get in petty little fights over some guy calling some guy a name and all this stuff. They're out for a good time now, right? It's all the underlings that do all the shit work, right? Know what I mean? So the big guys, we kind of, we're on a rapport with them too. They come in, "How ya doin', how ya doin'"? And it's a communications thing and it's not a friendship thing. We don't hang out. But when he comes in, he sees me, he's like "What's up"? and I'm like, "Like, hey," whoever the guy is, and we have a talk and I know they're not going to cause any trouble, unless like their life is threatened or something, right? Otherwise they respect us enough to take it out-side, right? For the most part and we've witnessed this, they've done that, and they've even helped us out in ways where "That's the guy you're looking for that did this" or whatever, "throw him out." (04: white male supervisor)

An approach adopted by some nightclub security supervisors is to co-opt former reformed gangsters and heavies to work as doormen. One su-pervisor told us, "We get a lot of hoods and a lot of gangsters and, you know, people that have reputations and stuff and the few people that are, they're known. So people respect us a little more, as to – you find in other bars bouncers have to fight a little more. Like, here we don't fight. No one really steps up to us. And that makes it sort of a weird environment, 'cause you know, we got the best out of life there ... we have some bad boys on our staff, but they're rehabilitated a little bit. And it all kind of works out" (05: white male supervisor).

Doorstaff understandably fear those who have little or no stake in con-formity, as one bouncer admitted: "There's three Hells Angels or what-ever in Halifax, I mean, the enforcer. And when you see a guy like that, you say to yourself, 'He doesn't care.' He may stab you. He may know he's going to jail but he doesn't give a damn. That's where situations are dangerous" (15: visible minority male doorstaff).

Gang-related fear of violence among doorstaff has a racial connota-tion that affects the overall organization of the nightclub (see also chap-ter 5):

The thing, that's what I hate most about my job, is dealing with the serious gangsters. Like people that make your fuckin' blood run cold. Like I'm talking, I don't know them personally, but I grew up here, and I know who who's in this whole city and, you know it, when you start dealing with the East Preston boys. And it's not a racial thing but it's just brutal. Like these guys are stone cold. Like this one guy, I won't say his name, but I had to bar him for a cou-ple of incidents and one night he comes in and basically can't come in, there's nothing I can do about that. And you know he rolls up his coat: "I'm not packin', my gun is outside." And now what am I gonna do, call the cops? Now I've got him running after me personally, right? He just had assumed, "You want me to make you call the cops on me? I'm making this personal. I'm comin' finding you!" And that's the shit I got no time for. Like 'cause I'm a single father and I mean like I make ten bucks an hour and I don't make enough to stand up to guys that I don't ... these guys are serious. (05: white male supervisor)

The repercussions of dealing with gang members extends outside of the nightclub. While a drunken patron may be only temporarily dangerous because he has overconsumed alcohol, gang members will hold a grudge and are more apt to use violence as a standard matter of recourse in their everyday dealings. For this reason, doorstaff only reluctantly approach them, and then do so cautiously, often with the assistance or threat of assistance from the police.

Like we've had the Hells Angels in here, we've had to deal with them. I've had situations where I had to stop them from beating up some young guy, you know? And they'll put me in my place. They'll tell me, like, "Listen man, this is none of your concern." I'll say, "I realize that, but can you at least take it around the side of the building?" you know? Like, Jesus Christ, you know like, what can I say? I'm gonna put myself in harm's way, you know, I only get paid x amount of dollars to do it? So is it worth my life, going up against this guy, who's, you know, somebody I do not want to be dealt with and dealing with in the future? ... And long after I'm out of this business, I'd hate to run into him or one of his cronies that wants to prove himself to this guy. (04: white male supervisor)

So we had an incident probably three months ago where there was a fight on the dance floor. And I recognized one of the guys. He was a coke dealer from Dartmouth. And there was probably eight of them. I mean there's twenty-two of us, I mean I don't need to be out in the street, or out with my girlfriend, or out with her mother, and [meet] one of these clowns on the street who happened to be fighting people, you know, over something that happened in the bar sometime. So you try not to personalize it, and again, working here for a period of time you know the tactics to use on these guys. You mention the police and that type of stuff, these guys are usually pretty good with the "I don't want any trouble with the cops, I'm going out the back door" and that's the way you're going. You're like, "Fine, if you're gonna walk out of here, then I don't care what door ya leave. As long as you leave, and that's fine with me." (15: visible minority doorstaff)

By way of example, one known violent criminal punched a doorman and two patrons in the face one evening, breaking a patron's nose. The supervisor only called the police the following week because he didn't want the gang member linking nightclub staff to the reporting of the incidents. Nonetheless, the police forced the supervisor to pronounce bannings against the individual.

The effect of nightly anxieties mixed with the excitement of mingling with partiers in a sexually charged environment can have a cumulative effect on doorstaff beyond a generalized state of vigilance. The experience can have lasting effects on bouncers' sensibilities. As one put it, "Maybe if I quit this job now and get a real job I might calm down and be this happy-go-lucky person again, but I doubt it" (01: white male doorstaff). Experienced doorstaff report that their initial fascination with dance clubs fizzled over time, replaced with a state of unease about their job, future prospects, and psychological health.

Oh, the first few years I worked, it was a great job. Crawling around on the ground with people and messing with them, it was interesting, a very interesting job. But then it seems like everything's different. Every time I went to a call, it was something different. But then I realized, "No it isn't." (01: white male doorstaff)

This is a dead-end job, there's no doubt about it, you know what I mean? Like, how long can you do this for? In all ser[iousness], I'm thirty-five, just at the most two or three more years, far as I can see. (05: white male doorstaff)

No one ever really talks about the whole, like, psychological aspect of being in a situation where you're getting paid a little bit more than minimum wage and you could potentially die at work. You know what I mean? No one ever talks about that. (19: white male doorstaff)

Of course, a psychological malaise about the job of bouncing was matched with other serious concerns about the cumulative effect of working in a nightclub:

Late nights, long hours, smoky environment … physically, those take a big toll on you … After, you know, a lot of time in the environment, you can feel it. In the summer I work five nights a week, I'm at school [now] so I [only] work three nights a week … and just the two nights' difference, like, you can physically feel that, you know? Actually breathe again, almost. Five nights working in this environment, your lungs are just jammed solid type thing. Your ears ring. You're half deaf. You know, you're physically – you can feel it. And again just basically drunkenness I'm not partial to. (02: white male supervisor)

What I hate about the job is the fact that I try to give my pump a rest, and by the time I get out of here it's morning, sometimes four-thirty, five o'clock in the morning. And, when I wake up the next day, one-thirty, two o'clock, I feel really, really drugged out. Like I had, like I have a hangover or something. It's just my body … hanging out that late at night. (16: white male doorstaff)

Over time some bouncers grow to have a cynical view of drunken patrons. One respondent said exasperatedly, "I think that's just me doing the job for so long … being stuck in a room full of really drunk people forty hours a week. When you're sober, it's just annoying. And you deal with the same things over and over and over again, and you start questioning, like, why don't these people understand that they can't do that?" (01: white male doorstaff)

While it is no doubt true that the end value of a bouncer may be measured by his ability to use violence when necessary, a requirement that prompts a suspension of judgment about new doorstaff until they prove themselves, it is also true that overzealous and non-communicative bouncers are of little value and a possible threat to other doorstaff. This cultural maxim may be read as: "Violence if necessary but not necessarily violence." In other words, doorstaff need to be just as capable of *talking down* as *taking down* belligerent or violent patrons. The art of talking down or cooling someone off verbally is a treasured skill among doorstaff and their supervisors. One common technique involves the threat of permanent banishment, or banning from the nightclub for up to one year. Certain nightclubs represented a *scene* that some club-goers had become dependent on for their leisure and sense of self. To threaten separation from this lifestyle was often received with great distress by patrons and met with promises of good behaviour in the future. Generally speaking, however, much violence could be averted merely through the delivery style of a doorman's request (Thomsen 2005). Simply treating

others with respect, giving them fair warning, and avoiding "power trips"
are more important than physical intimidation for stopping a fight before it has a chance to develop.

> I like to help people, if I can. I'd rather not have to kick people
> out all the time. Actually I give people the benefit of the doubt. Or
> you know, I'll, rather than tell somebody who's stood up on a chair,
> "You've gotta go home," I'm like, "Don't do it again." If they keep
> doing it and keep doing, there's not much you can do then.
> (11: white male doorstaff)

> If you go up and say, "Listen, you fucking asshole, get off the
> speaker," they're gonna be like, "Fuck you." You know what I
> mean? But if you say, "Excuse me, would you mind getting off the
> speaker?" they're gonna be like "Sure, no problem," whatever. So
> it's just, it's a mutual thing. If you show the people that are in the
> bar respect, they're gonna show you respect. (14: visible minority
> male doorstaff)

> I mean, I'm not very big. I mean I'm only 240. Compared to some
> doormen I know that are 400 pounds, I'm not really all that intimi-
> dating. But a word will go a long way, a lot longer than a fist will.
> (04: white male doorstaff)

> [Other doormen] want to be in a position of power, and like, it
> shouldn't be about a position of power. It should be about dealing
> with the public, and understanding the public. Like, we're, it
> should be a pay raise. I think they should be paid more so the facts,
> more real people enter the industry. You know what I mean? Like
> people that understand what they're dealing with. Not just people
> who're there to pick up their cheques and to beat up some kid on
> the weekend. You know what I mean? Like that's not cool. (10:
> white male doorstaff)

> I like to see, you know, the guys walkin' the guy out, and commu-
> nicating and saying, "Okay, listen, buddy, you're not barred or
> nothin', you're just out for the night. You had too much to drink."
> Communication, right? And just, stay away from the name-calling.
> A guy can call you everything in the book, he's not hurting ya. Now
> if he starts throwing swings at you, that's a different story, right?
> (04: white male supervisor)

Some of these cooling-off approaches are taught to doorstaff during training:

> My ... my training aspect, is I guess, more experience than anything. On the job, I consider myself a people person. I can talk to anybody. I can talk from a guy from deep Preston to a lawyer, to a business lady, to a prostitute. It don't matter. I can talk to anybody and I can, I can communicate and adjust with anybody's thinking. I find that's my biggest attribute. (03: white male supervisor)

> With this training that we've had, that's part of what they tried to get into your head, that you don't necessarily have to slam them on the ground, bounce their head off the cement. You can say, "You've got two ways to go, walk out and walk away, or we take you out." And a lot of people are opting for the "walk me out." Which is nice. (03: white female doorstaff)

> The book suggests that I should try coming over, maybe ask you if you'd come talk to me at the door. Talk to the staff at the door. Try and stay calm, and try to feel threatening, although it's difficult for most of the bar staff. (11: white male doorstaff)

A crucial tool for facilitating the ability to talk people down during the evening is to establish rapport very early on:

> I start at 9:00. I have a chance to just walk around and see what kind of people are in the bar and ... some people will approach me and talk to me and stop, so we kind of get a little bit of rapport then. So later on through the night, if anything happens it's, if you've already talked to the person, usually they're pretty good. (02: white female doorstaff)

> I don't have a hard time talking to people and I can usually interact with people fairly well. So, for me the job's, it's just like public relations, basically. You just go up and talk to people, basically and like if they have to go, they have to go. And sometimes you have to use force to get them out, but most of the time like you don't. So it's just basically talking. (14: visible minority male doorstaff)

> You see them arguing, you, tell them, "Listen, I'm watching you two. You guys separate. Don't go around each other no more, all

right?" And if you see them at it again you ask them to leave ...
Give them a chance. (08: white male doorstaff)

You can stand there grunting and groaning and basically being on a
power trip, and all people do is look at this guy and say, "Oh he's
just big oaf," you know, "Making his $5.50 an hour, trying, getting
respect by intimidating people." Or you can joke with people and
be more casual, and you know, maybe give people the benefit of the
doubt, maybe treat them with a little respect. It'll come back to ya.
(02: white male doorstaff)

The value of being a good communicator is evinced by experienced
doorstaff's lack of patience with younger bouncers who try to prove themselves physically, or doorstaff with short fuses.

You get this nineteen-year-old offensive lineman that's six foot six
and weights 290 pounds, sure he's going to make a great-looking
doorman, but if he's an idiot that has a temper with a fuse that's
only an inch long, then he's going to be a horrible doorman causing
all kinds of trouble. But don't ask me how you regulate it, how do
you filter these people out? No idea. (01: white male supervisor)

We have one guy here he speaks, what we call, like a cooler, you
know what I mean? One guy that I would very doubt that many
people in this town could stand up to him and come away walking
or whatever, 'cause he's that good. And so, I know he's there, and
he's sort of back here if need be. (05: white male supervisor)

I think you will find guys that are younger, and smaller, will have
more problems, and he'll have a tendency, like [Nightclub 4], where
you get a lot of young guys down there and all they have on their
mind is fighting and beating people up. They're still in that mode
where, "Hey that's cool, that's the thing to do." You can only do
that for so long. You talk to the majority of the guys here, that've
been here for three plus years or whatever, [C.] is one, [K.]'s another, [J.], you speak with those guys, they're not concerned with
beating people up or throwing people out. (15: visible minority male
doorstaff)

Indeed, not being involved in physical confrontations was a source of
pride among many more senior doorstaff:

Like me, I find I'm like one of the way most light doormen. And I notice like the difference between when I approach someone, another doorman approaches them, they thank me a lot of times. Like, "Thanks for being like that, and understanding my situation," whatever. (10: white male doorstaff)

In eight years I've never closed my fist and hit anybody. I don't see the reason for it. There's other ways to do it, but how in the minority am I? You know, how many doormen have closed their fist and punched somebody, people, for no reason, let alone a good reason? (01: white male doorstaff)

The last thing you want to do is throw somebody out. Or get in a fight. I'd rather sit here all night and do nothing and get paid. That's what I like doing – getting paid to do nothing. But if I have to do something, I have to. That's just how it is. (13: white male doorstaff)

The following respondent took pride in his handling of a potentially volatile event through the use of cool-headed communication and even flattery:

I worked in Pictou, at a beer party, and there was three fights and they should have been about fifteen fights. There was only three or four. And I broke every fight up, with words, and the people left ... Buddy said, "It's unbelievable, I never seen a guy that walked up to a guy that pissed off, who's out of turn, and have him shaking [his] hand." Like, I was wrestling with this big, big guy, hugging on to him so he couldn't hit me, and his sandals came off ... I'm sayin', "Look buddy, I don't want to fight you. I gotta go home." And next thing you know, this big huge drunk guy, he's, I felt the tension stop and I let him go and he just looks down, and he says, "I lost my sandals. Where're they [go]?" I found them, I gave them to him, he put them on and he shook my hand, said, "You're a nice guy" [and] walked away. You know what I whispered in his ear? I'd said, "Man, see, you're gonna fight and ruin your whole weekend," 'cause he [was] probably from there. I said, "I have a better idea." I said ... "Why don't you take your beautiful girlfriend ..." As soon as I said that, she shut her mouth. And I said, "Go home and [have] a good night, and then come back tomorrow and party." I said to him, you know, "Go home and [stay in]." And that's what stopped it. They stopped and I gave him his sandals and he shook my hand and then [they] walked away with arms around each other, and they were there the [next] night partying. Then he even apologized for acting like an asshole. (13: white male doorstaff)

Some doorstaff attribute differential use of force to different night-club cultures, hiring standards, and even pay scales:

It's just not good for business to go around hitting people. You'll lose customers. (06: white male supervisor)

Well, a lot of the other clubs, the guys are probably makin' six dol-lars an hour. I make eleven dollars an hour. So I mean you're gonna get a big difference between quality. Say you pay someone six dol-lars an hour, you're gonna get six dollars in work out of this person. If they think it's a whole lot easier to punch this guy in the head and drag him out, it pays to sit and talk to him for four or five minutes. And say, "Guy, listen, you gotta go," again and again type thing. Bad guys like that. (15: visible minority male doorstaff)

I've had a lot of incidents, and we've only had three times where we've had to fight in three years. And I really think that's pretty good in this line of work. At this bar, because we're open till four, three-thirty, we get all the drunk, obnoxious people. And we do good. I really believe that anyways. (02: white male supervisor)

The ones I've seen here, yeah, a lot of the guys are like that. Very patient. Very patient – like, a lot of chances. I've been in other bars, man, they give you half a chance and oof, you're all locked up and have four guys on ya. They're patient here. They'll ask you three or four times. And then you have to kind of tell them, "Look, it's time to go, you gotta go." (13: white male doorstaff)

Doorstaff who are too quick to use violence do not last long on the job:

There's been a couple guys we've had working in the past, they're too big, too aggressive, too mean, too whatever, and they just get worked out of the schedule very easily. It's like, sorry, buddy, can't help you. You don't wanna break it to him that, you know, he's got to get off the 'roids or whatever. (04: white male supervisor)

If somebody isn't doing their job right, they get fired, faster than they can spell their own name. That's good, because it keeps us all safe. (13: white male doorstaff)

You see these hotheads. There are some people they just shouldn't be bouncers. You know? And they don't last here. (16: white male doorstaff)

Despite their pride in talking someone down, for bouncers the unavoidable reality is that they must be perceived by their peers as capable of using force when called upon. When patrons see respectfulness and cordiality as a sign of weakness, then, according to both cultural mores and occupational expectations, bouncers should be able to handle themselves physically. Said one supervisor, "It's not a polite society we're dealing with a lot of times." Some patrons interpret politeness as a sign of weakness. "And you know, they'll use that to see how far they can push you" (06: white male supervisor). Said another, "I want somebody that's not very aggressive, but I want somebody that'll handle the situation, not shy away from it" (03: white male supervisor).

Solidarity and "Door Wars"

A common attribute among doorstaff, police officers, and the parapolice is a strong sense of occupational solidarity. We have already observed that among doorstaff group alienation, as measured by responses to Perrot's scale (1991; see also Perrott and Taylor 1994; Perrott and Taylor 1995), is statistically significantly higher than that of police officers, and that this attitude, moreover, implies strong subcultural bonds and especially feelings of dependence on fellow security staff. Of course, this can breed insularism and an "us-versus-them" mentality, but the subcultural bonds born out of mutual assistance are also based on trust and practical self-preservation. Bouncers look out for one another because they have to, enabling a sense of physical and emotional security. One doorman aptly put it, with a sense of gravity: "You're never alone" (11: white male doorstaff). Doorstaff need one another for many reasons, including acting as reliable witnesses for one another at trial: "I've learned that you have to be very careful as to how you get hold of witnesses," one respondent said. "You have to find somebody to back you up. Which is why I count on these guys the most" (05: white male doorstaff).

Unity among doorstaff takes many forms and may be as innocuous as buying coffee for everyone. Of course, this is in many ways similar to other occupational cultures. On more than one occasion, the compulsion to contribute equally to group solidarity resulted in person after person carrying in cartons of donuts and coffee for groggy co-workers starting to wind up for the evening.

In-group solidarity and a generalized suspicion of outsiders posed particular obstacles during the research process. As mentioned in chapter 1, on a few occasions my researchers and I had difficulty penetrating bouncer culture. Our questions about levels of violence and security procedures were met with considerable suspicion. On two occasions doorstaff intentionally kept two research assistants waiting for over an hour to conduct interviews, or simply acted in a rude or uncaring manner about the research. On another occasion, I was directly challenged by a doorstaff supervisor who wanted to know where I got off thinking that I knew something more about the best way to do security. I had to inform him that security was actually the aspect of bouncing in which I was least interested.

This attitude towards outsiders was not universal, and many doorstaff were quite eager to allow outside research. They were forthcoming about violent incidents and their feelings and thoughts on a wide range of issues related to bouncer culture. In some cases they appeared too interested, demanding to see fieldnotes: "So what the fuck do you write down anyway?" Eventually, this doorman was given some notes to peruse, although he could not make any sense of them.

When we had not visited one particular nightclub for over two weeks, the security supervisor greeted our return with barbs about our "being scared off." However, once we were accepted as part of the nightclub noise, as part of the scene, doorstaff would make use of our presence. Indeed, the more time we spent in the field, the more common it was for doorstaff to utilize us as an additional set of hands. I tried to avoid this as much as possible, but as it was more important to me to get access to the bouncer culture, I assisted where it seemed innocuous and unobtrusive to do so. One evening one of the research assistants was put to work almost immediately stamping the hands of incoming patrons. On another occasion he was asked to flash the emergency lights during a violent confrontation to alert other doorstaff. Our appearance typically confused patrons, who thought we were supervisors or additional doorstaff. It was not uncommon for us to guide club-goers toward the washrooms or point them in the direction of the snack bar or coat room. This was made even more problematic one evening when a research assistant donned a staff parka to keep warm in the subzero Halifax night. The same researcher was promised in jest by a doorman, pointing to a spot on the sidewalk outside the nightclub, that he would "kick the shit out of someone." He wanted to make it up to the researcher for enduring what he perceived to be an uneventful night. A recurrent theme among doorstaff was complaints about a lack of "action," which usually meant violence. They would apologize for slow nights and for the fact that we "hadn't seen anything yet." This seemed to contradict interview data where on a one-on-one basis doorstaff often measured good nights on the basis of a *lack* of violence. In some ways, doorstaff still wanted to put on a show for us, or at least talk as if violence was imminent, to make the evening more exciting.

Solidarity among doorstaff who work in the same nightclub is far stronger than a general sense of solidarity among doorstaff on simple occupational grounds. I believe that when they were answering questions concerning solidarity and interdependence on the alienation scale, they were understandably reporting on their feelings towards fellow doorstaff in their own nightclub. Had the questions asked about doorstaff generally and about those at the respondents' own workplace, it would be safe to surmise that – based on interview and observational data – the results might have varied. This localized allegiance manifests itself in various ways, but it was very common for doorstaff at one nightclub to point to the level of violence at another as proof of their lack of effectiveness. When I told doorstaff that other nightclubs were also involved in the ethnographic study, the typical response was either "things are more violent in that nightclub" or curiosity about their colleagues' procedures and levels of violence. There was a general sense that the respondents' own nightclub had things right, and that rival nightclubs were either "too strict" or "too lenient."

Even for doorstaff who had moved from one club to another, it was not uncommon to quickly change allegiance. We had interviewed one doorman (V.) who worked at the Galaxy three months earlier and was now employed at the Mansion. Asked why he left, he explained that he could "only hear the same bands play the same sets every weekend" for so long. It was the same reason he had left the Beacon. When pressed further, he also complained that the Galaxy staff had become "too uptight" and that he had become tired of it. He much preferred the less regimented style of the Mansion and the bands it attracted. However, we recalled that V. was part of a group of doormen at that Galaxy who had made several negative comments about the Mansion when we answered their queries about where we were off to next. In fact, it was V. who led most of the criticism about his current manager's security measures.

In some instances, doormen would compare the pugilistic capability of one nightclub's bouncers to their own. For example, a doorman at the Beacon thought his own staff was inferior in fighting skills to those at Nightclub 4. He argued that "one on their thugs" could probably beat up "four or five of our guys." This rivalry is said to have spilled over into what many doormen referred to as the "door wars" of the early 1990s. There was a strange mix of nostalgia and repugnance on the part of doorstaff at the idea of running turf wars between nightclub doorstaff. These stories seem incredible but have embedded themselves as part of the lore of doing nightclub security work in Halifax. Some rather fantastic stories circulated. The "door wars" included arranged fights in public parks of thirty or more doormen from competing nightclubs, the "invasion" of a nightclub by doormen from a rival establishment, or constant fights among doormen frequenting another nightclub.

Even today, rivalry between doorstaff at competing nightclub establishments spills over when doormen and bar staff get together on weeknights. On one Monday night we were told to anticipate fights between doormen from rival nightclubs and doorstaff at the Galaxy. In some instances even staff from the same nightclub would get involved in fisticuffs: "Bar staff are the worst. They think they own the place. Half of the staff from here will be pounded tonight, including assistant managers."

Animosity between rival nightclub doorstaff is always tempered by a reciprocity of privilege that manifests itself as immediate access akin to VIP status.

> We're open later than everybody else, right? So other bar staff that come up here after their bar has closed, we give them the same type of respect that we would like when we go to their bar on our night off type thing, right? So it's a mutual thing. So we get perks from when we go to different bars and whatever. (14: visible minority male doorstaff)

> We're open, we're a cabaret. A lot of bar staff come here. I mean Sunday nights we have a bar staff promotion where we, you know, give them specials so they have a taste of ... a lot of the door staff are Americans, and we just, you know, see them every night, "How ya doin?" (01: white male supervisor)

Different nightclubs rotate, each in turn providing hospitality, perks, and discounts to Halifax-area bar staff and doormen. These perks are the same otherwise granted VIPs. Doorstaff automatically become part of an "all-access" Halifax nightclub insider group.

> They use their bar status or whatever to get in. And when you go [to] their bar, you use the bar status to get in, and it's just like, sort of there's rotating nights where the different bars are busy. So if you go, say, to a bar that's busy on a Tuesday, you're talking to the door-man, bring to your bar on Saturday, he's going to talk to you, and then it becomes "Oh, this is my buddy here," and "This is my buddy here," and you just all sort of, end knowing each other just from always being in the bars. (19: white male doorstaff)

> You don't have to wait in line if you go in [unintelligible] bars. So many bar stops, and you don't have to pay cover charge. (06: white male doorstaff)

> You don't have wait in other line-ups at other bars. That would probably be the biggest perk of the job. You get to, get to meet different people, maybe some other people that you wouldn't meet when you were just a regular customer, something like that. When you're in other bars you get treated better, and maybe quicker service, than if you're just a regular customer. (18: white male doorstaff)

The ability carry on with limited regard to nightclub policy is another perk typically associated with VIPs. Visiting doorstaff, in effect, are given the same latitude. On the other hand, when visiting or off-duty doorstaff misbehave, they can put their comrades in a rather difficult position.

> And if you ever wind up in trouble in another bar, usually you're dealt with friendlier, usually, in most bars. Very few rare exceptions … I think one of the biggest perks is when you have a night off and come to party … you get away with a lot more, usually, than you should. (07: white male doorstaff)

> When your friends are down here too drunk, and you know you should toss them, you gotta find a way to disappear for a minute, and let somebody else take care of them. Or usually, once we're all friends, that's even harder to do 'cause, after a little while working here, your friends become friends with the other doormen. (07: white male doorstaff)

I recorded an example of an off-duty bartender placing his fellow bouncer in a precarious position by being boisterous and drunk in the nightclub:

> A bartender is in the nightclub on his day off, and it is apparent that he has been drinking heavily with one of his friends who also works at the same nightclub. J. tells me that if he continues to drink heavily he will "fire him out in the street" because "he's just another person." The situation is serious enough to warrant a brief meeting between three doormen and a supervisor. For the time being, no one is actually removed. The bartender's more sober friend is warned that if his friend does not pull himself together, they will both be ejected. J. threatens to throw him out once again and another doorman agrees that it's time to take him outside. Their decision is overruled by the supervisor in the hopes of maintaining the peace, but he also decides on a new policy: "I'm telling a manager no more staff drinking in the bar. He's done it before. They are the worst of the bunch. It's only forty-five minutes until closing, so let's just forget it." I wonder whether the bouncers would be as eager to remove him if he was a doorman rather than a bartender.

When doorstaff engage in violent activity – even in support of a fellow doorman – while on their night off, those on duty are not always thankful for this help. A doorman who is associated with the nightclub or visiting on an off-duty basis may still be determined to be acting legally at the behest of management or owner of the nightclub who can, in turn, be held liable for the employee's conduct (see chapter 3). A drunken, off-duty bouncer, therefore, can cause considerable difficulty for his fellow doorstaff by compromising their discretion and effectiveness.

As the reader may have already surmised, a general sense of doorstaff unity does not necessarily extend to other nightclub staff. Bouncers are often sceptical when bar staff ask them to remove a patron. The motivation behind the request is sometimes questioned, especially if it is suspected that the bartender is merely upset about being tipped poorly. In fact, at one particular establishment, the need of doorstaff to differentiate themselves from non-security nightclub staff resulted in a change of uniform. There, doormen were concerned that their shirts read: "STAFF" rather than "SECURITY." One doorman remarked dismissively, "I mean, a bartender could wear our shirts!" Perhaps part of the animosity towards other nightclub staff relates back to the issue of gratuities. Doormen, at least in policy, are not allowed to take money from persons wishing to jump the queue. Other bar employees, however, make quite a bit more money on tips.

You know, they make two hundred bucks a night, and I'm making whatever I make an hour, no more benefits or anything, you know, and I'm like "suck it up" – you know what I mean? And then they want a guy thrown out because he didn't tip them or something, the doorman has to do it, and that guy is gonna want to fight the doorman or spit on the doorman and call the doorman names when he's making the same wage I'm making. That pisses me off. (09: white male doorstaff)

It's kind of funny, you have a person who's a waiter, or a bartender somewhere, they'll say that they work in the industry. But if you have someone that was a doorman, he'll say he was a doorman. (04: white male doorstaff)

Doorstaff solidarity at work and the reciprocity of privilege, the exchange of social capital, extends to after-hours get-togethers and weekday outings. Bouncers, who are already at a younger, partying age, make their co-workers their prime social circle. This is reminiscent of other cultural analyses of occupational groups including, especially police officers.

We're always talking or just hanging around … Yep. We always do, like, work functions, like we went on a boat cruise in the harbour and out to McNabb's Island for a night, the bar and bar staff. So we always do a lot of stuff. Just going out for the night and stuff. (08: white male doorstaff)

It's just like you're buddies after a while. You become friends and stuff. We go out here and there. I usually, two days off, I just stay home and, lick my leaks, and bring the dog for walks and do stuff like that. (13: white male doorstaff)

There's certainly, you know, a core of people I hang out with outside of work. Who, I mean, if I stopped working here, I'd still probably hang out with. (19: white male doorstaff)

Doorstaff solidarity also requires backup when visiting another nightclub or bar. The occupational risk of being attacked by a slighted patron often necessitates that bouncers travel in groups when out for a drink:

> Doormen stick together. Especially on your own staff. If you ask, I'm sure it's the same for bartenders and waiters, but the doormen especially, if you go out drinking, you go out drinking in the bar that you work in, 'cause it's safest. You know, somebody's always watching our back. You know, we're surrounded by our friends and watching each others backs. You hope that your guy is going to know better than to be an idiot in a bar who's drinking anytime something happens. We stick together. Like, we don't always get along amongst ourselves, but when it comes down to it, we watch each other's backs. A lot of the time the only people you can hang out with are the people you work with, because of the schedule. You work nine to five, from nine at night till five in the morning. You're asleep all day. You get up. I've turned into a virtual vampire. I don't go out during the day. All kinds of people out there. I get up at four in the afternoon, you're lucky if I get up at two, but you gotta hang out with these people. I definitely, since I started bouncing, found it extremely interesting. I don't trust people, in general. (01: white male doorstaff)

> Tuesday is a staff night, we come out and we have a couple of cheap drinks. Have a laugh. The boys go camping on Tuesdays, Mondays and Tuesdays, sometimes. Things like that. Get out and unwind – but we go together. (11: white male doorstaff)

While drinking and partying is a common social activity among doormen, a great many more prefer quieter leisure activities away from work with fellow bouncers:

> Work out, meet and go for dinner, stuff like that. Nothing really partying or anything like that, just relaxing. (01: white male doorstaff)

> We go out drinking together, we just, we go watching wrestling together. We wrestle together. Like everything. (09: white male doorstaff)

> We go out for lunch … every once in a while. Or we'll go out to the door boss's place, watch football or something. (04: white male doorstaff)

In fact, a primary reason for not going drinking is sometimes a generalized antipathy towards the nightclub scene by long-term doormen who have seen it all. As one expressed it, "I don't like being out of control. I'll go out with the guys once in a while, once, maybe once a year, I think. Last year I think I came out down here, had a pop, had a beer maybe, carried the beer around till it was so warm I couldn't drink it anymore. You know what I mean, I'm just going, 'Yeah yeah, whoo hoo.' Yeah, you know. I guess when you do it, when you do do it for a job, you don't do it in your personal life, I guess. I don't, anyway. Maybe when I was younger I did, but not anymore" (03: white male supervisor).

Relationships between bouncers, however, vary considerably. New doormen are typically not included in social activities because they are not considered permanent. High staff turnover and seasonal variation result in core social groups of veteran doormen who only sparingly invite new members to their circle: "The friends I made out of long-term bouncers here, but the newer guys that come and go, I really don't hang out with them. It's just a few. And the guys I do hang out with, they do expect a little more from me as being their friend" (05: white male supervsor).

As far as supervisors were concerned, socializing was a necessary part of helping promote solidarity, but they engaged in it with some unease. They want to help promote a fun and social atmosphere, yet not compromise their authority:

Maybe a few days off camping, or whatever the case may be ... What happens in the social time and what happens here is two different things. I don't carry one over to the other. (01: white male supervisor)

I've gone to some football games for the guys, just to show the support thing, and the birthday party thing, or whatever. You know, just little things like that, but I don't go out of my way to hang out with them and you know, if I had nothing to do, I don't come over here hang out with them, it's not like that. (04: white male supervisor)

I have to keep a sort of a distance from them because of being a supervisor. (06: white male supervisor)

In one case, a doorstaff supervisor avoided socializing with his staff altogether. "I don't hang out with the guys here," he said. "There are some, you know, good guys who work here and guys that while I'm here

I can socialize with. And I enjoy coming to work to talk to them" (02: white male supervisor). Some doorstaff do not see the point of interaction and believe that they are not necessarily close to their co-workers: "I may stay if I need a drive home type of thing, or whatever, but very rarely do I go out with, I mean, people that I don't know very well. Maybe there are five or six guys that I'm pretty close with, and we golf and that type of thing. I mean maybe go out for something to eat or whatever, right? Sit at each other's house, watch a football game and that type of thing" (15: visible minority male doorstaff).

Much like the shift work involved in public policing, private security, and other twenty-four-hour services, the schedule itself conspires to delimit the bouncer's social circle. More often than not, group solidarity and socializing is formed not only through the need for self-preservation in public spaces – the opportunity for off-duty doormen to relax with like-minded "kinsmen in repose" (Van Maanen 1978) – but moreover revolves around the basic availability of companionship.

> Like, everybody here is really, really close. It's just weird, 'cause of the schedule that you work, that there's not very much time to do anything else. So it's like all my friends that I've had during school year work during the day during the summer, whereas I'm sleeping until three or four in the afternoon. Then I get up and come to work. Whereas they work all day, then there's like about three or four hours after they get off work, before I go to work, that I can see those friends. Then after that it's I go to work and they go to bed. You know what I mean? So on my days off, which would be like a Monday or a Tuesday, I'm basically up until like three or four anyway. So I sleep in the whole day. So I don't get to really do too much other than hang out with the bar staff that are off duty that night. So we end pretty much hanging out, like spending seven days a week together. So that's the way it goes. You end up getting pretty close after you spend that much time together. We're pretty close around here. Everybody gets along pretty well. So, every now and again we all go out together or whatever, go get a meal sometime and hang out. On a Tuesday night we all went to an abandoned campsite and camped out for the night. Had a few drinks, whatever, chatted it up. And I dunno, that's about it. We do that, like we do like a bunch of group activities. Like we'll go to the beach sometimes, a bunch of us will head down to the beach, afternoon or something, before work, just stuff like that. We always hang out together. It's not a big deal. (14: visible minority doorstaff)

Most other friends outside the nightclub industry are only available when doormen are otherwise working, even on the weekends. As we have seen, however, scheduling is only part of the reason why doorstaff socialize primarily with other doorstaff, often to the exclusion of others working similar shifts such as waiters and bartenders.

"Meatheads" and "Assholes"

An important barometer of group solidarity and insularism is group concern with and manipulation of public (and especially media) perception. This has been expertly documented by Peter Manning (1997) in the context of public policing, in what he identifies as the "dramaturgical context of police work" as a profound mechanism of subcultural solidarity. The construction of the police funeral, for example, lends credence to the notion that the public police are as much about dramatic social symbolism as they are about the mundanity of patrol.

Increasingly, bouncers and their trainers and supervisors are becoming more sensitive to public perception. They often feel misunderstood, underappreciated, and vilified as violence-prone "meatheads" pumped up on steroids. This sense of besiegement, of course, is common among both public (Chan 1996) and parapolice (Rigakos 2002b) organizations. Thus, doorstaff frequently criticize what they perceived to be hyperbolic media reporting about their jobs and who they are:

> I think there's actually a pretty comical aspect [to media reporting]. They're pretty humorous. There was an incident here where one of them, the men from across the street, came in wielding I think it was like maybe a two-and-a-half inch Swiss Army knife. And the way the newspaper portrayed it, it made it sound like he was in here swinging a machete … they just blow it out of proportion and make people, I think it makes them afraid to go to bars really … Then all of a sudden [there are] these stories like, "Didn't somebody die there last week?" And I mean, I worked here for almost two years, and I could count on my hands how many times I've been in situations where I've actually been worried that I might get hurt. (19: white male doorstaff)

> I don't think they have an adequate outlook on the bouncers. They're just taking the one side kind of story and they're making us look vicious, from what I've read. Like, out of control doormen.

Well, don't get me wrong. There are some doormen, and I will admit there are doormen in Halifax, that, yeah sure, they blow their temper way too much. Or they may have used way too much force. But not in this club … It only takes a few to ruin it for everybody else 'cause you just get classified. (18: white male doorstaff)

They try to paint us as steroid juicers and whatever. I mean like most of us, most of us here go to school, Saint Mary's, Dalhousie, a lot of universities. Just like part-time jobs for a couple of years. And they try to give the image of professional bouncers or something, which isn't the case at all. (07: white male doorstaff)

One respondent talked about how he was personally "upset" about the way he was depicted in a newspaper article: "They were extremely biased against me. They brought up the fact that I played football in high school. They made implications that I was just some big idiot, that I was looking for trouble type of thing. And they painted this guy as a peace-loving, you know, no-problem kind of guy. So I was really upset, 'cause it was totally not the story at all. It was not the story, and I think often it's not. I think if people really knew the whole story, they would think differently" (05: white male doorstaff). The perception is widespread that the local media only cover and sensationalize the most negative of incidents. Doorstaff feel unappreciated because the general hospitality and policing work that they offer largely goes unnoticed. As one woman pointed out, "It would have been nice – like even during the Tall Ships, when we had so much business, would have been a really nice time for them to do a positive story" (03: white female doorstaff).

When stories about nightclub incidents are reported in the local newspapers, doorstaff complain that the whole story is never told and that reporters typically cast bouncers in a negative light. An episode that captured headlines during our research included media criticism of doormen who refused entry to a patron who was brandishing a knife. They were criticized for failing to notify the police in a timely fashion, even though they reported that they called immediately. Shortly after the knife-wielding man was refused entry, he attacked a pedestrian outside of the nightclub. A doorman at the club maintained that it was bouncers who saved the victim's life: "The last thing in the newspaper was probably the stabbing that happened here. But you always see things in the paper, fights, that occurred in bars. People I think, generally look negatively at bars … what it exactly said in the newspaper was that we had 'comforted' [the victim], when in essence we'd actually saved his life. It was a doorman that went with him to the hospital. And was with him [when] he actually went into surgery to close the wound … We called an ambulance, he would have died before the ambulance got there anyways. We have a first aid kit there at the front door, and he was actually cut in his aorta, he was bleeding out, and we just stopped the bleeding" (04: white male doorstaff).

In situations where doormen have clearly used excessive force, the common refrain among bouncers is that "the guy didn't know what he was doing." In one incident a doorman placed a patron in a chokehold and ended up crushing his windpipe, resulting in the man's death. Repeated reliance on chokeholds, however, is a somewhat troubling development, especially in light of the following respondent's reference to this maneuver as a standard measure:

I had a little fella upstairs who was fighting. And he's barred from some of the other bars around town, he's, you know, a known troublemaker. And he was going crazy. I had three doorman dragging him out. He was resisting the whole way, grabbing onto things, and stair railings and one of the doormen was six foot four, 275 pounds. The other one was about five foot seven, three hundred pounds, and the other one was two hundred pounds, six feet tall. And they were struggling like crazy with this guy. He was going nuts. He punched one of them in the face and they were having a really hard time. And I just stepped in and took him and put him to sleep and said, "Okay, carry him out." And saved them a lot of trouble. You know one of them could have been injured, they could have injured him severely struggling with him like that. That's why I insist on training. Because there's, you know, eight hundred pounds of doormen there and they're having trouble with a 150 pound guy, taking him out. That is why I always say there is no point in getting into a brawl, just put him to sleep. And it is often a lot safer for you and for him if you put him to sleep, because next, he wakes up and he's already outside and the patrons inside are much safer. He's not inside going crazy. (06: white male doorstaff)

But despite the perceived public antipathy towards bouncers, they are nonetheless coaxed for the latest scandal, fight, or drama with all its "gory details": "People are usually interested. Like they want to know all the gory details, like they want to hear all the war stories, 'Oh lord, were you there that night the guy died?' and stuff like that" (19: white male doorstaff).

The media are considered only part of the wider public misunderstanding of the bouncer's role. Doorstaff have come to believe that the general public view them as meatheads with little to offer except incivility and muscle:

"You make $5.50 an hour, you're just a dumb jockey" – you know, it's commonplace. (02: white male supervisor)

I would think the way we're portrayed, a lot of people think of us as just some stupid idiot that [the] only, you know, job he can do, because he's big and he can throw people out, [is] intimidate people. You know, a lot of us aren't like that. Most of us have our degrees and, you know, we're striving to better ourselves. This is just a means of doing something, and people just don't realize it's just a job, we're not here to ... (04: white male doorstaff)

I think that, [in] people's minds, most doormen are meatheads, you know, they're they're "mindless enforcers," I guess you call them. But I mean, like I said, this job is judgmental, and if you don't have good judgment, you can't do this job. So I'd say the general perception is that they're just "door dummies" ... Most guys, I mean the guys that work here, most of them, everyone's going to school, just getting away from the school. The last thing they want is trouble. They don't want to beat people up, they just want to get through school. I don't think anybody wants to be a career doorman, it's not a career job, that's for sure. So that'd be the biggest thing I guess for people to understand (01: white male supervisor)

This lack of public respect is believed to be worse than for other private security agents such as armed guards. One respondent told us, "I have a buddy of mine that went from here, he actually got laid off from here, and he went to Brinks – not Brinks, um, Pinkertons or Brinks or one of them security firms? He says, 'You know, I get more respect there, at five-fifty an hour, than I got working for you for nine.' Just because people think of bouncers in the negative way. Hopefully I'm working to change that attitude" (03: white male supervisor).

Doorstaff believe that the public only sees part of the incident and typically misses what led up to the rough handling of a patron:

The public only sees the tail-end of the situation. So they see like maybe the guy saying, "One more thing," and me going [punching and making smacking sound] and all of a sudden I'll push him out the door. And putting him in like a bar hold and taking him outside, and that's all they see. And they're thinking, "Why is that doorman getting so pissed off?" Or like, "It's that one little word." But it's not that one little word, you know what I mean? You know, it's that ten million words before that. Crazy. (10: white male doorstaff)

Some guy beats someone on the head with a bottle and then plows two girls over with punches and, know what I mean? They don't tell that part of it. Or you probably wouldn't hear all of it. People think you're an asshole and they don't know you. You're a real nerd. It's just stereotyping. They think every doorman's a big asshole who just wants to throw everybody out. That's the last thing we want to do. (13: white male doorstaff)

The only part of our job that they see is usually when we do bad. When you're in a bar, you don't usually see the doormen until something happens. They're that person standing next to the wall, and usually they stay there and you don't really see them move around too much until it hits the fan and all of a sudden all they see is three big guys pulling one little guy out and think it's an unfair fight, having never had to do it themselves. So I would have to say the general public's outlook at us is we're just a bunch of door dummies and meatheads. They have no idea, most people have no idea, what we do for a living. Don't have a clue, think we check IDs and beat people up, and it's nowhere near that. (01: white male doorstaff)

Doorstaff report that they feel misunderstood and stereotyped both after the fact and during the handling of an incident:

When you're asking somebody to leave, you've got people telling you not to hurt him, yelling at you, getting in your way. Really don't know the whole situation, like they might not have known that he was over in the corner beatin' up his girlfriend. Smacked her around a few times, and you're taking him out 'cause you want to get him out of the bar and he's resisting. And you're having to put a chokehold on him or something like that, right? 'Cause he's resisting, and the easiest way to get somebody out of the bar is just to choke them out. That's the easiest way. Just put a choke on somebody, he drops to the ground. But the thing is, there's a lot of people, like what happened at [another nightclub], they tried to put a choke on him, but the guy that was doing it didn't know what he was doing. (14: visible minority male doorstaff)

It's the most unappreciated job I've ever heard of in my life. Like, you know in eight years of bouncing, I think I can count on my finger how many times somebody said thanks at the end of the night. You know, "Thanks, you helped me with this." Like, you know, even when you go in and you help somebody with a big problem and once it's solved and they're having a good night again, they just forget you exist again. Very unappreciated ... I don't know, there's not many perks to the job. (01: white male doorstaff)

This lack of appreciation and respect, however, some doorstaff concede is earned through the brutish acts of fellow bouncers: "It's these guys that literally just run in 'cause the guy slipped on a wet spot on the carpet, pick him up, choke him out, throw him through a wall – those guys are making it look bad for the rest of us. I'd like to think that this is a job that should have respect, but everybody keeps taking it away from us. And we're the ones taking it away from ourselves, as far as I'm concerned. Other doormen make us look bad" (01: white male doorstaff).

Although they perceive themselves to be disparaged by the media and the public at large, some doorstaff believe the role of the bouncer is nonetheless very much respected in the Halifax nighttime economy:

I get a lot more freedom, I have a lot more respect, I guess. I'm just being honest, you know. I got like twenty-seven goons under me, you know what I mean ... it's about the closest thing I can say of actually having a little army, like a little platoon of your own sort of thing. (02: white male supervisor)

Like I said, we get the bad. Like out all the bars in town I'd say we get, we get the baddest. And I mean all the way from Hells Angels to whatever. And as long as you're straight up with them and they understand that these are our rules – and our rules are so simple, you don't do drugs, you don't fight, gotta get along – they respect that. (05: white male supervisor)

The creation of in-group solidarity has always historically been linked to the construction of suitable (outsider) enemies (Christie 1986). In the case of law-enforcement, these distinctions between civil and incivil members of society have long been the subject of subcultural analyses and contemporary critiques surrounding profiling. As doorstaff work in close proximity with police officers and often rely on them for support in handling the same subjects, it should come as no surprise that a common feature of bouncer culture is a general disdain for drunken troublemakers, punks, ruffians, and "assholes." This broad categorizing is not necessarily endemic to any one social grouping yet nonetheless is most often attributed to those who have little or no material or social capital. Indeed, bouncers sometimes identified their primary function as "just to make sure everybody has a good time, keep the assholes out, and anyone who wants to have a good time can stay ..." (06: white male doorstaff).

In any case, a lack of patience with those patrons who demonstrated disrespect towards doorstaff was not confined to revellers of presumably lower socioeconomic standing. One nightclub supervisor told me that the "biggest assholes are actually VIPs," who were seen as demanding, critical, and condescending towards doormen because they thought themselves to be "upper class." In light of this, he only assigned his best doormen to work in the VIP lounge – those who had an even temperament, a "very thick skin," and a very good memory for faces, because VIPs were offended if asked for identification. A local celebrity tried to enter with a group of friends and after a brief exchange was turned away. When I asked the doorman why he didn't allow the man in, he responded, "Because he's an idiot. Write that down. He's an idiot!" I asked if there was any other reason and he responded, "No ... I don't want to embarrass him." Despite the man's standing as a well-known celebrity, his treatment of doorstaff precluded him from entering. He was relegated to the "asshole" category.

These types of pronouncements were commonplace. In another instance, by almost identical reasoning (or lack thereof), when I asked a doorman, "Why did you toss him?" he responded, "Well, let me explain it to you ... he's a piece of shit" (09: white male doorstaff). In fact, this was not the only occasion where I would hear the call go out over the radio, "Don't let that guy in, he's a piece of shit."

The police were sympathetic to bouncers insofar as they were dealing with the same problem population. Bouncers reciprocated this sentiment:

A cop came down – a guy smashed a window – came down, arrested him. Shoot, afterwards he just said, "You know, I have no idea how you guys do this." You know, dealing with all these drunk idiots. (09: white male doorstaff)

[I'm] standing here, in my outfit, going, you know, "You're bother-ing us, could you take off please?" and all I get is, you know, "F you, screw you," you know, and other perusals. The police do their jobs and the same thing happens, you know, that they get accused of excessive force and a slew of other things. Again, people don't see what's predisposed the whole turn of events or series of events. (02: white male supervisor)

There was thus an obvious aversion to criminal types who became bel-ligerent, unruly, and a threat to doorstaff and patrons:

All those guys that were killed there, a group of four guys came in here all the time. Those guys that were intimidated would let these guys back into the bar. I mean these guys were accused of murder – I mean, these alcoholic guys. You don't let people like that in the bar, right? (15: white male doorstaff)

Guys that have reputations around town as being big gangster kind of guys – trying to get them out, that's a bad situation. (18: white male doorstaff)

Those who showed disrespect toward bouncers were immediately rel-egated to the asshole category:

As long as you're honest and straightforward with me and you don't fuck me personally, or fuck us at work. (06: white male supervisor)

Yeah, until you have to throw them out. And then it's, "Oh yeah, you're a fuckin' goof, you're a fat pig, you're on juice, dah dah dah," "Screw you, I'm just tryin' to have fun." Or "Leave me alone, I did-n't know that I was going to involve that person, I was drunk." You know what I mean, it depends. But if they want something, they have nothing but respect for you, but if you're doing something they don't like, they're going to throw everything they got at you. You know, so … we have the nights where someone'll come in, and as they're leavin' it'll be, "Yeah, thanks a lot, that was a great night, blah blah blah blah," you know. If you do some stuff to … But the next weekend when they show up, they're like, "Hey! Remember me, I met you, can I get in?" you know, "without payin'? Can I slide by cover"? Like that. And you get the people who always offer money too. Like if a show's sold out, like if it's a sold-out show,

they'll come up, "Oh oh oh yeah, you well, you need fifty bucks!"
"Can me and my friend get in?" They'll, "Oh come on, buddy!"
Those are the same people, who will like four hours later [say],
we're not allowed to talk to them, "You're an asshole!" (19: white
male doorstaff)

Basically anyone who fights in the bar will be not welcome back.
For quite some time. If they fight with a staff member, they're never
welcome back. As long as they live. (04: white male doorstaff)

The type of derogatory name-calling that arises on the job can heighten
a doorman's sense of antipathy toward patrons and he immediately cate-
gorizes them:

They say to me, "Oh, door dummy," and "He's not smart enough
to be in school, so you're doing this job," whatever. "This is a nice
career," all these kind of comments that come at ya ... (01: white
male supervisor)

[Some of these] fuckers walk past ... the staff and as they're walking
past just kind of, under their breath, say things like "faggot" or you
know, just things to irritate ... to see if they can get under your
skin. (11: white male doorstaff)

General incivility or misbehaviour need not be directed at doormen
at all. In fact, bouncers harboured an unflattering view of many patrons
in nightclubs, viewing them as childish drunkards that need babysitting.
In this way, bouncers constantly moralized about appropriate nightclub
behaviour and, by extension if not by accident, the virtues of sobriety:

I'm an adult babysitter. Make sure the babies don't fight. That's
about it. (10: white male doorstaff)

You can have the nicest people in the world, but when they get
drunk, uh, Michael Moriarty was thrown out of here for uh – we
asked him to leave, he asked the security guard if he'd seen a large
bag of, of marijuana. And Michael Moriaty already really wasn't
very happy, but he left along with his security guard. He left the
Shoe Shop in a police car. (06: white male security supervisor)

You know, it's like they're children, you're the adult, you can't play anymore. And, you know, they resent that, and, I can understand them resenting that – just, you know, we got liquor laws and I've got bosses I've got to answer to. (06: white male supervisor)

It's just whatever, you would think, I mean, an asshole would mean. That type of person. Some of them are ignorant pigs, yelling and screaming and fighting. The childish thing wouldn't be a big deal, but the fighting. It's your job to be a big deal, and then these big screaming people. (15: visible minority male doorstaff)

Alcohol helps explain a wide gamut of incivility for doormen, particularly when "nice" patrons become belligerent and unpredictable. The fact that anyone could turn on a doorman at any time after having a few pints of beer creates an atmosphere of social uncertainty and a generalized mistrust, even of regulars:

The customers who come in and you see them, once a week, then all of a sudden it's twice, three times, and then it's, oh no, that stupid guy, like, why does he get drunk and stupid like that? (10: white male doorstaff)

You walk them out the door and you take the extra time because they're patrons, they're regulars and you want their business back, but they're the same people that'll spit on you, literally, from time to time … Oh yeah, I've been spit on many times. And usually from one of our regular customers that you see on a regular basis that's really nice, and they figure they're immune to the rules, and you throw them out and they spit on you. (01: white male doorstaff)

The perception of contingent niceties and its easy slippage into incivility and violence can wear on a doorman's worldview, turning him into a borderline misanthropist and agoraphobic:

That's just how I feel. I hate people. I obviously hate people in general. Individually people are great. I like talking to people. But as a whole? Can't stand 'em. There's there's, and it really sucks because I can't go out to buskers. I can't go walking around or I'll feel like killing somebody that's standing next to me. It's people annoy me … the young guys, "Oh the girls in here" and I'm like, I don't see any girls in here, I see a bunch of drunken people. That's now I'm in charge of babysitting them and being nice to them. And I'm nice to them. I'm not going to be rude to people I don't feel [unintelligible] … But I keep that in mind. You haven't done anything to me yet, but you [have] every potential in the world to. I'm a cynic now, and I really happen to think this job does that to you. You don't trust young people. (01: white male doorstaff)

Even when alcohol and bravado turn a whole crew of sailors into belligerents, there is some respite in the sober afterthought of acknowledgment from their superior – a moralizing sentiment that clarifies the role and legitimacy of the bouncer:

The way it went that night was, we each grabbed a guy. If you do it right you can prevent – like, sometimes with a bigger group, if you do it right, you can prevent all them from jumping in. So what you want to do in the situation, you want to stop the guys, first of all, who're going to fight back and just kind of hold the guys who're just jumping in to help their friends. They're not necessarily going to fight with you; you just got to hold them back. That type of thing. We were lucky that night, 'cause we were outnumbered for sure. But they … actually the captain of the ship came down about an hour and a half later and apologized to us, and I assume those guys were in dire circumstances on the way back. (05: white male doorstaff)

This chapter began with a statistical analysis showing the level of alienation among and bouncers – positively correlated to experience of workplace violence – to be significantly higher than that among the public police on whom they may depend to enforce social order in the nighttime economy. The "us versus them" mentality among bouncers indicates a culture more manifest and entrenched than police culture.

From this focus on bouncer culture within the context of the occupational milieu, the following three chapters shift to a view of the nightclub from the perspective of the experience of its patrons. Thus, having studied bouncers as a constitutive and productive part in the manufacture of the nightclub scene, we now move to examine the product.

5

Getting In

This chapter is the first of three chronological examinations of "experiencing" the nightclub as a risk market – as a site of aesthetic production saturated by consumption, risk, and security in late capitalism. Whereas up to this point I have focused on the bouncer as a worker in role and his relationship to the police, management, patrons, and other bouncers, these chapters discursively reposition the bouncer within the broader theoretical context of the spectacle of the nightclub. We thus move from the eye of the bouncer to the spectacle of consumption as a whole, considering the nightclub chronologically from the eye of the patron.

Tantamount to the input-processing-output of a factory, the nightclub as a risk market can be understood from the three stages of getting in, getting noticed, and getting home. In the words of one nightclub manager, "The line, my friend, is the whole story. These faces, their colours, how they dress, the way they act, the way they carry themselves – this makes or breaks us. We know from these faces whether it's going to work."

If the queue makes or breaks the nightclub, then the vetting of those populations wishing to enter it is the most important constituent component in its production – an issue of security, to be sure, but even more telling by extension of these very same principles of risk management, its very creation as spectacle. Depending on the theme that is being created through music, ambience, advertising, and marketing promotions, the nightclub becomes those who populate it. In this way, who gets in will always matter as a basic first step in its production. The act of defining the nightclub, of creating a sense of place for a subculture or genre to display itself, is a delimiting process.

Sentry-dataveillance

The security posture of doormen at a nightclub can best be characterized as "sentry-dataveillant" (Rigakos 2006, 283–91) – a notion I have used elsewhere to describe one aspect of the overlapping labours of public and private policing. Sentry-dataveillance is particularly characteristic of checking identification at the door and making judgments about potential patrons' suitability for entry. This age-old notion of "keeping the watch" and guarding against intrusion is a core activity of bouncers and, as we have seen, also of the public police who assist bouncers nightly and engage in similar activities in various contexts.

One of the essential characteristics of sentry-dataveillance is its polymorphous manifestation in which physical security is augmented by technology. In most corporate settings, pass-key technologies have largely replaced the need for physical identification, beginning in the late 1970s. Since identities can be feigned and pass-cards stolen, new biometric technologies have been developed that now replace our historical reliance on face-to-face identification. Instead, products utilize digital renderings of facial, ocular, and physiognomatic characteristics that are akin to fingerprinting entrants. Of course, this is the commodification of the most basic of policing activities – the supplanting of an essential human security labour with a series of material commodities. It is a more efficient system that ostensibly allows for faster flows of population, more productivity, and more accuracy.

While shorter wait times, accurate and accelerated identification, and the replacement of labour with surveillance machinery is the "effectiveness-and-efficiency" purpose of these technologies, the nightclub has no issue with elongated queues. Long lineups, remember, signal desire and exclusivity. This slow coralling and processing of potential punters, therefore, is a security measure, to be sure, but security becomes a legitimation of the line itself serving its purposes in performance and crass marketing. One doorman told us, "You can stretch the line now, big time, if you take your time on the search. People think it's just for the search so they're not mad anymore if they're standing in the cold and the club is empty. You tell him, 'It's for your own security, man!'" (11: white male doorstaff).

Three white men in their twenties were patted down in front of me before being allowed to enter. This was a common practice at the Beacon but especially on theme nights when hip-hop or rave music was being played. Vigilance was dependent on the anticipated crowd. At the front door of one nightclub there are two signs. One reads, "Patrons subject to search," and the other "Video surveillance. Patrons subject to metal detection." Maintaining one access and egress point is particularly important. The use of multiple entrances and exits causes considerable difficulty for doorstaff, because they must relate information about persons being ejected to doormen at the other entry points. Typically, this is done through radio communication but in some instances descriptions are vague or not related quickly enough, and a troublemaker slips back in. In one nightclub with multiple entrances, steps had been taken to eliminate three access points.

The corralling of patrons, in any case, is a sight in itself. Albeit mundane on one level, it is a performance and ritual of inclusion at another. I recorded in my fieldnotes:

> I step outside of the nightclub to see what is happening. It's still empty inside and I'm wondering when things will pick up. As I exit the nightclub I am surprised to see a mass of party-goers shuffling from side to side in the cold as they queue up. The wait seems grossly disproportionate to the amount of available space inside. The doormen are creating, it seems to me, an unnecessary lineup. I watch three doormen process the crowd. One is using a metal detector wand. Another watches the line and directs patrons to the box office. The third (T.) stamps hands as he checks identification. Having been corralled, clubbers are now inspected, branded, and let in to feed.
>
> As if reading my mind, two young men start baaing like sheep and laugh as T. barks out orders. His instructions are clear: "Keep the sidewalk open, please! Up against the wall. Look up into the camera when you are being frisked!"
>
> As time passes, I continue to watch the queue. Men and women arrive separately in groups. They start to eye each other and strike up conversations even before they are inside the nightclub. "I heard the DJ is awesome!" says a male raver to a group of younger women. One of the women responds, winking towards the doormen, "Yeah, I hear the bouncers are hot too!" T. smiles: "Flattery will get you everything." Another white male with blue dyed hair is sporting baggy clothing, apparently the evening's theme-wear. He offers the doormen five dollars each to allow him in despite his lack of identification. They scoff at the raver and point towards the camera, claiming that they "are being watched." Of course, their reasoning for declining his bribe is disingenuous as I have seen them take money from others outside the camera's sight-lines. "We can't take

any money," they add, and T. leans in close toward me to add, "Especially from people with blue hair!"

In other cities, electronic monitoring has reached new heights. A software program known as BarWatch (see www.barlink.ca) creates a database of nightclub visitors while verifying their identification. Other surveillance mechanisms can link public police with correctional services and nightclub bouncers. A pilot project launched in Edmonton was designed to keep criminals out of nightclubs and alert authorities if they were breaching conditions of parole either by violating curfew or visiting licensed premises. This technology was being considered for Halifax during the time of my field research. In Edmonton, when a patron is banned from a nightclub, he is blacklisted on the database and will be denied entry to all other participating nightclubs. He is, in effect, banished from the nighttime economy.

Doorstaff told us better communication between night clubs and police was needed. "I think communications between the bars, in regards to who you throw out, would be a lot better. Could be a lot better. My brother stepped out for a night on a pub crawl. About twenty-five guys who had just been thrown out of [Nightclub 6] for fighting, and nobody called it in, they knew that they were coming down here, this was their next stop, and no body bothered to call ahead. [My brother] was by himself, and he got jumped" (05: white male doorstaff).

Although it isn't common practice, some doormen will share information with other nightclubs when it is in their interest. When a stamp and pad were stolen from the Galaxy, phone calls were made to other nightclubs informing them of the theft and requesting their assistance in case something turned up. Communication between police officers and among bouncers in different nightclubs already takes place on a more informal level. Indeed, once potential patrons have been corralled into holding pens awaiting access to nighttime "transgression" (Presdee 2000), they are easy targets of passive surveillance by the state. Oftentimes the police, outside nightclubs on a paid-duty basis, use these nocturnal choke points in order to facilitate state interests.

Like sometimes they'll look for the people, show us pictures. "If you see this guy let us know," or "He's known to frequent bars," or "Don't let this guy, if he comes in." Sometimes we'll see people going in the bar, and we'll say "That's so and so," known criminal or whatever. (white male supervisor)

They keep the uncertain element, the people that should be out anyway, right, they see the cops at the front door and they figure, Okay, you know, if we go in there tonight, we gotta be really good, 'cause they're that close. And they won't have a chance to get away kind of thing. Or the cops even know certain people and they just stop them at the door and say, "Listen, you're, you've been charged with so many counts of assault," or whatever. They don't really have to explain themselves, they just say, "We're not letting you in tonight. We don't want any trouble from you." And they know who the bad guys are. And it helps us out too. (visible minority male supervisor)

The vetting techniques and technologies deployed outside nightclubs range from the arbitrary to the mundane to the technologically sophisticated. Metal detectors, CCTV cameras, electronic card readers and books of the banned happily coexist with "I don't like your face" and "Get lost, punk." There is a general tendency to perceive technological "advancements" as less arbitrary, fairer, and somehow binding on the gatekeeper. Of course, this isn't so. Discretion, for better or worse, is still the primary vetting tool of doormen.

CCTV cameras are located throughout the nightclub and next to ATM machines and above cash registers. But they also appear at door entrances and even point down towards the sidewalk bordering the nightclub. Interestingly, patrons' cell phones and cameras are not allowed in the nightclub; countersurveillance is outlawed by nightclub management. Security gadgets of all sorts have now made their way into each and every Halifax nightclub. Even at the Mansion where security measures were relatively lax at the start of our field research, metal detectors, security cameras, and personal radios with transparent earpieces were all in use by the time we had completed the ethnography. However, although the technology to maintain databases on banned persons is currently employed in other locales, most Halifax nightclubs still largely rely on their doorstaff's memory. "Known troublemakers" are now digitally recorded at two nightclubs, but most doormen can easily identify persons whom they have ejected in the past.

Metal detector wands are another staple of nightclub security access. Even so, these gadgets also have limits. One nightclub owned a number of metal detector wands but they were only used in milder weather because cold conditions made them far too sensitive. Even with the presence of metal detectors, doormen were instructed to conduct "pat-downs."

These are used to legitimize longer lines, giving the appearance of higher demand even though the club may be relatively empty. The security reason, of course, is that pat-downs are more effective at detecting weapons, because even metal detectors can be circumvented. One doorman told me that a handgun with the right amount of cloth wrapped around it can fool the metal detector. In this sense, the frisking of patrons is used both as a method of risk management and to create the appearance of high demand for the nightclub. Indeed, there was a perception among doormen that mere word of mouth managed to keep out many patrons who might be planning to carry guns or knives. Some patrons were scrutinized more than others despite the presence of detectors and pat-downs. For example, on at least two occasions, black patrons who appeared to be wearing gang and/or hip-hop paraphernalia were searched more carefully and directly asked, "Are you carrying anything tonight?" "I mean nine times out of ten the guy's just gonna turn and walk away, right, 'cause he's been arrested already" (15: visible minority male doorstaff).

A new security gadget introduced during our field research was a hand-held card reader that checked the age of patrons by lifting the magnetic imprint on the black strip of government identification such as driver's licences. It looked similar to a debit machine card reader, and for me it had a similar symbolic effect and purpose. The Galaxy had three of these readers in operation. A digital readout on the instrument displayed the age of the patron and allow this to be quickly cross-referenced with information on the physical ID card. On one busy Saturday night, one of the doorstaff stationed at the entrance used the ID reader in a unique way. A drunk patron known to the doorman approached the bar entrance. Expecting that the patron would insist that he was not inebriated, the doorman held out the ID reader and affixed a straw to the AC power slot on the side of the gadget. He turned to the patron and said, "You have to blow in this before getting in. We've got us see how much you've had to drink." Sure enough, the man leaned over and blew as hard as he could into the straw while the doorman held it. The doorman told him to stop, pressed a button to display the time, and held it in front of the man. The doorman showed the inebriated patron. "1:02. See this? You're waaaay over the limit. We can't let you in." The drunk man shrugged his shoulders and left without incident. This doorman now carries straws in his pocket for future use.

A relatively simple and effective way to minimize the chance of weapons and illegal substances in a nightclub is to institute a coat-check policy. Along with the patrons' physical unbundling, the persistent consumption-security-risk nexus is here metaphorically also laid bare. On the one hand, a forced coat-check policy connotes a sense of decorum. Patrons in heavy coats are not an attractive aesthetic. On the other hand, the coat-check is an effective security measure that pays off. Patrons must pay for the service.

> We had a coat check that was implemented. There's people in here with guns. That's why the coat check is here. It's not to try and make extra money or that type of thing. And I tell people at times, "That coat check's there 'cause I mean we've had people in here with guns and knives." I mean, we were moving people, a gun falls out of somebody's pocket. You're like, you're jumping on trying to grab it out of this guy's hand type of thing. That's the reason that coat check's there. But people really don't know, and we say, "Oh no, it's just there," I mean to club people. I mean that's the real reason it's there and management is not gonna tell ya, "That's the reason why the coat check's there." (15: visible minority male doorstaff)

> Throughout the fall, winter, spring months, we often enforce the coat-check rule, especially the long coats. The people at the door are always watching, to make sure nobody's – hopefully they can spot something a person's carrying. (05: white male doorstaff)

One of the secret delights of doorstaff supervisors was to show me their collection of fake identification – a "Book of the Banned," as one of them called it. Each successive page of the laminated album, like a chronological display of advancing print technology, revealed yet another innovation into desktop computing, scanners, and colour printers. The ability to spot fake ID was a prized occupational skill among doorstaff, akin to police officers spotting a "joint body" or stolen car (Skolnick and Fyfe 1993). Doorstaff routinely confiscated identification cards, simply holding onto those they thought suspicious or counterfeit. They managed this primarily by calling the bluff of prospective patrons. Some would feign calling the police on their personal radios to verify the authenticity of the identification card. Threatened with the possibility of criminal charges such as identity theft and/or fraud, the suspected patron would choose to leave, and the doorman would add another bogus card to his album of the banned. At least two nightclubs kept such books, and another was planning to start one.

> I think they should have pictures or maybe a little bio on people that are problem people. Troublemakers, that type of thing. It

would just give us more power at the door. I mean if we know a background, or a history on somebody and say maybe he isn't the kind of guy you want in the bar. (15: visible minority male doorstaff)

Now like them guys are barred for life, and I put them on the list and I put "indefinite." And there's no pictures or nothin' but I might start a book of the, I call it the, p.o.s. Book … Piece of Shit. [*laughter*] The p.o.s. Book. (03: white male supervisor)

In lieu of threatening to call the police, another doorman immediately pocketed a potential patron's identification card. When the man demanded the return of his government ID, the doorman calmly asked a co-worker for a pen, then scratched and lifted the faux facing of the card to reveal the original underneath. "Man, I knew it was fake as soon as you took it out of your pocket. The scan is too grainy. You're too used to getting into the Galaxy!" The doorman finally returned the underage patron's handiwork and engaged in friendly banter with him for the next five minutes while they smoked. Having been caught red-handed, the young man gave up all pretense and eventually left in a jovial mood.

Working the Door as Production

In a strictly Marxist economic sense, bouncers are unproductive labourers in the generally unproductive service sector economy. Like police officers, security guards, clowns, and menial servants, they make no material commodity for exchange; their labour-time leaves no surplus-value and no capitalist reaps the benefits of their exploited labour. According to Marx, "The mere direct exchange of money for labour therefore does not transform money into capital or labour into productive labour" (1972, 403). One doorman aptly put it: "Security's just an expense. We're overhead that you don't really need until something happens. So, security I find always gets cut back, cut back, cut back" (06: white male supervisor).

I have already argued, however, that bouncers help "make" the scene and that within the spectacle (Debord 1995) of the nightclub, itself within the variegated consumable spaces of the night (Lefebvre 1991), the bouncer is indeed eminently productive. Patrons too are no less commodified, even though, again within a strict Marxist economic rendition, this is utter nonsense outside slavery. The nightclub as a pleasure factory is a cacophony of imagery imparted at a price for entry, augmented with a fee for its amplification through alcohol or drugs. Late capitalism everywhere replicates its commodifying principles, attempting to colonize every aspect of the nighttime frontier (Melbin 1978), fetishizing human interaction by hiding its productive logics. It is everywhere and therefore invisible.

This section elucidates the productive role of the bouncer in this frenzied, crowded, postmodern factory floor. Bouncers are, in an iconographic sense, the last vanguard of de-industrialized blue-collar machismo, trading hardhat for headset as union jobs are outsourced and factories move offshore. They are now aesthetic engineers, part of the pulse of the nighttime economy, vetting patrons into desirables and undesirables, VIPs and riff-raff, regulars and newbies. The aesthetic engineers are working in spaces that are themselves constantly being re-engineered:

> In a one nightclub during the ethnography we were told that renovations were underway in order to attract a "better crowd." The changes to the style, architecture, and music to be played in the new section of the nightclub was aimed at "getting in the bad element out" and "attracting more spenders." As part of the renovation process, changes were also being made to increase security by limiting the number of access points and installing CCTV cameras at the entrances in order that all members of the public entering could be recorded. Many of the changes to layout were intended to eliminate "many nooks and hiding spots throughout the bar … which made it difficult for removals" and hindered the ability to relay descriptions of banned individuals to other doorstaff. The construction of the new space was going hand in hand with security concerns. On the flip side, of course, removing persons from segregated spaces obscures the spectacle of violence from other patrons in the nightclub.

Targeted dress codes, music genres, and marketing strategies are in the end negotiated by the bouncer all within competing material, social, and cultural capitals of the night. While these considerations are invariably perforated throughout by age, class, gender, and race (Messerschmidt 1997), so much as this is possible this section holds in abeyance direct commentary on these intersections, for they deserve and receive their own treatment soon after.

How important are bouncers in making the nightclub a site of aesthetic production? Managers, owners, and, of course, doorstaff themselves thought them central to creating a mood or impression for the nightclub. If one sees the nightclub as an attraction, then a burly and surly bouncer is counterproductive: "You know, you get a 350 pound guy standing at the door, you know, grunting and groaning for IDs and things like that, and people gonna go in with a negative attitude. You know, whereas you put someone a little less physically intimidating and maybe with a little bit more personality at the front door and you're gonna, hopefully start things off on a more positive note and people are gonna, you know, go in [the Galaxy] with a smile on their face rather than going, 'That's a hick.' So the end result, hopefully, will reflect the person's first impression as well" (02: white male supervisor). Trying to illustrate the social skills of his fellow staff, one respondent noted, "This bar is like kind of an attraction, like one of the best bars to work at. We have about twelve doormen and at least five of them could be head doorman" (10: white male doorstaff).

In any case, no matter how cordial the doorstaff, potential patrons are reminded that they are being scrutinized. Increasingly, the entrances to nightclubs are posted with a variety of signs ranging from a reminder of the establishment's zero tolerance policy on drugs to fire permits/capacity codes. There are also reminders of the presence of cameras with notices that read: "Smile for the camera" and "Notice: our premises are under video surveillance." Patrons are reminded that they will be under the gaze of nightclub patrons and security staff and recorded by CCTV cameras. They should therefore act accordingly. The ideal nightclub doorstaff puts people at ease and signals their transition into an exclusive area of consumption, risk, and security. In this way the bouncer is an iconographic symbol of prestige in the nighttime urban economy. Knowing the bouncer is a powerful manifestation of social capital.

There are actually two lines at the front of most nightclubs: the regular box office queue and the VIP line. The former is for everyone who cannot muster any particular form of capital to gain privileged access, while the latter is for VIP pass-holders, walk-up celebrities, bar staff persons on guest lists, and those who have already been stamped. Of course, there is always the possibility of entry by simply "juicing" or tipping the doorman. I witnessed innumerable attempts by persons from all walks of life trying to get VIP passes from doorstaff, but these were usually handed out sparingly, at the bouncers' discretion. Those who received passes were able to bypass paying a cover charge and feel special. Those who were not favoured with a pass – or worse, who had their passes revoked – were variably shocked, angered, and humiliated because part of their self-worth was tied to being "someone" in the nightclub. Regulars, celebrities, and important people were waved right in: they were the "in crowd" both literally-spatially and figuratively-symbolically. And on both those levels the gatekeeper, of course, was the bouncer. One evening a security supervisor arrived at the front entrance of a nightclub I was visiting to inform the doorstaff that two celebrities, Kevin Spacey and Brian Bosworth, were on their way to the bar. He told them that the celebrities would be brought in through the back door. When I asked what the nightclub's procedure was for VIPs, I was told that such special persons had their own security personnel. The VIPs' security agencies contact the nightclub ahead of time to warn of their impending arrival. The nightclub then assigns one door-man to join the security entourage when they are admitted.

Dress codes are an indicator of exclusivity, of a particular set of aes-thetics, of constituting ambience; they are also a mechanism by which to attract and dissuade potential patrons through their self-identification with various representational stagings. Couched within a notion of the representation of self through consumption and the concomitant effects of such representations on risk and security, these ordering schemes are far more ubiquitous to the nightclub as aesthetic production and specta-cle than may be realized. Dress codes force preparatory work for inclu-sion: they invoke a mindset, they build expectation, they produce chatter about appropriateness. They also empower the doorstaff: they are the first instance in the disciplining of patrons, reaching out and gripping them by their collared and cologned shirts well before they leave home. Dress codes, guest lists, and cover charges are constitutive of space, manifestos of gender, class, and race cleavages. They carve the night into discrete pockets of consumption status and risk, presumably through anticipated associations of like-minded, like-dressed, and like-aspiring punters. A posted dress code could surely be the frontispiece of the night's violent confessional.

DRESS CODE

NO

Athletic wear or shorts

Camouflage wear

Ripped clothing

Jersey style shirts

Hats/headwear

Cut-off pants or shorts

Muscle shirts (men)

Towels

Some of the items on the above list were included to prevent specific sub-cultural elements (read: black hip-hop crowds) from entering. Some items were added so that there would not appear to be a double standard.

For example, disallowing "hats/headwear," more generally rather than baseball caps specifically can be read as the nightclub's attempt to avoid publicly targeting a particular group. In fact, at one bar the dress code was being amended to make the rules appear more vague and thus place more discretionary authority in the hands of doorstaff. One doorman told me it allowed them to dismiss "a lot of people from coming into the bar that we feel might be problems. We have a pretty extensive dress code, and we're allowed to use that at our own discretion." I asked if the dress code prevented people who might be trouble from coming in. "Yeah, for the most part," he responded. "It prevents a lot of people that, you know, that you wouldn't want in the bar. And if there's something that we could pick out on them, that we you know, besides saying that "we don't want you in the bar ..." (04: white male doorstaff)

Not specifying particular subcultural groups such as "hip-hoppers" or the "Goth crowd" or the group's attire and accoutrements helps depoliticize exclusion. Another doorman explained, "If you're turning them away because they don't meet the dress code that the bar has, then you get in all the pissed-off situations, right? They're gonna stand their ground. I mean the majority of time it's pretty positive, because it applies to everyone. You usually end up turning away, I mean "I'm sorry, I don't make up the dress code, I'm just here to enforce the policy," and so you get a pretty good response from people. Like I mean, you approach it in a half-decent manner then" (15: visible minority doorstaff).

Some patrons appeal to managers on the basis of the policies posted. They literally point to posted dress codes, complaining that a doorman has inappropriately interpreted the directive. Men are asked to check any denim, leather, or suede coats. Anything other than a shell or dress jacket must be given to the coat girl. No ripped clothes, headwear, track pants, work boots, or gold chains worn outside of shirts are permitted. The last of these curious rules was apparently implemented because it "was intimidating female patrons."

On rave nights the dress code is slackened because "these types of people have a style all their own" and because, in Halifax, "many of them are black." A supervisor told me that on rave nights they are far more likely to let the dress code slide a little bit. They allow baseball caps, for example, because people on Ecstasy like to hide their eyes. In order to reward patrons who return after changing their clothing because they did not originally meet the dress code, most doormen allow them into the nightclub without paying cover charge. And when business is slow, dress codes seem to slacken: "It's hard where you have to – where you want to fill the place," one doorman admitted. "If somebody just got off work from an oil rig, say they've got grease all over their clothes, you know, we don't care, we're not gonna let you in the bar. It's not the image we want to portray in the bar."

So the dress code wasn't totally about preventing violence in the bars? I asked. "Well, I think there are certain images, of course," he replied.

At one of the nightclubs we included in the ethnography, there appeared to be no discernible dress code. At first I thought this rather odd and in conflict with my notion that nightclubs were "produced," as it were, through rules of exclusivity and inclusivity. One evening when a man entered that same nightclub and turned to ask, "Do I have to take off my hat?" the doorman responded, "Oh, don't worry about it, man. Do whatever you want." When I asked the doorman, "Is there any dress code here?" he responded with a rather an emphatic "No!" – because "that would ruin the place. Hey, we see all sorts of people in here. Some people look like they just got off the plane from the Bayou!" And it was true. As I scanned the crowd, it was obvious that ripped jeans comfortably circulated amongst business suits. But the nightclub's eclectic mix and its "freaks" were its draw. No dress code was the code here:

> It's so low key and that's what draws people, I think, to it. Some people think it's a freak show, but I kind of like the freak show, I guess. I dunno. 'Cause I mean some people are weird, coming in with mohawks, purple hair, and, just being themselves. And that's the coolest thing about it, right? (04: white male supervisor)

> People come here because we let everybody in. I know some of these guys and they only dress up to come to our club. They're weekend freaks! [*laughter*] (11: white male doorstaff)

Music is expressive, it is both social and anomic, freeing, motivating, sexy. It is political even when – perhaps especially when – it attempts to be apolitical. From hippie acid trips to punk rock mosh pits to inner-city rap dens to rhythmic pogoing in a hangar full of lollipop-sucking ravers, music comes to define successive generational rebellion, culture and counter-culture.[1] While I have no intention of conducting an historical analysis of the potential for oppression or liberation in the musicology of a good beat or rhyme, it is impossible to analyze clubbing without being confronted with that most favoured of contemporary, supposedly counter-cultural carnivals of the postmodern theorist: the rave. Raves, rave or techno music, and their development have received tremendous attention from both criminal justice alarmists (e.g., Rintoul 2001) and critical cultural enthusiasts (e.g., Jackson 2004), the former focusing mainly on sexual assualt and death by Ecstacy, the latter on the liberating principles of raving. Those who tend to exalt the rave experience do so in the context of its "mystique of happening" (Presdee 2000, 120) because "in all its forms [it] continues the postmodern theme of fascination with sensation ... without sense or meaning" (121).

For Presdee, among others (e.g., Jackson 2004; Malbon 1999), the rave comes to symbolize an ultimate form of consumption, an expressive and "unregulated carnivalesque atmosphere" (120). He argues: "Rave culture becomes the perfect form of consumption without context of content, an apolitical and safe form of nothingness that challenges and shocks by its very concentration on the ecstatic out-of-mind experience that places the hedonism of the 'body' before the logic of the mind" (Presdee 2000, 121). Presdee recognizes that this ostensibly freeing, countercultural space where the rave occurs is increasingly regulated by the state through policing and licensing until, regrettably, the "unofficial second life of the people is driven deeper from view and comprehension" (135). This is a lamentable development, to be sure, but only because, first, we are to believe that raves are or were somehow "liberating" and second, that the state's (nocturnal) awakening only now usurps this transgressional potential.

These two assertions strategically ignore the alarming presence of *private* policing. Let's not forget about the gate-keeping of the bouncer, the usher, the bus driver, someone, anyone, standing by with a stamp and ink pad collecting cover. Why privilege the state? Moreover, why regard licensing laws as the rave's obituary? Raves are more prevalent now than ever, free, tourist-destination raves even more so. Are raves thus now more than ever a "perfect commodity" by virtue of their own lack of historical awareness, a "golden age" of raves ignored, forgotten, or ill respected? Doesn't the rave's contemporary ahistoricism, villification, and criminalization therefore make it even more transgressional, more potentially liberating by virtue of its reluctant politicization?

This hamster wheel of theoretical nonsense is of my own making (certainly not Presdee's), so let me jump off to offer that *raves and rave music are nothing special*. In fact, raves by virtue of their characteristically frenzied yet nonetheless placid love-stupours are anything but transgressional or potentially freeing. They have easily been swallowed up not by the state's late-night stumblings but by nightclubs already well equipped to strategically market to ravers, promote DJs, and, above all else, offer some semblance of organized policing. Raves today are usually just one more theme night – tomorrow, Seventies music, Thursday, alternative punk rock (whatever that has become), Friday, hip-hop. We are thus left to nostalgize about some long-lost movement whose "nothingness" was abruptly absorbed and recirculated with astonishing ease.[2] The rave has been swallowed up and spit out by that same circulating morass of symbols it sought to swim against; glow-sticks and Skittles now float alongside hip-huggers, biker jackets, Mohawks, mop-tops, and Raider's jackets, just another prop in the spectacle of the nightclub.

This supposed pluralism of nightclub music, this multiculturalism, actually everywhere seeks to exclude by style because rebellion sells (Heath and Potter 2005). Music genres are soundtracks for age, race, class, and gender. Nightclubs play types of music to include and exclude. They produce through dress code, cover charge, aesthetics, and music a type of personality for themselves. They create a comfort zone for some by dissuading others. One doorman told us, "Oh they're not gonna tell ya the reason why the bands are here. It's to cut down on black people in the bar. That's the reason why it's there. It's not stated or said anywhere, but that's the reason why it's there. You know what I mean? The bars close early on certain days. That again is for a reason … to keep out a certain crowd of people that're coming from different bars. That's why things are there. I mean, a lot these guys, they pussy-foot around, but you know, I try and say it how it is, right? I mean you're not gonna get that from a lot of people around, to be honest and to be up front. It's all about keeping black people out" (15: visible minority male doorstaff).

The connection between aesthetics and comfort makes the reputation of a nightclub. Nightclubs self-select by providing ambience for targeted populations: the intimate connection between music, the logo-ized wardrobe styles that are associated with different genres, and the types of people that wear such clothing. This became abundantly clear one Saturday night when I asked a club-goer in Toronto for suggestions for bars: "Over there," he pointed out to me, "is actually, that club is way Benetton, mixed. That other one down the street is totally Abercrombie: all white bread all the time. If you want to see the whiggers and brothers, you know, iced out, chains and Enyce, [*pointing*] turn right at [Main] Street. The top-end club – red carpet, limos, Armani boys, hotties – doesn't open until 11:30."

Are artificial lineups really artificial? On the face of it, the answer is an obvious "yes," because there is an abundant supply of space relative to the demand. Nightclubs may open their doors at 9 P.M. and a club may be deserted up until 11 P.M. or later; nonetheless, patrons wait patiently outside under the direction of doormen. This is of course a familiar ritual.

But the logic of the queue is only evident if we consider that the product is not the nightclub per se but those who populate it. In analyzing the screening of VIPs, gangsters, cuties, b-boys, ravers, and the like as essential to constituting the nightclub, we have also witnessed the theoretical intersections of security and consumption (and risk). Dress codes, ambience, cover charges, music – these all discipline the patron to behave in particular ways. But perhaps what reveals the patron as product and aesthetic labourer above all else is the empty nightclub. Why bother? Why stay? "This place is dead." A stage is meaningless without an audience; bar stools and railings are worthless without voyeurs and dancers. Line-ups are thus never artificial in this sense: they are essential for producing critical mass and mass appeal. The queue is the first assembly station in producing the nightclub itself.

One doorman told me that because his nightclub has cut back in staff from twenty to fourteen people on busy nights, this has actually cost them more money. Since one of the main doors to the nightclub may not be opened and more people spend time in line rather than drinking, he surmised that this had resulted in less income for the establishment. On a slow night, a supervisor stationed on the sidewalk looked inside the bar. "We're losing a lot of people to cover. I'm going to start saying 'You pay and your friend gets in for free.'" Demand matters. A young white male in khakis arrived at 2 A.M. outside the Beacon. "I've got no ID, but I've got all this shit," he said while offering of assortment of cards from his wallet. "I'll look at shit. Shit is lookable," responded the doorman. The patron was eventually allowed in.

Age, Class, Gender, Race ...

Under régimes of risk, security, and consumption, the management of populations becomes the defining techne for ensuring success. Risk markets lend themselves quite naturally to decision-making based on the statistical principles of population characteristics. This process can be as ubiquitous and seemingly innocuous as "market research" (Miller and Rose 1997) and insurance assessments (Doyle and Ericson 2004) or as targeted and politically charged as anti-terrorist profiling measures (Armoore 2006). In any case, these forms of risk assessment rely on aggregate knowledge of characteristics of categories of peoples. Whether these categorizations are empirically calculable or the product of bias cannot belie their politicizing and moralizing nature.

Core social identities of age, class, gender, and race (in no particular order) are categorizations of consumers and risk that are amplified rather than vitiated in the nighttime economy. This section gives particular attention to the roles of these identities in constituting the nightclub, notwithstanding that throughout this book, age, class, gender, race, and sexual orientation[3] impact the analysis. I want to consider these identities, moreover, not only in a general theoretical and discursive sense but both concretely and empirically through the words and actions of nightclub bouncers themselves. These are often unflattering, sometimes racist, prejudiced, and dehumanizing constructions. It is important to remember that these identities are cast, however, in the context of nightclub appeal, consumption, and risk. Even so, they are sometimes playful and even sympathetic.

Knowing the bouncer and maintaining a good rapport is a precious commodity in the nighttime economy. Other forms of identity seem to give way in the face of a nod of approval by a doorman, a social capital manifested in the form of "vouching for someone." When a group of intoxicated frat-boy types tried to gain entry to the nightclub, I was certain that they were just the type of individuals who would be sent on their way. As it turned out, they were familiar with the doorman, and he turned to one of their group and said, "You're not going to get in any trouble in there, are you? Because you're a little drunk and you were beaking off out here a little earlier." After some assurances, the group was allowed in. On another night, when a group of eight drunk football players approached the nightclub, they were given guest passes despite being boisterous and shouting profanities. Another doorman allowed his cousin to enter on the condition that he buy him three beers. A young man with no apparent connections who appeared to be in his mid-twenties took one bouncer aside and asked if there was "any chance of getting in tonight." The doorman, who didn't know or trust the youth implying the bribe, flippantly responded, "Yup, if you stand in line and pay cover charge, lots." A woman unsuccessfully tried to drop a name and was informed she was "outta luck" because the doorman she was asking for no longer worked at that nightclub. She was instructed to pay cover charge or leave.

The predominant function of doormen in downtown Halifax, as in most other nightclubs, is the inspection of identification cards primarily for the purpose of keeping out underage patrons. Violating the drinking age can place the nightclub at serious risk of having its licence suspended. Moreover, underage drinking could result in lawsuits. Doorstaff must be diligent enough to leave a good impression with the liquor inspector. As an example, my conversation with a doorman was interrupted one evening outside of the Mansion by a supervisor who stuck his head out the door and barked, "ID, ID, ID, and when in doubt, more ID." Concerned about recent visits from the liquor inspector, he was reminding doorstaff that when unsure of the validity of a first offering of identification, they should ask for another.

In one case a woman well known to doorstaff was not allowed in because she did not have identification, even though staff knew that she was thirty-eight years old and a frequent guest. Young women, nonetheless, were far less likely to be asked for identification than men. On certain nights, it was clear to me that doormen were far more vigilant against men than they were women. I recorded in my fieldnotes:

> It is 20 below as I stand shivering outside the nightclub shortly after midnight. I am occasionally ducking under the heaters despite my heavy coat. There is a stiff breeze howling up Brunswick Street, and I feel as if my eyes will freeze shut. Yet I am stunned to see four very young-looking women queue up with barely anything to protect them from the frigid night air. Not even a jacket? Their exposed shoulders and backs turn bright red. They are shivering but they need only be in line for a few moments. The doorman standing next to me has already motioned them into the club, and the girls bat their eyes as they whisk past the others in line. One of them stops to give the doorman a kiss. "Why did you let them in before the others?" I ask, already guessing at the answer. "The poor girls had nipple-itis," he responds with a smile.

Whether the doorman was motivated by a sense of chivalry or the fact that without an abundant supply of attractive women, a nightclub would flounder, young scantily clad women were often hustled through the front door without been questioned. I asked another doorman why he refused to allow a young-looking patron to enter. He responded, "She's ugly. I don't like ugly people." After some prompting he admitted that the patron's ID was expired.

Race and crime are inextricably linked not only in the mindset of the general public but also that of police and doorstaff. The particular problem that race poses for a doorman relates back to negotiating the nightclub as a risk market. Hip-hop music, gangsta rap, and even popular dance music attract "a certain element" clearly not welcome in some downtown nightclubs. This is because the music itself and the genre's style links itself to organized crime and gangster life. Black men who emulate rap and hip-hop artists style themselves in a fashion that seems aggressive or intimidating to the average student pub-goer.

Some doormen, however, readily concede that the connection between black criminality and nightclub violence is exaggerated, pointing instead to the problems caused by whites: "I'd say probably 99.9 per cent of the problems [are caused by] white people, and the other per cent is other black people, Indian, Chinese, or whatever else. So it's not a big problem. And I don't see them doing, changes, or having changes like I mean [clubs are playing] … white music" (15: visible minority male doorstaff).

Indeed, in one nightclub we were told that renovations were underway in order to attract a "better crowd." The changes to the style, architecture, and music to be played in the new section were aimed at "getting the bad element out" and "attracting more spenders." As part of the renovation process, changes were also being made to increase security, limiting the number of access points and installing CCTV cameras at the entrances so that all members of the public entering the nightclub could be recorded. Improving the nightclub's aesthetic and upgrading the security system were a means to an end: making some patrons feel more comfortable while excluding others. Often these decisions were linked to race:

> That's the one thing I hate … it's a racial barrier. And I mean … a lot of people have negative sides towards maybe black people and I think that is unfortunate. So that's a part of this job that I don't like. (20: visible minority male doorstaff)

> We have a lot of different racial groups coming down here. Sometimes you get a few fights, that happens …well we had to remove, it's usually remove a couple of people, and then they have a whole group who follows them out. That's usually what it is. We've had a few cases like that. We had to bar, like, probably twenty, I can't remember, there were about twenty, twenty people in the bar. A lot of cultures. We get a lot of Lebanese and Greeks and a lot of cultures. (08: white male doorstaff)

Doorstaff supervisors, of course, report that they have no tolerance for racial epithets or racist attitudes among their bouncers:

> I don't like racists, don't like anybody that's got that attitude. We had this one guy that was working here for a while, and he came to the back door all lit up, and he was "nigger" this, "nigger" that, and I said, "Where are you going with that mouth? Are you taking that

mouth into this bar? You work here? You've gotta work with people that are black and stuff, and you're going in there with a lip like that on you? That doesn't make sense to me. You go in there and say something like that to one of these guys, and I don't care if they pop you! You bring it on yourself." And he worked here. He's toned it down now, and he's only working here one night a week, but he's not even doorstaff now, he's bussing now. (04: white male supervisor)

While doormen concede that problems in a nightclub often have nothing to do with race, it is nonetheless also true that black gang members are a source of tremendous tension and potential violence:

[You] don't know everybody, I mean we've thrown out groups of people who've been from Toronto and they've turned out to be criminals who've had guns, you know, we had no idea. But they always find out the next day, you know, through the grapevine, they were carrying guns or whatever. (06: white male supervisor)

I had some blacks that spit on me a couple of weeks ago. They spit on my lap. (10: white male doorstaff)

[We] try to run a clean bar. We keep troublemakers, criminals, out of the bar, to keep it safe inside. And that involves, you know, keeping organized crime out, and people, you know, charged with crimes, or people we know from talk on the street they're committing crimes and they haven't [unintelligible]. You know, these guys, basically, a lot of them have nothing to lose. And when you're telling someone that no, they can't come in, and this is important to them to get in here, and they, you know, either they're drug dealers or they've killed people in the past, and things like that ... If you don't know who the criminals are, then you're putting yourself in more danger. Uh, because you have to handle them a certain way, you have to handle them a little differently than you would, say a twenty-year-old college student who's here and wants to drink. (06: male white supervisor)

A group of black men in a nightclub can heighten the overall level of tension for doorstaff and change the general complexion of the nightclub – particularly when such groups become a visible contingent populating one section of the nightclub. "It may appear more that there's problems with the blacks and we deal with them, because as we say, we got eyes ...

But I mean … the highest crime rates in Nova Scotia are not by black people," one doorman admitted. However, "It just seems like there's sections, when a lot of black people come around the bars, I mean, you've got unfortunately small clusters … in certain parts of the bar. And maybe that's good, because that's where they're happy … but then the whole nightclub, it gets changed. Like there's a certain part of [the nightclub] named 'the hood' … It's not right, but that's the way that it's done, right?" (20: white male doorstaff)

Doormen were often implored to make sure that identification cards were valid before allowing anyone entry, yet it seemed evident that bias in the form of discretion was routinely being exercised. I observed in my fieldnotes,

> Two black couples are at the front entrance by the box office. The bouncer is asking them questions. A woman in her late twenties says that she only has her ID from Acadia University and that her and her friends from Kenya do not have other Canadian identification. She is told that she cannot enter without government identification. Visibly upset, she is holding up her notification card once again and saying, "Do you think I could fake this ID, look at the picture!" The response is simple: "Sorry, but it has to be a government ID. You can't get in here tonight." Annoyed, the woman leaves with her friends, while her male friend adds, "You guys are going to lose our business." The two bouncers sarcastically respond, "Whooooooooo. Think we care? No …" Right after the incident with the group of Kenyans, several well-dressed white women approach the entrance. Without checking their identification, the doormen smile and give them guest passes.

While race continues to play a significant role in nightclubs and especially in the discourse of bouncers, it is important to contextualize the nature of the exchange. My fieldnote below describes how racial epithets are sometimes strangely both a source of alienation and exclusion while only moments later they are half-mocked as a way to create camaraderie and inclusion. It is also telling that the social capital of "being known" to the bouncer and the patron's class position plays a significant mitigating role when it comes to race:

> It's a cool but comfortable night as I stand by the main entrance once again. Shortly after 1:05 A.M., two fashionably dressed black

men queue up in the VIP line. One of the two immediately gestures towards the doormen with a nod: "Gotta be careful of you white guys!" "Yeah, we're greasy fucks!" replies the doorman with a smile. They obviously know each other and continue to exchange greetings. "What happened to [Pender's]?" asks the patron. "Ah, we got rid of it to keep the black guys out," answers another doorman. "You buy them shoes?" fires back the black man. The doormen laugh and hand the two patrons guest passes ... Once they have passed, they shake their heads in amusement. The two doormen now point in the direction of a co-worker, a doorman of native descent. "Check out the haircut crew," one says to the other. I take it they are mocking the close haircuts of the three native men dressed in hip-hop attire who are chatting with the native doorman. The two bouncers share a quiet laugh as one turns to the other with his palm raised and says: "How!" "How, yeah, he's the chief," the other responds. They exchange smirks of self-satisfaction as they turn to attend the patrons approaching the bar ... An hour later the two black men make their way out of the nightclub. As they exit the front entrance, two doormen are conducting pat-downs of patrons still entering. Much to the surprise and confusion of those in the queue, one of the black men yells out, "Make sure you check the white man! Check the white man!" The doorstaff smile and shake their heads, saluting the men as they leave.

The object of the surveillance capacities of the nightclub is to render the patron as known as possible. Despite all the technology, the best method of detecting possible troublemakers is the doorman's own memory. Nightclub managers often hired bouncers from areas where they believed gang activity was more common. For example, one of the more senior and well-respected doormen was born and raised in Spryfield, often known for black criminality. He was invaluable for his ability to recognize "known persons" in Halifax's underworld and traded on this knowledge for his own benefit. Indeed, he was well on his way to receiving a degree from Dalhousie University and becoming a correctional officer. This particular doorman became fed up with having to deny access or remove his own acquaintances, so he moved to another nightclub that was unpopular with his childhood crowd. He said he could no longer work in such locations because everyone would be saying, "Hey, cuz, can you let me and the boys in for free?" He added that he much preferred anonymity: "I like the strangers," he told me, "I like the strangers."

Nonetheless, knowledge of local toughs was an asset sought after by nightclub managers:

> I pretty much know all the bad boys, all the people that we barred. See, with this job so many [doorman] are transient, they come and they go, it's hard to keep track of, that's my biggest thing. (04: white male supervisor)

> 'Cause, like the criminal mind, when he's out there, like, they're changing their looks. These guys are growing their hair, growing beards, they're doing, it's just like they got this evil thing in them, that just doesn't stop, and they just gotta go out, cause trouble all the time, you know what I mean? And, they'll try like, Halloween would have been a perfect night for them to come out, you know, they can come in and they can joke to their friends, "Yeah, I was in the Mansion, I was all dressed up" or whatever, right? So then he'll try to get back in again. And like we had some big, big friggin' guys come in here and really disrupt this place, eh, like knocking people out. On the way out the door. Like literally animals, eh. (04: white male supervisor)

> I was the same way growing up, I had some bad experiences with different doormen and stuff, I mean throughout the city, and whether it's racism, or whatever else, you know, I was exposed to it myself. And I mean there were certain doormen that I knew that were a good group of guys, and other guys that were big company people, they were assholes or whatever else. But now I know the guys I grew up with so ... (15: visible minority male doorstaff)

Black patrons are particularly suspect for carrying weapons, especially if they may have gang affiliations. For this reason, they are given special attention during frisks and thoroughly examined by metal detectors. In Halifax there is limited lustre attached to gang affiliation. Doorstaff see gang members as instant trouble, loose cannons that need to be checked almost immediately. Knowledge about local gangsters and their friends is an asset among doorstaff. When the girlfriends of gang members are seen in the nightclub, a call goes out to the doorstaff to keep a watch for the arrival of their boyfriends. Typically, this also involves informing the police. One tactic often used by doormen is to target and scrutinize one aspect of one member of a group. If somebody has inadequate ID, he can be disallowed entry based on the dress code, or if he is being belligerent and/or disrespectful to the doorman, he may be singled out in an attempt to keep the entire group from entering. When one member of a group is disallowed entry, the others will also typically leave. On one occasion a "rough-looking" black man known to be a gang member and recently released from jail was in the nightclub. A doorman asked him twice to leave because he "kept taking his hat off and putting it back on." When a group of his friends pulled up in front of the nightclub to join him, doorstaff decided to pat down and ID all of them. This was done in order to keep them from entering, since "those guys don't carry any ID in case they get picked up by the cops." The group was dismissed as a bunch of "Fairview skids."

We have already witnessed how visible minority doormen have a different attitude towards black Nova Scotians. In some cases, the fact they come from the same communities they are asked to police puts them in a difficult position. One final aspect of race and nightclub culture involves the perception by some doorstaff that their own backgrounds affect how they are perceived by others:

> The thing is, where I'm from ... there's like three really big groups. There's like all the English people, all the French people, and all the natives. So the natives hang with the natives, the English hang with the English, the French hang with the French. And so it's really big groups. And wherever you go, you get clashes between all three groups. Like, I never had any problems with anybody, cause I'm native, French, and English. My mom's English, my dad's got French in him and native, so I've never had any problems with anybody. So whenever I'm home, everybody knows who I am and like all three groups know who I am, and so I get along with everybody home, so I've never had any problems like that. But that's the way it is. (14: visible minority male doorstaff)

> People find out that I have German in me. I have a shaved head, and they'll make [racial slurs] and I'll laugh at it. But it's not funny, the way they talk to me, because [they think they know] what I'm like, but they don't know. (20: white male doorstaff)

The connection between race and gender is manifold and always augmented in the context of a nightclub. Feminists have long understood the binary distinctions under patriarchy that have produced a madonna/whore dichotomy. Hegemonic masculinity, of course, adds to this the notion of women who are deserving and undeserving of protection. Often, this deservedness intersects with class and race.

There was these two black girls, and they're like, they're kind of known around town, they've been barred from most bars in town … a little aggressive. [They] like to fight all the time. I heard they actually stabbed some girl downtown about a year and a half ago. But anyway, they had a party here, at the function it was mostly black people in the bars, hip-hop bar, or hip-hop party. And there was three white girls that were dancing and I seen these two black girls were going to be a problem. Like I was watching the crowd and they were doing stupid things. Like flicking cigarette butts at the white girls, and like they're like talking blah blah blah [*making hand gestures*]. I knew there was something going to happen, it was just a matter of time, guaranteed. So I turned my head for like, I dunno, two, a second, I turn back around, all I see is just three black girls are just pounding on this poor white girl. They're like ripping her hair around, it was crazy, like they were pulling her by her hair. So I jump up the stage, tried to separate them off, but the girl wouldn't let go of the girl's hair, and like really wouldn't let it go, so I had to ah, put her arm up, then I went straight up like this [*motioning upwards*], but [they were] still holding onto the girl's hair. I had to put her arm over my shoulder, right here. So like just hook back on it. Like if I keep getting, you could get, you could like dislocate her arm. Right, but I would never do that. I just put pressure: "Let go, let go, let go," just to the point where it hurts her so much that she has to let go. So eventually she lets go and then I put her in a full Nelson and carried her out. And her sister was behind me. And all of a sudden I hear this bottle smash, I turn around, her sister's running at me with a broken bottle. Like, "I'm gonna fucking stab you, blah blah blah, you blah blah blah," just going crazy, right? Like I've been stabbed before, like I'm not gone get stabbed again … Like if this chick comes within like five feet, I'm gonna take her head off with this chair, who cares, she's got a knife … with a knife if you get little cut here, to your artery … you bleed to death like in a minute. There's no joking around if it comes that close. So when I picked up the chair she stopped. Like she was running at me, then she stopped. I'm kinda like: what am I gonna do? And then a friend came up behind her and tried to grab her arm. As soon as I seen her friend grab her arm, I knew she couldn't do anything, so I gave her a fast [*makes smacking gestures*], grabbed the bottle, yanked it out of her wrist. Then I threw her out. Then her sister … I had them both out and [by the way] that's the chick that spit in my face, like [*makes spitting sound*]. What the hell, man … like?! (10: white male doorstaff)

Women who do not play by the rules of femininity relinquish their right to special treatment. In fact, they become the subjects of increased vigilance. Hegemonic notions of beauty and "ladylike behaviour" come to define how bouncers will react in given situations. Women who dress the part and flirt with doormen stand a better chance of gaining entry. Women who are viewed as unattractive and overweight are commonly referred to as "fuglies" (fat and ugly) while those who appeared promiscuous are called "skanks" or "whores." The attractiveness of a woman is an important cultural capital that augments the aesthetics of the nightclub. I recorded:

It's already 12:58 A.M. and my legs are aching as I lean up against a wall just inside the entrance. For some time now I have been watching doorstaff hand out guest passes to selected patrons arriving outside. Some are already reserved for scheduled pub crawlers wearing T-shirts. Others are given to VIPs and local bar staff. I am also informed, however, that passes are given to women with "tight shirts or big nipples." To emphasize the point, one doorman acts out the process. He pretends he is staring at a woman's breasts while holding her invisible ID in a strategic position. He feigns a locked stare toward imaginary breasts. "Hey, you get in free!" Another bouncer jokingly adds: "Yeah, and your ugly friend, she has to pay … no, as a matter of fact, she's banned." They laugh for a few seconds before one of them turns to me and adds with some degree of seriousness: "Basically anyone with their shirts open trying to get attention [gets in]." Only fifteen minutes later a group of women in their early twenties approach the bar entrance hopping from side to side in spaghetti-strap tops, as if elated. They smile at one of the doormen, flirt outrageously, and mention that a few of their friends will be coming shortly. The doorman examines their IDs, slyly exchanges smiles with them, and hands the entire bubbly group guest passes for free entrance into the nightclub.

On another occasion, a group of ten women approached the VIP side of the entrance dressed in leather outfits and jackets. One woman spoke to the doorman and mentioned that the entire group were her friends. She requested and received guest passes for each of them. The prospect of bringing in ten women in leather was a "no-brainer" for the doorman. She gave the doorman a hug, smiled, and flirted while her friends filed behind her into the nightclub. A few moments later she joined them.

Women who are inappropriate or disrespectful, however, will be denied access regardless of their dress or attractiveness. I watched as an attractive woman who was once a "cage dancer" at the nightclub was told that she was no longer a VIP and had been removed from the list. She protested out of a real sense of desperation but was told that her conduct was inexcusable: she had called a doorman an "asshole." She vehemently denied this and tried to negotiate a pass for herself. Obviously distressed, she eventually ended up paying for her own cover charge but vowed to clear her name and restore her VIP status.

Women like to spit in your face. But men hardly ever do it, but women do it all the time. (07: white male supervisor)

After dealing with these people for so long, they really fit into categories. You know like, this girl's gonna cause us a problem. She's talking loud, she's dressed like this, and you know she, well, if she gets drunk, it only amplifies things. (01: white male doorstaff)

Like, girls sit there and cry. You know what I mean? I take their ID, they're about seventeen-year-old kids, they'll cry. I'm like, "You think that's gonna work?" No. I've had like five girls crying in front of me tonight. I don't care. You know what I mean? Then there's this, stupidest girls. Like some of them, they're the worst off to skip line. Guys go out and try to skip by me, nope, not gonna tell ya, yep. Girls will be like the ones [to] skip line. There's a way to think about it, and show your tits? No. That's not gonna pay any bill. Some of them, they show off their boobs, like I don't care about that, you know, that doesn't bother me any. We had a girl whipped down her pants one day. Two weekends ago … I get a kick out of it. Like they're trash, you know, no offence with you, I expect, but I think that's trash. (10: white male doorstaff)

Another woman was removed from the nightclub because she had thrown up all over herself. Her hair, arms, shirt, and the floor around her were soaked in vomit. When she was escorted to the washroom to clean herself up by a female doorstaff, she begged to stay. She even asked, "If I clean it up, can I stay?" Her offer was refused. I recorded in my fieldnotes,

A well-dressed and attractive woman enters the nightclub with a group of friends and is told to pay cover charge. She is simply ignoring the doorman. Finally, the doorman raises his voice and says, "Do you want to come in here tonight?" She answers "No" half-jokingly and changes her answer quickly to "Yes" when the question is repeated. "Then don't fuck around!" This leads to a rather heated argument about respect from both patron and doorman. "You don't have to swear at me just because you're a bouncer." She is taking the role of offended party and eventually, after offering to simply let her pay and enter, the supervisor says "You know what? Get out!" More arguing ensues and he finally tells her she can "do it one of two ways." She demands to speak to the owner, but the doorman grabs her and forces her out the door. Once outside, she amazingly spins and punches the doorman in the face. He doesn't retaliate and radios her description to the other doormen. When someone on the radio asks why, he responds, "Because she's a fucking alcoholic and a bitch."

In chapter 4 we discussed how removing a woman from a nightclub is a distasteful and difficult situation for some doormen because it either paints them as unchivalrous or places them at risk of "getting beat up by a girl." One way to legitimize the rough treatment of women is to first dehumanize them through labelling: "Last night was the night of the crazy bitches." After closing time, one doorman informed me that three women had attempted to gain entry by flashing him. One of the women unzipped the front of her pants and revealed she did not have on any underwear. He said he maintained eye contact with the woman, whom he believed was a call girl, and simply responded, "What, you think I haven't seen c*** before?" He told us, "Because if you look, they think you're a perv [and] if you don't, they're still pissed off," which creates "a no-win situation."

Class matters in a nightclub. More specifically, class and social capital are just as much passports in the nighttime economy as in the workaday world. Doormen develop strong stereotypes about problem patrons that centre around class. These attitudes are often evidenced through their common use of epithets such as "skids" or "trash." In fact, doormen were candid about their putting class at the forefront when determining access. When class intersected with gender, they were even more judgmental:

The people I try to [eliminate] … people on welfare, four kids, different fathers, collecting welfare, come down here getting drunk. Tattoos all over them, gross looking, kinda. They're just skid. Like people who're, live in trailer parks, I guess, and swear a lot. (08: white male doorstaff)

Girls will sit there and "Ah, are you gonna [let me in]? Do I have to wait in that line?" "Yeah you gotta wait in line." "Why?" "Because everybody else does, why you so special? You bar staff?" "No." "Then wait in line." "But yet these …" "Wait in line." You know, like, you know? They'll bitch and go on, and like, sometimes you're sitting here and they'll use the washroom, or all stayed at [another club]. I'm like, I'm like, "ha," you know what I mean? I'm just, it's … trash. I hate trash! They got five pounds of makeup on, a ring on every finger, all perked up. You know what I mean? Fat hanging out of their sides, big gut hanging out, and they think they're cock of the walk. And they're all skids. (09: white male doorstaff)

Perhaps the most obvious sign of differential treatment for those who possess either social or material capital is the VIP line. VIPs are never searched. Elegantly dressed women are never searched. There is a general "hands-off" policy when it comes to those on the guest list, VIPs, celebrities, and persons known to the bouncers. I observe,

Tonight the doormen are not frisking everyone. Most of the women are let through without pat-downs. It seems anyone with oversized clothing, typically black males, are being scrutinized with the metal detector. While a group of men are being patted down at the front of the queue – the first such frisking in a while – three young black men quickly get out of the middle of the lineup saying, "This is bullshit!" Some time later a group of boisterous young women arrive at the nightclub entrance. They are using profanity and appear to have been drinking. A doorman asks one of the girls to walk in a straight line in order to prove her sobriety. We all watch rather bemused as she repeatedly steps to her side to regain her balance. "I'm sorry, you've had too much to drink. You can't come in," says the doorman. "I'm SORRY, but I walked that line!" comes the indignant response. "I'm sorry, but you're going to have to go somewhere else." Of course, neither party is particularly sorry, and the young woman walks away with her reluctantly supportive friends in tow to find another nightclub. As she leaves she starts to hurl insults at the bouncers and the bar. Another bouncer mutters, "So fucking ghetto …"

While doormen were reluctant to admit it, quick access to a nightclub was often secured by "greasing the palm" of the bouncer. "I'm not saying it might not happen there," one respondent told us. "They could still pay me to get in the front of the line. Sure. Get in front of the people that are waiting anyway … Guys will pay twenty bucks to go in the back door. [The] manager, he'll set them up. He'll send someone down around back with twenty dollars and they'll 'Let me in and here's twenty bucks.' Guy says, 'Yes,' he's fired. (09: white male doorstaff)

Even though members of other nightclubs and staff from establishments that catered to the needs of bouncers were given special privileges, this did not erase class positioning. For example, late-night pizza delivery boys often provided doorstaff with free pizza. In exchange, they would not be required to pay cover charge. Nonetheless, doorstaff typically referred to them as "pizza skids" because of their dress, their poor tipping and their habit of nursing one beer for many hours.

That many doormen were derisive of persons who were not known to them, who appeared badly dressed, or who were somehow less refined or simply poor may seem odd, given that they are not exactly high income earners themselves. Doorstaff, however, typically identified with producing the nightclub as an aesthetic site of consumption – their primary task. Achieving such an aesthetic meant the continuous exercise of both policy and discretion in order to keep out undesirables identified on the basis of intersections of race, class, gender, and age. Despite this mandate, some doormen seemed to sense that those who did not always "fit in" were usually the least likely to cause a security problem:

They control themselves, you know what I mean? Like, they'll beat up on themselves. Like they'll mosh and everything else, but they're not looking out for the little girl in the white dress, you know, [*makes smacking sound*] popping her in the head. It just doesn't happen that way. I used to work at a bar on the Primrose, like an industrial graphic bar, we'd get all kinds of, like in my opinion called "freaks." You know, the more oxen-like, just really strange-looking people, right? And the thing is, they never started fights. And you know, you'd think they would. It's always like the first-year university kids who never drank before, they'd come into the bar, get loaded, and like "Look at the freak, man, haa haa haa." They'd start the fights, right? It's always the clean-cut pretty boys has the tendency to always … (10: white male doorstaff)

Managing access to a nightclub puts doorstaff in the spatially contradictory position of being on the street but no longer of the street. While they may have grown up in tough neighborhoods that make them a desirable addition to the nightclub's security staff, they are asked to turn away those childhood friends and acquaintances. In an even less flattering scenario, doorstaff who have developed minimal local connections other than through university enrolment, varsity football, and lifting weights with a small cohort of friends, and have never been of the street in the first place, perhaps find it far too easy to mock those they think of are lessers. One of the unfortunate effects of working as a doorman is the development of a targeted misanthropy towards those who look like trouble and must be excluded. The effects would be comical if they weren't ugly. I recorded an incident in my fieldnotes:

> A well-known homeless man arrives at the bar entrance with a bucket in hand and starts panhandling. The doormen allow him to beg for a while before they start to tease and mock him. The man, who is physically impaired and has difficulty speaking coherently, jokes back. Finally, the man slowly takes off his jacket and passes his bucket and coat to one of the bouncers. He turns to the other doorman and raises his fists, challenging him to a mock fight. Laughter erupts from the queue. Despite his disability, the man is certainly a crafty play-fighter.

We have seen, therefore, that identification is amplified in a nightclub in order to negotiate access. Identification can oftentimes be juxtaposed with identities. These identities are constituted by generalized categories such as race, class, gender, and age but may also include subcultural groupings based on music genres. I found it odd that in order to gain temporary access to the nightclub, patrons often will leave their identification card or wallet with the doorman – an identity collateral for temporary entry. In one case, a black man entered the nightclub to look for a friend and offered his ring as collateral.

The bouncers sometimes shared "ID stories" with the liquor inspector. A doorman's sister had her identification stolen; another young woman who tried to enter the nightclub a few days later using that same stolen identification was recognized by a fellow doorman. He "had a good laugh" before he confiscated the card.

The liquor inspector joined the storytelling. He received a call from his insurer that his card had been confiscated at a Halifax nightclub. He found it amusing, telling the insurance representative that he was, in fact, the liquor inspector. Another doorman topped that story by describing his own incredible incident. He had lost his driver's licence in the nightclub the previous year, and few months after he had misplaced it, was surprised when it was presented to him for entry. He laughed at the club-goer, saying, "This can't be you because it's ME!"

Patrons became so frustrated at not being allowed entry to the night-club because their identification cards were not considered valid that they committed a form of identification suicide: "It was her Nova Scotia drivers licence and it was ripped, like the top plastic was ripped, and you could barely see the face, but I was, you know, 'You have any ID besides? A school ID, and then I can help you out.' But all she had was [driver's] ID. And I was like 'I'm sorry, you know, for tonight I can't let you in, go to DMV tomorrow, get a new ID, and see for the weekend.' Well, she freaked out. Like 'This is blah blah blah,' throwing around the words and stuff, and I just went 'Sorry now, none of ya's are getting in.' So she took the ID card, ripped the whole front of it off of it, so then she now has no ID at all. (03: white female doorstaff)

This chapter has examined "getting in" to a nightclub in the context of negotiating surveillance technology and identities such as age, class, gender, race, and age. Through their sentry-dataveillance roles, doorstaff produce the nightclub through the vetting of populations and by actively constructing a nightclub aesthetic. Thus, doorstaff are not only prime policing agents in the nighttime economy but, more importantly, they are manufacturers of an urban risk market – a site of circumscribed transgression and consumption that begins at the door. The following chapter moves us from the door to the interior of the nightclub, theorizing the dynamics that make nightclubs sites of aesthetic production in late capitalism.

6

Getting Noticed

Having presented our VIP passes and cleared the queue, we enter the nightclub itself: a frenzy of activities, dramas, and power plays where identities are refigured and hierarchies of social capital violently reasserted. The point now is to see and be seen, to grease the gears of desire and the desire to be desired within the machinery of surveillance.[1]

According to Michel Foucault (1977), a history of surveillance is no less than a genealogical investigation of the "governing of the soul." Under this rather ambitious and far-reaching theoretical backdrop, Foucault interrogates Jeremy Bentham's infamous architectural design of the panopticon, a prison that governs and disciplines through the unrelenting gaze of a supposed watcher. The panopticon, with its interior tower and cells set about its perimetre, sillouettes the prisoner against his cell window, unable to tell when he is being watched. The architectural design of the prison thus makes the need for a perpetual physical gaze unnecessary. It disciplines the prisoner automatically. For Foucault, Bentham's panopticon marks an historical transition from the use of extreme, ceremonial spectacles of deterrence – epitomized by the public execution and confessional – to the mundane, recognized, and ubiquitous security measures of modernity. We transition from the many watching the few to the few watching the many.

While agreeing with the relative importance of the panopticon to the genealogy of surveillance and social order, Mathiesen (1997) has nonetheless criticized Foucault for creating a stark theoretical rupture between these two supposedly antipodal surveillance regimes. He argues that contemporary spectacles persist and that the media (despite their affinity with power elites) and the criminal justice system do participate in the prosecution of celebrity criminals and politicians, publicize the execution of serial killers, and even investigate and expose CEOS, CFOS, and the like. While it is true that surveillance and power (for Foucault, "biopower") have become ubiquitous and routinized, the deterrent spectacle persists, and the many still watch the few even while the few watch the many. This dynamic process Mathiesen labels the "synopticon."

There are at least two important aspects emanating from Mathiesen's contemporary critique of Foucault that resonate with what I will discuss in this chapter. First, while bouncers and managers indeed increasingly rely on surveillance technologies such as CCTV, hand-held ID card readers, and metal detector wands to augment the old-fashioned panoptic watching of patrons through natural observation, the nightclub remains a powerful spectacle wherein not only are all participants – including the bouncer – subject to surveillance but so is the optic orgy, the *spectacle*, which itself is centrally constitutive of the nightclub as a space. The spectacle must therefore be synoptic to function. Indeed, it is a synoptic frenzy.

Second, it very much suits the analysis in this chapter that the exemplar cited for marking the transition to routinized surveillance is Bentham's panopticon. I want here to intentionally overstate the surveillance connection between *panoptic* prison as a disciplining-punishing-factory and the nightclub as a *synoptic* disciplining-pleasuring-factory. Of course, I realize that it may be belittling to the experiences of prisoners to create such analogy but I do so apologetically to make my point about power, space, "optical violence," and crises of respect as a counterpoint to the rather celebratory and emancipatory depictions of nightclub culture and raves. I know of few other places other than prisons and nightclubs where crowding, bumping, stepping on another's shoes, and even eye contact can be interpreted as signs of disrespect legitimately creating conditions for violent confrontation within the logic of that space. Indeed, it strikes me as particularly illustrative that a sizable minority of bouncers were either already qualified or undergoing training as correctional officers.

[We] did that IAT training. I have a lot of prison-guard trained guys. And that's good, and it's bad, you know. They're trained for a convicted criminal. They're trained for a person with, that has just about no rights. These people in bars have all the rights in the world. So that's the only thing you've got to turn them off of, 'cause they're all going in and extracting people from cells and batons and shields and, you know what I mean. If we got [to] extract somebody here, it's calm, it's quiet, it's get people, get a person out. (03: white male doorstaff)

It's like anything: if you come to work within the prison system, you have to treat people with respect, but they have to also know, if they step over the line that, you know, whatever's going to happen. (04: white male doorstaff)

This chapter empirically examines the synoptic frenzy of the night-club through an analysis of the various manifestations of "optic violence," including rational risk-reducing surveillance, the sexual, voyeuristic, and seductive gaze and its power, and especially the iconographic, masculine role of the bouncer relative to this power and desire. Through the use of interview data and ethnographic accounts I hope to shed light on this synoptic frenzy in motion. Towards the end of the chapter I consider how bouncers read crises of respect signalled by moves against personal space and identity, and the role of inebriation (or "liquid courage") in making this possible.

Synoptic Frenzy

What I have been referring to as the synoptic frenzy of the nightclub as a risk market has up to this point evaded any substantive explanation. Inside the nightclub space, the optic orgy of seeing and being seen is valorized as a productive process. Surveillance of patrons becomes a productive activity insofar as it creates aesthetic spaces of optic consumption, of privilege, distinction, and hierarchies of symbolic capital. The desires of the nightclub – what draws bodies and collects them – becomes its own machinery, a veritable "smoothing machine" (Bogard 2000) wherein the chaff is thrown off, bodies discarded and reorganized for consumption. Once past the queue, the patron is scrutinized by bouncers, cameras, and other patrons. There is an incessant disciplining of bodies, a compulsion to sway and go with the flow, to party, to drink, to indulge. The few watch the many as the many watch the few. VIPs and celebrities are roped off in display pens, privileging the scene with their injection of elite social capital, and we are in turn made special by the space vested with this distinction. Patrons are extolled to valorize the symbolic, the superficial, the material. Depth of communication is intentionally stunted, manipulated in deference to the optic spectacle – to turn down the music would only undermine this alienating power. Describing the synoptic frenzy of the nightclub, therefore, involves mapping the multitude of optic factors that are its base, always shifting nonetheless. These lines may be alternately fleeting or ponderous, managerial or voyeuristic, but aggregately serve to fuse surveillance and consumption as a principal constitutive feature of the nightclub as a risk market.

The synoptic frenzy of the nightclub is best explained through empirical example. Below, I offer my ethnographic account of this synoptic frenzy in motion.

It wasn't a particularly eventful evening. A tour of the nightclub; an examination of its CCTV camera system; a chat with the doorstaff supervisor; and a rather awkward run-in with a former student. I put my notebook in my pocket and leaned up against the railing as I overlooked the dance floor. Bored, I scanned the mass of patrons as they gyrated and swayed to the music on the dance floor. One by one, individual bodies were swallowed up, absorbed by an organic mass. They went out of focus as I gazed through them. They slowly became an amorphous, pulsating blob. I must have held my stupefied look for quite some time … until, like a laser, a brilliant light suddenly pierced through the haze of my peripheral vision. A man shouldering an oversized video camera was making his way through the mass of dancing patrons. The powerful spotlight atop his camera shot forth a brilliant white beacon that strangely cauterized the dancing blob. The spotlight collected bodies, both cutting through and pinching the blob wherever it turned. Dancing patrons crowded into the light like moths. Wherever the camera pointed, the crowd coalesced and its movement became more frenzied, more heated.

Finally, the cameraman settled his lens on an attractive young blond woman in a halter top. She was literally "lit up" by the candlepower of the camera's hot white light; her dancing, her smile, her entire persona also figuratively "lit up" in its warm, admiring glow. The dancer became more animated, more evocative. Her hip movements exaggerated as her arms snaked above her head, striking poses expertly in rhythm with the music. The song rattled through our skeletons. Wow! Now, the entire nightclub lit up. Whooping and clapping. Cheers and whistles. But even as the dancer played to the camera, her eyes looked elsewhere. Others around her too kept looking in the same direction. I followed their sight lines and immediately remembered the large screen above the dance floor. The dancer was being projected. Larger than life, towering over the dance floor, she was being spliced in with the Madonna video: "Come on, vogue. Let your body move to the music (move to the music). Hey, hey, hey. Come on, vogue …"

A group of young men to my right started chanting, sporadically at first but then in loud unison: "Jump up and down! Jump up and down!" Almost immediately a bouncer tapped one of them on the shoulder, and I watched as they all turned to face him, their smiles now broken and ready for confrontation. The doorman in his bright yellow shirt put his finger across his lips: "Ssshhh!" he motioned, gesturing that the men should calm down. But he left them with a wink, a smile, and redirected their gaze back to the screen, nudging one of them with a friendly chuckle. I scanned the rest of the nightclub. Patrons watched the screen and then the dancer, then each other for reaction, back to Madonna. The bouncers in their luminescent yellow shirts looked on, watching the show and the crowd. And, in turn, we watched the bouncers watching us. CCTV surveillance cameras nestled unseen in the roof cavity monitored us from above. The dancer continued sizing herself up on the big-screen. A bouncer off to her left was projected onto the screen too, and he immediately smiled, pulled up his sleeve and flexed his bicep. A mixture of boos from the men and cheers from the women followed. Quickly, however, the camera turned back to the attractive blond: bouncer – dancing girl – Madonna, and back again. The dancer watched the bouncer watch her as he nodded approvingly in the background. Three women off to my left along the railing began to make sour faces, holding their noses, mocking the performance of the blond patron, and gesturing "thumbs down" as they watched with disapproval. The cameraman occasionally focused on other women dancing or even a group of men but invariably returned back to the nightclub's favourite iconographic, sexy, blond dancer. Even Madonna paled next to her suggestive movements. More cheers and yelps of approval.

Finally, the song was over and the hot white light of the camera was extinguished. There was, I think, a sense of momentary disorientation, silence in the nightclub's post-climactic confusion. We all seemed to furtively glance at each other, sheepishly looking for something else to look at.

We were, of course, all part of a synoptic frenzy, each optically devouring the other, surveillance, voyeurism, and consumption all becoming one. We embraced the thrall of our ridiculousness, our excess. We became the nightclub's spectacle and its alibi as we recovered from our post-synoptic spike:

The dancing mass began to re-form itself around our momentary starlet. Through the darkness she sustained a fading glow. Like a slowly extinguishing ember, Madonna's co-star still managed to give off heat. She was now the subject of an after-buzz as raised glasses, thumbs up, and nods of approval were quickly followed by hand shaking, pats on the back and one uncomfortable and presumably unwelcome hug from a man who either thought himself familiar enough or wanted to clumsily stake some territory. The dancer's deportment changed in the cool of the dark. She became smaller, blushed frequently, looked down as she danced and held her arms closer to her body as her friends began intercepting unwanted attention. I strained my eyes now to make her out as the darkness closed around her. The strobe lights flashed violently and re-smoothed my attention back to the throng. They were like thousands of flash bulbs freezing and glamorizing the nightclub by illuminating its individual parts, its spectacular moments. But these instants were so many and so simultaneous, hundreds of little dramas, crises, and power-plays as individually profound and brilliant to their participants as they were inconsequential and invisible to that callous blob that would again reclaim them.

I want to contrast this aspect of the spectacle of the nightclub, this synoptic frenzy as I have described it, with the emancipatory power of the carnival gleaned by Bakhtin (1984) through his seminal analysis of the works of medieval French writer Francois Rabelais. In an enthusiastic tone prophesizing more contemporary analyses of the Situationist (Debord 1995) movement and rave culture to follow, Bakhtin (1984, 7) asserted that the medieval carnival depicted "belongs to the borderline between art and life. In reality, it is life itself, but shaped according to a certain pattern of play." So powerful, freeing and expressive was the clowning and debauchery of the medieval carnival that it created "a second world and a second life outside officialdom" – an assertion foreshadowing Jackson's (2004) and Wilson's (2006) celebratory analysis of contemporary rave culture. The notion is that for the raver, the "habitus is temporarily erased" (Jackson 2004, 4–5). We shall return to the emancipatory potential of the current carnivalesque again, but for now it serves us to more closely examine Bakhtin's explanation of the confluence of art and life as a precondition of this expressive and freeing second life. He argues, "carnival does not know footlights, in the sense that it does not acknowledge any distinction between actors and spectators" (Bakhtin 1984, 7). Indeed, "footlights would destroy a carnival, as the absence of footlights would destroy a theatrical performance" for "carnival is not a spectacle seen by the people." Instead "they live in it, and everyone participates because its very idea embraces all the people."

This notion of spectacle stands in stark contrast to the voyeuristic, regulated, and exclusionary pulsations of the synoptic frenzy. Of course, the nightclub too creates a symbiosis of spectator and actor, but footlights are indeed everywhere and thus nowhere. Bouncers, dancers, CCTV, risk management, and so on, along with a concomitant push for aesthetic rebellion, all seem to extol an existing security-risk-consumption nexus: each is embedded in the other, and each act of lewdness is greedily devoured by the spectacle for its own consumption, for the valorization of capital. Unlike the medieval carnival, the nightclub's intersecting optic trajectories reinforce rather than temporarily elude the overarching mode of production, let alone challenge existing power relations.

One is also tempted to view this description of a synoptic frenzy in motion as an exceptional case. After all, the projected image of the "synoptic blond," Madonna, and the bouncers are a neat but rather rare bundle of circumstances that conveniently make the surveillance-consumption link *exceptionally* obvious and tangible. But is this the *common* machinery of the nightclub? While this case is particularly illustrative, my point is actually the mundanity of this spectacle within the logic of the larger nightclub spectacle which is absolutely ubiquitous. I think it is not an exceptional case, just an exceptionally revealing one. The synoptic frenzy, and especially CCTV, may conflate its voyeuristic, commercial, and security functions in multiple locales. In exotic dance clubs, where owners tell dancers the security cameras are present "to keep dancers safe from unruly customers," the systems are also used to prevent dancers from "going too far" or "cheating the club" – important economic and legal risk management measures (Egan 2004, 306). One should not, however, infer from my analysis of the synoptic frenzy nor from my description of optic violence to follow that these structural aspects of nightclub production alone create violence, that somehow peaceable and happy punters are refigured into angry voyeurs by the risk-security-consumption machinery of the nightclub. On the contrary, there are numerous examples throughout this book of the eruption of violence from existing grudges, the settling of gang-related scores, the continuing rivalry of cliques, and the exposure of love triangles. Still, it bears attention that despite their pre-existence, these animosities seem to be violently expressed and effortlessly reanimated within the spectacle of the nightclub.

As if the synoptic frenzy were not omnipresent and powerful on its simple terms, one nightclub installed a million-candlepower spotlight overlooking the dance floor. This new equipment was touted as an enhanced security measure. The purpose of the spotlight was to quickly "light up" any fights that might occur. This made all altercations visible, and enabled a quick response by doorstaff as they would scramble to the beacon's target. Here we have yet another manifestation of the spectacle of the nightclub: in this case violence was being highlighted in the midst of all other forms of optic consumption. Security surveillance technology was literally wedding the two, and it is to this aspect of the nightclub we now turn.

Optic Violence

The voyeuristic delights offered by the synoptic frenzy are, of course, part of the more general optic milieu that is at the same time inherently alienating, competitive, and violent. This violence manifests itself in manifold ways, flourishing within the overarching logic of spectacle and its "lonely crowds" as described by Debord. The nightclub valorizes visual communication largely by subjugating other forms. Nightclubs produce alienation and fetishize bodies because depth is undermined when the surface is exalted. Patrons must assess each other, the nightclub, and the scene, as it were, based on these manufactured aesthetics, these innumerable visual cues. Patrons may be pre-screened at the door for entry but no matter how much subcultural uniformity is theoretically achieved, subdivisions and hierarchies force a need to "close the gap" (Foucault 1977) even further. And when the scene is eclectic, insufficient differentiation from the workaday world is demanded: "the wilder, the better" becomes its own normalizing mechanism. Patrons are judged and judge others by the advertising symbolism attached to their style and their logos, which are completely divorced from the plight of domestic and overseas sweatshop workers (Klein 2000). Fashion, style, and garments – the central signifiers of social capital in a nightclub – are therefore as fetishized as their production is mystified to the buyer and observer.

Afloat in this sea of material alienation, optic violence manifests itself in at least four ways, by (1) managing, (2) staring, (3) cutting, and (4) leering. First, there is the routine, rational, and managerial optic violence of security. This form is born out of Benthamite panoptic surveillance and the disciplining of bodies for the management of sight lines through the use of advanced technology and even clandestine organizational espionage on bar workers and bouncers themselves. Second, we have the very atavistic display of optic power that comes merely from making eye contact and "staring down" an adversary. This base compulsion to establish dominance is a favourite technique of bouncers. A stern look or stare is often enough to elicit compliance to nightclub codes of conduct. Third, whereas dominance may be established optically by way of targeted intimidation, it can also be just as effective and potentially humiliating through looks that are disapproving, scoffing, and dismissive: what I call giving someone the "cut eye." Looks of disdain are far more penetrating and exaggerated within the spectacle of the nightclub because one's presence is performance, one's worth is merely aesthetic, and one's ability to communicate, to overcome barriers and connect, is intentionally stunted. *Fourth*, while the synoptic frenzy produces the pleasure of voyeurism for the nightclub viewer, it can do so only by first producing objects for consumption. Hegemonic heterosexual masculinities and femininities are reified and produce leering. Race and class are exaggerated even further. Multiple forms of social and subcultural capital are celebrated so that the entire evening's style and music can be thematized. A fresh and changing nightclub normativity, no matter how opposed to daytime lifestyles and geared to its own bounded transgressionalism, manufactures exclusivity, frustration, and the potential for violence. The nightclub seduction and its ability to create desire, therefore, objectifies, dehumanizes, and produces a litany of scorned courtiers of the night – it must do so as a precondition of its exclusivity, its sense of place, and its very existence. I consider each of these four forms of optic violence more comprehensively in the remainder of this section.

Once inside, nightclub surveillance appears self-evident: CCTV cameras, bouncers, and DJs looking about (oftentimes in panoptically elevated positions), bartenders and servers keeping an eye out for troublesome and/or inebriated patrons, and even other patrons inviting the intervention of bouncers to settle disputes. Surveillance is obvious and sometimes intentionally obtrusive: bouncers in illuminated T-shirts *want* to be seen because they are a deterrent. Often, they are strategically stationed under pot lights, lit up through the haze of the nightclub to remind patrons, staff, and other bouncers of their presence. The doorstaff, too, are objects of aesthetic consumption. Depending on the nightclub, they may be uniformed in bright yellow polo shirts with "SECURITY" emblazoned across the back or black T-shirts with white lettering. There is, of course, no single uniform of nightclub security; this varies depending on sponsorship and whatever ambience or aesthetic the nightclub wishes to project. To further reinforce the conflation between security and consumption, security staff are often bedecked with sponsored "security shirts" that display advertising for beer companies.

At the urging of a doorman I also took up position at panoptic vantage points: "Up here, you can get a great view of how the bar works, how it moves," I was told. "You know, if you can been seen, you know, it's less likely it's gonna happen. Fights aren't gonna start … if they think they're being watched everywhere they go. I'd rather have bodies there, a set of eyes that can see things" (01: white male supervisor).

The security eye aggregates, looking for vacillations in tempo that are a cue to deviation: "I always joke around, when I watch the dance floor, [that] I don't see a group of people, I see a *kata*," one doorman told me. "You can't individualize them anymore. When you're staring at a crowd, you don't – I used to sit down and stare at the person, person to person, then you're missing too much. I just generally stare at everything and you watch the movement. Everything that happens bad in here speeds up" (01: white male doorstaff).

All nightclubs invariably had CCTV surveillance cameras at access and egress points. Most incidents developed there or ended up becoming particularly violent and potentially litigious at this point. Moreover, CCTV surveillance cameras "at the gate" ensured that prospective patrons were identified for later litigation or for the purposes of future banning. These managerial risk-reducing activities are oppressive only insofar as they circumscribe behaviour, discipline bodies, and are the basis for violent removal. The camera is managerial because it circumscribes risk. It acts as witness to offset litigation:

> If it's on camera, then it's evidence to say, "Listen, you, you're on camera." I mean you want that. "You attempted to strike this individual, you were grabbed for that reason." I mean it wasn't what you said, I mean, like you went to the door and asked to come in and "the guy punched me in the head, or grabbed me right away." It's good that way. We had a guy … he's actually our boss, he had to deal with a girl, an ex-girlfriend of one of the employees here, and he asked her to leave. And she put up a big thing or whatever, and he said, "Well, you have to leave." [He] looked at her, walked behind her and shut the door, didn't grab her … and [the camera] shows him, he's coming out back, so you see the different camera shots and her going out the door. She calls the bar the next day and said she was grabbed by the guy and he broke one of her ribs at the front door. So you see this all on camera and you say, "Well, listen, there's nothing. Not at any time were you grabbed. I mean other than you were restrained by your elbows or whatever." So I mean it covered that guy's ass … That's where it comes in handy. (15: visible minority male doorstaff)

Cameras also threaten to uncover excesses by doormen as a means of workplace control: "Anytime you even kick someone out, it's reviewed. Or if anything like, if it's anything serious, especially, it's on tape, so like you can't do anything too bad, you can't just go punch out a bunch of kids. You gotta go hide behind somebody. Like it's, everything's on tape, like there's no room for any messing around. (12: white male doorstaff)

Even in the case of softer or surreptitious surveillance such as the use of "secret shoppers," managerial espionage on bar staff and doormen is disquieting and intimidating.

They sort of walk around to make sure everyone's in their spot, but, I dunno, like management's even more fucked up than we are. I mean, to be perfectly honest. It's really, I dunno, they don't really do anything. We're sort of more like self-policed. It's more like, who're working probably realize that if something bad happens, you sort of need each other. And I mean you'll occasionally get to give each other a lecture and stuff. There's more self-policing than there is management. Like, holding onto the reins. (19: white male doorstaff)

There's a little tiny guy, the bar manager, that runs around and spies on us. Not really spies on us, but he always seems to be everywhere, every time we're doing something wrong. And that'll keep you on your toes. And other than that, they pretty much give us free rein … We have – the owners bring in a group of secret shoppers, every two weeks. But I don't think it's really acted on, because every week it comes back, "The tables were dirty, the ashtrays weren't done, the bathrooms were messy." They've done a few things, the janitors were in through the night instead of just at the end of the night. And they went around and cleaned up, but there's still hundreds of thousands of bottles kickin' around, and there's three thousand people in the bar. It's impossible to keep up with all the people. (04: white male doorstaff)

Indeed, as the watchers are watched, they develop a suspicion about surveillance, understanding that it can both indict and exonerate them for their actions:

I think the door staff here are scapegoats for a lot. Now I don't particularly like that – again, being a supervisor I don't get the brunt of it. I'm kind of exempt, to a point, from it, but I still have to go back to my peers, or the guys I supervise, and tell them that, you know, management feels that you screwed up. (02: white male supervisor)

It just so happens that the management will come along and see the tail end of it. Or a customer will come along and say, "I just saw that doorman hit that guy in the face." But he didn't see the customer hit the doorman in the face. And you know that's happened occasionally. I mean I deal with my staff, I'm "What the hell's going on here?" and then, you know, watched the video later and seen the customer take a swing at the doorman first. (06: white male supervisor)

[They] do have secret shoppers that come in here. And they'll inter-act with door, they do it for all staff. But they have this special form for doorstaff. Interact with the door, interact inside, ask questions. Maybe witness some confrontations with doorstaff with other patrons. This gets reported back to the management, upper man-agement, and they respond accordingly. (01: white male supervisor)

Panoptic sight lines are crucial to bouncer safety and security. They provide a central mode of communication through hand signals and eye contact, ensuring action is taken to follow up on missing, displaced, or mobilizing comrades. The pattern of distribution of doorstaff through-out the nightclub ensures that there is a direct line of sight between at least two co-workers at any given time. The most important position of responsibility in the nightclub usually goes to the doorman who is in charge of overseeing the dance floor. In two of the nightclubs we exam-ined, there were designated stations set up above the crowd for bouncers to overlook what was happening.

Other nightclub staff also became implicated in security. Bartenders flash lights behind the bar if they are being harassed or spot problems. DJs will call out and identify fights in progress: "Code 111" represents the dance floor, "Code 10 10 10" represents the VIP lounge. Busboys and wait-resses will call over the bouncer if they believe there are problems brew-ing. Coat-check girls may flick emergency lights above the doorways from their booth. And, of course, patrons themselves will come to the aid of doormen or inform them of potential problems. In this sense, all actors are securitized (Loader 2002), co-opted by risk reduction as an overrid-ing mobilizing phenomenon. They are observed by the same technool-ogy they rely on to observe others. One night I recorded:

It is shortly after midnight and I have emerged from a putrid nightclub washroom. I intentionally drag my feet trying to scrape the slime and urine from the soles of my shoes. Trading the stench of human waste for the sting of tobacco, I make my way toward the entrance. A man who was previously allowed into the nightclub has been asked to go back to the entrance. He is wearing jeans, a T-shirt, and has long hair with a goatee and looks rather bewildered. The doormen are unsure about whether this individual had been previously banned. As I pass the coat-check area, I see photocopied IDs and various mug shots of banned individuals displayed on the inside wall. I wonder whether they will use this ad hoc "wanted" board to make their determination. I am informed that they have brought the man back outside to conduct another pat-down, checking for weapons. They ask the suspicious patron to look up into the digital camera facing the street. A manager and security supervisor are apparently viewing developments through a CCTV feed piped into the security office. After approximately five minutes, a supervisor arrives at the entrance to inform the man that he has been banned from the nightclub. He leaves without incident, not even bothering with the pretense of indignation. After the man is sent on his way, I inquire about the reasoning behind the ban. According to the doormen, the man had grabbed a waitress's behind and caused a fight in the bar three months ago. I ask another doorman if they used a book of banned individuals or somehow compared him to a photograph. He replied, "Nope, you always remember assholes."

Security tapes, I am later to discover, are started at 10 P.M. and run for eight hours until 6 A.M. They remain on file in digital format for up to a month. Important incidents are archived longer: "And after that guy was piped out front, you heard about that, eh? That's the big reason they put all the cameras in the street. They had one, I mean, at the front doors you need it. Probably more for customer service reasons, you want them on the front doors ... I mean, cover-charge girls were stealing money, that type of idea. But the reason why they're outside and throughout the bar now is more to protect the employees against confronting stupid complaints or whatever type thing" (15: visible minority doorstaff).

These risk-reducing observational vectors criss-cross the synoptic frenzy of the nightclub – a crude nexus of security vision, rationally integrated within the club's transgressional delights. Doormen are supposed to maintain constant visual contact with one another:

First thing is, make sure that you can see each others at all times. (07: white male doorstaff)

There's always one, most often two people, beside you. And when I move, I have to wave off as well. And I can't move until I wave off. If I do move without waving off to one of them, he's gonna come looking for me. And you don't want to call wolf too many times, because they might not come, in danger. So we've got a really effective type of hand-signal type system. Not all the guys have combative training, I don't think. (11: white male doorstaff)

Wherever you go, there's two people with their eyes on you, watching you. So that makes your chances of anything happening to you, or the reaction time of other guys getting to a situation, a lot less. 'Cause if they can see you going into a situation, two guys are watching you. And something happens there, those two guys are going to be on you right away. And once those two guys go, the two guys that're watching them are gonna go too, right? (14: white male doorstaff)

The sentry-dataveillant, monitoring, and panoptic responsibility of bouncers working inside the nightclub led respondents to liken their role to that of a CCTV camera:

We know if somebody spins their hand, I know if something's wrong, there's signals for something wrong. There's signals for saying, "I'm going for a walk, don't worry about me." And it's basically, you have to learn the signals. The lights mean things. Sometimes the lights flash and that means there's a fight. And there's codes ... *I'm like a video camera*, I sit there and I turn my head back and forth. Make sure you watch, you look at your guys at least every twenty, thirty seconds at the longest. Make sure that they're still there. If they're gone, you go and see why they're not there, 'cause they should have let you know they were going for a reason. So you go and check it out. (13: white male doorstaff, my emphasis)

The one thing I do is I look for people who're drunk, I look for people who're being obnoxious and just like at the beginning of the night think in my head, who're gonna be the ones that I'm going to have to watch for the rest of the night, and just sort of always look side to side, keep my eye on everybody. Like some guys are just staring off into space. For the most part *I try to keep my head sort of swivelling, looking aroun*d. (19: white male doorstaff, my emphasis)

The second act of optic violence in the nightclub is the "stare-down."

Staring someone down is a signal of domination. The act carries with it the threat of impending violence: "Either conform, defer, or suffer the consequences." The term implies an active attempt to degrade, to make someone smaller, to establish status and elevation. I recorded:

A muscle-bound white patron with a torn pinstripe shirt is pacing in front of the nightclub entrance. Only moments earlier he had been removed by four doormen. I missed the altercation but can see from his appearance – the red blotches on his freckled face, his torn shirt, and a growing welt on his cheek – that he didn't leave willingly. He continues to pace, growling and mumbling. A friend tries to pull him away, but the angry redheaded patron shrugs off his grip and marches toward the closest doorman at the front entrance. As he approaches us, I realize that he is a formidable man: 6′2″ with large forearms now tensed with anger. He is only inches away from J.'s face, who is three inches shorter. He slowly raises his right hand and points right into the bouncer's nose: "I'm going to fuck you up! I swear, I'm going to kill you, you fuck!"

J. holds his ground and says nothing. He stares back into the furious redhead's eyes. The other doormen start towards J. to flank him. The patron barks through clenched teeth: "You need your buddies, don't you, you pussy!" J. continues to stare at the man, finally replying after a long silence. "Nope, just you and me." He continues his steely stare at the enraged patron as he subtly waves away his comrades behind him. The doormen at his flanks take a step back and smile. This is a standoff. J. has called the man's bluff. "I'm going to beat you so bad you'll go blind!" threatens the patron as he steps back as if to begin his assault. J. doesn't assume a defensive posture. Instead he fills in the gap vacated by the bigger man and continues his unblinking stare. The tension is unbearable. Finally, the patron breaks. He feigns a smile, waves his hands in disgust, and complains as he walks down the street: "Ah, your punk friends would probably jump in anyway." J. takes the victory and decides not to respond.

There were innumerable instances where doormen stared at a potential troublemaker. If a bouncer had warned a patron and was not confident that his caution would be heeded, it was quite common for him to eye the patron suspiciously throughout the evening. I saw one bouncer approach a troublesome patron who was in the midst of a heated argument, only to stand two feet away with hands crossed and glare straight at him. The obnoxious patron immediately apologized to both the bouncer and the other patron and promised to desist from getting into future arguments. The doorman lifted two fingers as if indicating "two strikes" and left without ever having said a word.

The third form of optic violence is "cut eye." One August Saturday evening at a bustling, overpriced Toronto restaurant, I attempted to explain to a group of club-hopping friends what I was discovering during my field research on bouncers and nightclubs. Enthusiastically starting on my idea of "optic violence," I was sooned faced with looks of confusion. Despite my increasing loss of confidence in the notion, I forged ahead, hoping for a breakthrough. I finally offered an example with an accompanying demonstration. I mimicked the looks of disdain that I had often seen during my nightclub visits. Across the table, Niki, an experienced nightclub attendee, stopped twirling her hair for a moment to interrupt me: "Cut eye! You're talking about cut eye!" Turning to receive relieved nods of understanding from the rest of our party, she repeated with triumphant glee as if she had just cracked the Enigma code, "Cut eye! He's talking about cut eye!"

Cut eye, I now believe, is a particularly apt term to describe the intrinsic violence of these once-over, sideways looks of disapproval. They are not trivial. Physical altercations in nightclubs notoriously start with rhetorical challenges such as: "What are you looking at?" or "You got a problem?" in response to cut eye. The metaphorical "cut" is, of course, more than skin deep. It penetrates to the core of self-identity, self-importance, and belonging. It is an exponentially more provocative act in a nightclub because optics are valorized and fetishized, and subjects are alienated by design, colourful palettes on which others may project their desire – or disapproval.

The hierarchized treatment of celebrities and VIPs adds an important internal layer of exclusivity within the exclusivity of the nightclub. Even when inside, patrons are reminded in blatant visual terms that they are not all at par. It is no coincidence that red-carpeted "VIP lounges" and roped-off "celebrity pens" are invariably elevated. The spaces are architecturally symbolic of power – a form of optic violence achieved through the constant reaffirmation and reification of social and material capital found in a multiplicity of other common spectacles where the viewers are just as much on display as the main event. A significant reason why the Mansion became a hot spot for Halifax club-goers was that movie stars such as Harrison Ford would frequent it while in town filming. The manager told me that the nightclub started to gain prominence as patrons told others whom they had seen that night.

Finally, while leering is a form of optic violence in its own right, objectification is often necessary for eliciting sexual desire. More than the three previous forms of optic violence, this final, largely gendered form necessitates elucidation. The synoptic frenzy furnishes and exaggerates this consuming passion. The nightclub's voyeuristic impulse can be playful, sexy, and exciting but also saddening, disgusting, and dehumanizing. Bouncers are of course, part of a masculine subculture, and it is standard linguistic fare for such occupational groups, in both public and private sectors, to cultivate sometimes unflattering narratives about women. The objectification of women in a nightclub produces leering – a form of optic violence that may connote unpredictable, predatory behaviour on a more general continuum of violence and potential risk against women (Chan and Rigakos 2002; Stanko 1997). Women must negotiate this potential risk in the context of drug use and their desired projection of femininity (cf. Hutton 2004). The same type of attention may also be merely flattering but nonetheless a requisite part of the synoptic frenzy, its character varying based on context and object.

Bouncer banter is replete with sexual overtones. A large component of each shift is taken up by spotting, pointing out, and inviting others to view and evaluate the appearance of female patrons. These conversations can be lustful, predatory, judgmental, and derogatory, but in any case, they are dehumanizing and almost always degrading. This is especially so when the conversation turns to fantasies of sexual intercourse. The sometimes pornographic fantasies of sexual serendipity described here are merely an ethnographic sampling of what is clearly a more generalized, desirous, gaze of hyper-heterosexuality. Albeit commonplace among male-dominated occupational groups, such narratives are dramatically amplified in the doing of nightclub security.[2] I was often nudged to look in the direction of women a doorman considered attractive: "Man, look at them over there. They are just exquisite." This form of masculine objectification was part of the routine of being a doorman but was moreover an essential part of the heterosexual nightclub.

Women, I was told, were "one of the major perks of working as a bouncer." I recorded:

J. tugs at my arm once again to point out the rock band that has just taken the stage. The female lead singer is wearing an orange bra-top too small for her ample bosom. "Check THAT out," he says, as he points in her direction. "How about that?" he asks, giving me a nod and smiling. I return his smile ... Two hours later, three young women approach J., and after paying a cover charge, make their way into the nightclub. He smiles again in my direction and nods approvingly as he makes no attempt to conceal the fact he is leering at their bodies. Only moments later, he lunges across the entranceway to get my attention. This time he is enamoured with a twenty-something who has just come upstairs wearing hip-hugger jeans, sporting an exposed midriff and a skin-tight white T-shirt. "Did you see that!?" he asks. He doesn't give me enough time to answer as I look over. "Oh, you missed it," he continues. "You should have seen her from the front!" He continues to describe her as a regular who often wears tight shirts without a bra. His careful description utilizes hand motions, tracing hourglass shapes in the air and virtually cupping imaginary breasts in mime. This display continues despite my discomfort and even while he stamps club-goers as they enter. I am more than a little embarrassed and decide to move off to another location ...

At approximately 1:05 A.M. I find myself back at the entranceway talking to another doorman about a recent episode with the Hell's Angels, but we are interrupted by J. who turns our attention toward yet another female client. This time I don't even bother ... I'm elbowed and nudged so many times by an assortment of burly bouncers to look at women that my ribs and upper arms feel sore ... One hour later, a group of five women enter the bar. They are elegantly dressed and in their thirties. J. flirts with one of the women, holding onto her hand after he has stamped it and saying, "I just couldn't let go." I feel like gagging. The woman smiles and continues on her way and J. wonders whether they "were working girls" but laughingly surmises, "It probably wouldn't be a good idea to ask them." This continues all night ... 3:00 A.M.: "There's an amazing amount of woman here tonight, eh?" he says, raising his brows and pointing in the direction of a petite woman wearing a black evening dress ... 3:15 A.M.: "Wow, look at that ass!" And on it has continued, even at closing, as women file past the doormen ... more nudges, raised brows ... I probably have bruised ribs by now.

The doing of gender (Fenstermaker and West 2002) demands the masculine defence of virtuous women and the construction of girlfriends as protected property. I recorded an instance in which a doorman tried to exclude a woman because of his relationship to her:

Later in the evening I notice commotion at the front entrance. Two of the doorstaff working the entrance are agitated and exchanging words. A supervisor comes over and asks his co-worker to follow him outside. One of the doormen is outraged because his recent ex-girlfriend is sitting at the bar with her new boyfriend. The doorman felt humiliated and wanted them both removed. For the time being, the couple is allowed to stay.

Given this backdrop, and since bouncing is an almost exclusively male-dominated occupation, toward the end of my time in the field, I made a request to patrol with a female member of the security staff. When I was introduced to the woman I was to accompany, the doorman who walked me over to her immediately sexualized our introduction: "Maybe if you're lucky she'll show you her tits!" Later on our patrol the conversation turned to nicknames, and when I asked her if she had one herself, she said, "Yes, but it's bad." Of course, such behaviour was commonplace:

A group of doormen huddle around reading the latest instalment of "Savage Love" – a ribald sex-education column appearing in the last few pages of Halifax's entertainment weekly, *The Coast*. There is unapologetic sex talk, and the female cashier is laughing as the subject moves to pornographic movies. A coat-check girl arrives on the scene just as "t*** licking" becomes the new topic of conversation. The cashier greets her co-worker with "great timing!" Everyone laughs.

The most combustible combination for potential violence in a night-club usually consists of a woman perceived to be flirtatious or cheating by a jealous and/or humiliated male partner. Often, even the perception that another man is eyeing someone's girlfriend will lead to a physical confrontation. "I'd have to say the girlfriend/boyfriend thing is at least half of the arguments that pop up," I was told. "But that can break off into how many different things, you know, 'I saw you talking to this guy, or dancing with this girl.' It's just silliness, but you have to be a media-tor, and you know, I hear one person's side and the other person's side and then you make a decision on what happens, I like doing that" (01: white male doorstaff).

Two doormen related a story to me about a couple who had been in the nightclub the previous evening. The man arrived with his girlfriend, who started to flirt with someone else. The boyfriend confronted her and got so angry that he punched a wall, breaking his hand. The bouncers re-move both him and his girlfriend, who took him to the hospital. The punchline of this episode is that the woman returned later, "ditching the guy at the hospital" to continue her night out. "What an idiot," they laughed. I observed a similar situation that escalated into a brawl:

A man in a white T-shirt is quarrelling with a blond woman at the bar. They are both visibly upset and arguing loudly. The woman, apparently having had enough, slaps the man across the face. It is a rather loud smack and has the attention of most of the patrons in this section of the nightclub. A doorman moves over to her, taps her on the shoulder, and asks her to leave. As she leaves, she is followed by the white T-shirted man she has just slapped, and his friend, also in a white T-shirt. The argument continues outside, spilling onto the street corner in front of the nightclub.

Another man wearing a leather jacket and a baseball cap, who is also outside, decides to join the argument. I do not understand his relationship to any of the three parties involved in the original argument. Nonetheless, he starts to challenge the original man in the white T-shirt to a fight. Is this chivalry? I am not sure why he is involved. Two bouncers leave the front entrance and attempt to calm everybody down, but they have left the front entrance unchecked and patrons start to stream into the bar. At one point a man looks at me, assuming that I am a bouncer and asks, "What do we do?" "Stay there!" I reply and the man holds the line. Eventually, the doormen return to the front entrance, having separated the aggrieved parties. But only a few moments later the same woman approaches the front entrance along with the man in the leather jacket, asking to re-enter to get her coat and friends. I now assume she must have some relationship to the man in the leather jacket.

The two men in the white T-shirts have followed her from the corner to continue the argument with the man in the leather jacket. This is an argument about a woman and personal honour – a potentially violent cocktail. The bouncers' permission to allow her to get her jacket is drowned out by the three men now in another heated yelling match. Each is standing with his fists clenched, ready to fight. I step behind the rope divider as the situation looks like it will escalate. Without warning, one of the white T-shirted men throws a punch at the man in a leather jacket, hitting him square in the jaw. The punch was so hard that he bloodies the man almost immediately. The sound of the smack is audible to all of those queued patrons, including a horrified group of female pubcrawlers.

The man in a leather jacket responds: "Is that the best you can do?" Before the bouncers can move in, the group of three men have launched at each other, starting a violent fist fight.

Four bouncers quickly reach the men, attempting to place a headlock on the bigger of the T-shirted men. They are struggling with neck locks as they fall over the rope divider, smashing into the brick wall outside of the nightclub. The doorman who grappled with the man in the leather jacket now hip-throws him to the ground in a neck choke. The final bouncer is trying to control the other man in a white T-shirt but cannot bring him to the ground. There is chaos and screams from the people involved as well as from shocked onlookers. One of the doormen realizes that the fight is getting out of control and yells to me to run inside and flick the emergency lights. Without hesitation, I go through the front door and tell the coat-check girl to flick the lights. She is already in the process of calling the police and asks me where exactly the fight is taking place. "Just outside this door on the sidewalk." Only seconds later, ten bouncers stream out the doors of the nightclub. It seems that each of them is joining a bouncer already involved in a melee. Bodies are being jostled and throttled all over the sidewalk. The man in the leather jacket is being restrained by three doormen and his face is as red as a beet from his struggle to breathe and yell at the same time. "Let me go, man! Let me go!" His blood is pooling on the sidewalk and is splattered up against a car parked next to the curb. Both of the men in T-shirts have also been pinned, one against the wall of the nightclub, the other on the sidewalk about five metres down from me. His jeans are ripped from the waist to the knee.

A police car approaches and is flagged down by one of the doorstaff who has only now made his way onto the sidewalk. Three more police cars and a paddy wagon arrive in quick succession. Very cautiously, each of the combatants is let out of their restraining holds. One police officer approaches the patrons in line, asking, "What happened?" The bar manager has joined the crowd outside. The police are continuing to gather information about the fight. The man in the leather jacket is complaining to police about the chokehold used against him by the doorman. He cannot be calmed down. Finally, the police arrest the two men in T-shirts for assault and threaten to arrest the man in the leather jacket if he doesn't "shut up." Almost immediately, the doormen look to each other, commenting on what type of hold they had on their respective combatant and how he was struggling. One of the doormen thanks me for raising the alarm and mentions that it was "much appreciated."

The blond woman who was apparently the spark that ignited the fight has returned to the front entrance with her friends and is complaining to them in earshot of the doorstaff for "choking a guy when he's on the ground." She hurls more insults at the doorstaff until one of the doormen finally responds, "Shut up and go elsewhere." She responds, "You've got bigger tits than me!" and turns to her friends to repeat herself. "He's got better-looking tits than me!"

I found it fascinating that after all of the bravado, storytelling, and even blood and violence, the woman's most visceral verbal attack was aimed at feminizing the burly bouncer who pinned her friend to the sidewalk. Perhaps she intuitively knew that the entire fracas hinged on masculinity, chivalry, and paternalism. She sullied the entire episode by refusing to play the role of the grateful damsel in distress. She was, in effect, unworthy of the fight and therefore had made it about anything other than herself. If anyone ever thought it was so in the first place, the fight was no longer heroic, no longer meaningful other than for the valorization of the violent spectacle for its own sake. Love triangles were the source of numerous episodes:

As I idle at the entrance with another doorman, a quiet Middle Eastern male who looks to be in his early thirties, comes out of the nightclub and, mistaking me for a bouncer, asks if he can leave the bar for a minute. This has happened before. I tell him that I do not work there but that as long as he has a stamp he is allowed to re-enter. He stands beside me and points to a couple kissing and embracing against a wall down the street. After about five minutes he tells me that the woman is actually his girlfriend. It certainly doesn't look that way to me. The man decides to head off down the street and confront the couple. I watch him stride deliberately but nonetheless tentatively as I turn toward the doorman to inform him of these recent developments. We sit back and watch.

The doorman is unconcerned because it is activity away from the premises. The doorman informs me that the man kissing the patron's girlfriend is a bartender at the Galaxy, who has a reputation for this sort of thing. After a heated discussion, the Middle Eastern patron throws off his satin jacket and tries half-heartedly to get at the other man. It is largely posturing, as his girlfriend has little difficulty separating him from her new interest. Eventually, the new couple make their way down the street to another nightclub.

The Middle Eastern patron then comes back to the bar and, calmly as can be, asks if he can come back in. "Are you going to behave inside?" asks P. The man apologizes for any trouble he has caused and reiterates his situation. P. waves him in. "Go ahead and drown your sorrows." … Some time later the couple whom the jealous boyfriend went after comes back to the bar to see if he is still there. His "girlfriend" wants to meet up with him again. To my surprise, the doorman shrugs and says that the man is still inside but that he doesn't think they should go in. They do, and eventually the reunited couple leave together without further incident.

Nightclub titillations seemed everywhere linked back to surveillance, and women were the primary targets. They represented not only the primary draw, a voyeuristic attraction, but were viewed as most potentially at risk and therefore in need of protection. Oftentimes, the riskier the behaviour, the more thrilling, the more dangerous the potential repercussions. The desire to be desired produced gender-specific risks that doormen both appreciated and worried about.

From my panoptic position, these attempts to draw attention to oneself sometimes played themselves out in rather ribald fashion:

I am quite enjoying my elevated vantage point as the dance music thumps through my organs. I notice a group of women who appear intoxicated. One of them looks vaguely familiar. I think she's a student. They are all perspiring heavily, despite their breezy outfits. She motions to a man dancing next to her and fans herself with her hand as if saying "It's hot!" He acknowledges her comment and lifts up his shirt to fan his chest. Then, to my own and the crowd's surprise, the woman pulls down her tank top shirt exposing her breasts. I look over to J. with what probably is a rather amazed look, and he shouts back, "It's her birthday!" She has become an instant source of entertainment and attention. Shortly thereafter, the woman dons a jacket and her friends whisk her away into the night. We carefully watch over her exit. "There's some really hot ***** here tonight!" N. finally nods.

An inordinant amount of girl or "fox" watching, however, is not tolerated by other doormen if it jeopardizes their safety or compromises the overall security of the nightclub. One complained, "Some guys, this pisses me off ... say, 'I get paid to stand and watch girls dance'" (01: white male doorstaff). Another said, disapprovingly, "They talk to women, don't watch the guys" (11: white male doorstaff).

The problem can become such that it demands managerial intervention:

> You get hit on a lot like when you're a doorman, right? 'Cause girls want to get into the bar free. 'Cause they know who you are and all that stuff, right? So guys who come into the bar, like, "Hey listen, I'm the doorman." Whatever. All these girls are talking to me, or whatever, if you're just going to spend all your time there talking to girls, then you're not going to be a doorman for very long, 'cause you're not watching out for the people that're watching out for you, right? So something happens, and somebody ends up getting their face beat off, 'cause you're up there talking to some girl, you're not gonna last. (14: visible minority male doorstaff)

> Yeah, I monitor them quite heavily. I mean, I don't like them talking to girls too long, you know what I mean? The doormen, like, the shirt and the radio, it's a chick magnet for the young guys and stuff, and that's what I don't want. So I'll walk around, and if you're talking to a girl at the back bar and I'll just walk by, I won't say nothing. If I come back in another twenty minutes and you're still talking to the girl at the back bar? Then I'll say something. I'll say, "Jay, you come here," and I'll say something. I will never ever yell at anybody in front of everybody, I never will do that. I'll just say, "okay, you were talking to her a little long, watch your people." I've had girls, – like, they rotate every half hour? I've had girls follow them in rotation. (03: white male supervisor)

As iconographic representations of hegemonic masculinity in a nightclub, doormen receive consistent attention from female patrons. Bouncers too are therefore part of the objectification process:

> I got a ton of girls hangin' on me [at] night, that after two months you don't pay attention to it. Like, my girlfriend comes down sometimes, just like, she'll bring me a pizza or something. Outside, if she's going out that night. The girls hit on me. If she's there, she gets mad at me. But at the same time I don't even pay attention to them, you know, 'cause it's so constant. Like you know what I mean? They're a joke anyway. (09: white male doorstaff)

It was Saturday, it was kind of raining, and girls walk by, they'll grab your butt or something. You're like, "Fuck off … This girl pinched my ass. Like she didn't – that got me in trouble. (09: white male doorstaff)

In some cases bouncers apparently find the unsolicited attention from the opposite sex discomforting. The constant availability of flirtatious women and the realization that they too are being leered at and objectified may in some small way contribute to their vociferous degradation of women whom they find unattractive or unworthy of reciprocating attention. Women who do not fit a stereotypical image of femininity and beauty are met with derision in the nightclub, and doormen are active participants. They are just as apt to comment on an attractive woman as they are to comment on what they perceive to be an unattractive woman. When there is an inadequate number of what they perceive to be attractive women in the nightclub, bouncers complain that there's "not much skin in here tonight." "Unless you're into fat, ugly women," agreed his co-worker, "yeah, donkey, tonight." From my fieldnotes:

It is just past midnight and the nightclub is beginning to fill up. For some unknown reason, a group of revellers at a nearby table break out into a rendition of Bon Jovi's "Bad Medicine" during a slow song. J. warns a woman about using her cell phone inside the nightclub and then motions towards a group of middle-aged women at the bar. "What really grosses me out is when the fat women sitting at the bar talk about me when I walk past." I wonder how often that happens …

Doormen held conservative views about whether certain women deserved equal protection. Women who received unwanted attention from men they approached seemed less likely to garner sympathy from doormen. I observed,

It's 3:15 A.M. as I watch a young, attractive woman sitting at the bar move over two bar stools to her left in order to join two men who offered to buy her a shot. I still haven't lost interest in these last-ditch nightclub courting rituals, so I watch attentively. Over my shoulder, I realize the two doormen I have been talking to are also watching the same development. My concentration is broken when one turns to the other and says: "And then women wonder why they get treated like sluts," adding, "And when he starts following her home, she'll wonder why he won't go away."

My point in this section has been that the synoptic frenzy of the nightclub produces at least four forms of optic violence: managing, staring, cutting, and leering. These visual modalities seem always to run parallel with (in)security, risk, and consumption. At the same time as these optics objectify, degrade, and disempower, they also titillate, extol and empower, eliciting both digust and desire. When other forms of communication are subjugated, when depth is undermined and the surface is exalted, the visual is consumed fetishistically, producing alienation and valorizing the spectacle.

Crises of Respect and "Liquid Courage"

From my position overlooking the dance floor I can see a break-dancing circle open up. In the middle of the clearing is a man in his late twenties with a stocking cap. People are cheering him on as he makes some rather fantastic body movements. But after a minute or so another man in a blue shirt, probably in his early twenties, cuts right through the diameter of the circle, intentionally bumping into the break-dancer. From his prone position the break-dancer looks up and gives the intruder the finger. They crowd each other in order to intimidate, neither shoving nor grappling yet. Two doormen leave their positions and race between the two men. The man in the blue shirt looks angry and belligerent and is given a sharp push by one of the doormen as he refuses to calm down. From my vantage point I can see him pointing directly in the face of the younger man, warning him. Finally, the two are separated and, surprisingly, are both allowed to stay in the nightclub. The spectacle within the spectacle was interrupted violently. It all seemed rather territorial, belittling, atavistic ...

Panoptic vantage points, communication systems, training seminars, and self-defence courses all make up important aspects of the doorman's security repertoire. And while it is true that managerial protocols, dress codes, and surveillance strategies have a dramatic impact on how a nightclub is constituted, what we risk overlooking in our description of the synoptic frenzy and its various forms of optic violence is the role of doorstaff experience and their general "feel" for or "reading" of the crowd that develops over time.

The simple act of approaching a patron for removal from the nightclub is an affront. The suggestion of public humiliation and disempowerment is unavoidable but can be significantly mitigated by giving the subject of removal space to leave. "Let him keep his dignity and leave the place" is the credo of most intelligent doormen. One security supervisor felt that it was better to "give the guy room, let him mouth off to you and have his say" in order to avoid an escalation in violence. We have already acknowledged that the ability to talk someone down is a valued skill among doormen, but only insofar as this is backed up by the ability to use force when necessary. Indeed, "giving him an out and never cornering him" recognizes the fact that an approach by a doorman is easily construed as a loss of face producing a potential crisis of respect. The synoptic frenzy's judgment can be biting, and the evening's dramas potentially humiliating. These produce hundreds of crises of respect in the nightclub.

Jostling bodies, alcohol consumption, and status frustration coupled with the intrinsic powder-keg violence of the nightclub spectacle necessitate a keen pre-emptive eye from bouncers. Anything out of the ordinary such as sounds of broken glass or quick movements draw the immediate attention of doorstaff. "Anything can happen in a second. Like, somebody drops a beer bottle on somebody's foot, they get mad, and boom, so it can happen that fast." (01: white male doorstaff). In one instance, the lead singer for a local punk band started screaming, "Fuck you, Fuck you!" while pointing to a group in the crowd. The bouncers leapt to attention, then realized that this was part of the singer's routine.

Most of the reasons why fights develop are puerile:

Beating their own egos. A lot of guys, they take everything personally ... They gotta show off to, like, the other guys, they gotta show off to the girls in the bar ... (10: white male doorstaff)

There's just stupid things like, you know, "Well I was here first." And then, "*I* was here first." It's stupid, retarded, what people fight about. (04: white male doorstaff)

Something happens out of nowhere and you're thinking, "Well, they were just talking to each other." And "What's wrong"? Generally, if you see somebody who's walking around, and they're bump-

ing into people and you know, you can normally tell if somebody
else is not in the mood. And constantly looking at the crowd so
sometimes people stand out. And you can see things certainly before they happen. People who are talking and don't seem to be talking very friendly. Which is why it starts. Women, for example, who
are, who keep continuously moving away from a man, because he
keeps getting closer, and the girl feels that he shouldn't. Things like
that you can see. (11: white male doorstaff)

Bouncers scan the crowd looking for facial expressions that will top
them off about someone's attitude: (After spending hours scanning the
crowds and talking to bouncers, I too became attuned to changes in atmosphere. From my perch in a panoptic position I often could tell when
a fight was developing.)

I just look at everyone's faces. When I comb over a crowd, I'm looking at everybody's face. Because a lot is said in someone's face. And
if you're in argument with some person, you have that look on your
face. Like there's been plenty of times where someone will be drunk
and you have those guys that get drunk and they act like a tough
guy with their friends. Like, they approach their friends acting like
a tough guy, and then all of a sudden they're hugging and kissing
and stuff. And there's been plenty of times when I'm like, "Hey
buddy, have you got a problem?" He's like, "No, no, I know this
guy," right? But I look at faces and usually what sets off my alarm
is the expression on a person's face. What the other person's doing.
How other people are looking at those two people around them,
because if you're mouthing off I might not be able to hear them,
but the people around them can hear them. And if they're swearing
and like laying down threats, that will attract the attention of other
people, and they'll look. And when a lot of people are looking, then
you know that something's happening. That's what I look for. (18:
white male doorstaff)

Just maybe staggering, and he looks like, you'll see him, some guy
will walk by him, will rub shoulders, and just the way they'll turn
around and look at them, you'll go, "Okay, this guy looks like he
wants to fight somebody." Just keep an eye on them and then, you
know, "Oh, he has a beer." He's drinking a beer. And that way if he
does screw up I know on my way he has a beer bottle. So I know to

watch out for his beer bottle. But just, there's not much you can do besides that. They do all the safeguarding for us. (13: white male doorstaff)

Oh you usually tell. I mean, you'll get guys puffin' out their chests, bumpin' into people, talking shit to people they bump into. Starin' people down. You know, you can tell. Like, you can tell they're obviously trying to act tough. And you can tell guys who're like, there's two different types too. They're guys that go out, you know, are crazy, you know, they're tough guys, you know, they're heavies. (19: Male White Doorstaff)

Despite the seemingly universal and objective signs of aggression that will mobilize a bouncer, subcultural cues that hinge on race and ethnicity remain large factors in assessing danger. Oftentimes, these are nothing more than racially segregated nightclub cliques.

Like at this other club, it was like a map of the world. Like there was, like, the Vietnamese guys there, Spanish guys over here, black guys over there at the bar. You knew that there was going to be a problem. A little problem would become a big problem. Halifax isn't as ethnically diverse. You'll see the Gap guys get [it] on with the guys in leather jackets or the guys in super baggy jeans. (19: white male doorstafff)

It's a Wednesday night and every brother in the world is standing on the dance floor. We say to each other, you know, "No matter what happens, we fight them all or grab them all, because those guys are going to jump us. If one guy goes, they all go." You know what I mean? We already knew what we're going to do, because black guys fight in packs. (09: white male doorstaff)

Crises of respect, losing face, and attempts to reassert power are constantly amplified by alcohol. Alcohol is the fuel, the central social lubricant for both a good time and violence in the nightclub. The perceived loss of inhibition from taking alcohol, the cultural expectations surrounding its consumption (Heath 1987; Lindman and Lang 1994), and the debate about its actual violent potential being chemical or social need not concern us here.[3] But alcohol's accepted effects on motor skills, speech, and perception are, of course, perfectly suited to nightclub dramas, amplifying some inputs and blunting others, either socially or chemically eliciting disinhibition. These effects produce a sense of confidence and bravado often described by bouncers as "liquid courage." I record:

> A young white male patron who has been drinking heavily is being escorted from the nightclub. He is not resisting but is visibly enraged at this indignity. He has been accused of harassing various women and is so intoxicated it is difficult to make sense of what he is saying. "The fucking bouncer broke my chain." In his frustration he begins punching the door through which he has been escorted by the doorman. He is a smaller fellow, and it doesn't appear as if he is drunk enough to challenge the bouncers. Finally, one of the doormen asks him what his problem is. He responds sheepishly, "No problem. I just need to find my hat." Someone is sent to fetch his hat from the nightclub but he continues to punch the door. "Somebody tell that asshole to stop banging on the door before he gets himself seriously hurt," yells out one of the doormen. A supervisor walks over and threatens to call a police wagon if the drunken reveller does not calm down ... He is joined by a friend and the two of them begin to utter threats towards the doormen. They are mumbling under their breath, muttering, even growling as they avoid eye contact. The doormen hear them but dismiss the smaller men's taunts. "Liquid courage," one of them laughs.

Generally speaking, bouncers hold the popular conception that alcohol produces violent situations by creating frames of mind where anything is possible. Alcohol "just puts people in a frame of mind where they don't know what they're gonna do" (02: white male supervisor). Said another doorman, "Alcohol amplifies a person's personality. It definitely does. You see a lot of that, a person when they're sober who fights, they're gonna be a lot of problems" (01: white male doorstaff).

When patrons do not know their own limits and apparently lose their inhibitions, they believe that they can resolve perceived slights through violence. They become less aware of how they affect others and seem hypersensitive to how others perceive them. In a sexualized nightclub awash in synoptic tensions, optic violence, and the bombardment of visual cues, it is no wonder that many drunks are angry people who want to take on the world. One bouncer disgustedly observed, "There's a lot of people that, once they have too many drinks, they feel like they can take on the world ... very gullible young nineteen year olds, and they get tough, and they wanna go out and fight? And you're like, 'Buddy, you have to find all your friends, find a gym, do something,' you know? It's just fucked" (08: white male doorstaff).

Bouncers are also very much aware of the potential for litigation if they fail to act in cases of inebriated patrons:

Drunk people suck ... You have to deal with a lot of stupid people. And here the liquor laws are a little bit more relaxed than they are in Ontario. Like in Ontario it's illegal to be drunk in a bar? So if someone's like obviously drunk, you have to throw them out. Here's it's pretty much if they're drunk and they still have money in their pockets, it's totally fine. If they're drunk and they're broke, then they gotta go. But like here I've seen where, you know, a guy will be sleeping, they're like, "Oh, wake him, give him a Coke," you know what I mean? Get him, like, a glass of coffee, it's all right, don't worry about him. And Ontario, it's like, the way you have to pay for a cab or you're gonna get sued. And you know, get fined, perhaps do time. You know what I mean, they deal with it a lot more seriously there. Here it's more relaxed and just, everyone loves to drink in Halifax. You know what I mean, it's like the whole city is based on drinking. You know. (19: white male doorstaff)

You're less inhibited than you would be when you're sober. You know, you don't jump up on a table and start dancing, you [don't] stand up on a chair to see if somebody's there. And you don't realize it but being drunk, that's pretty dangerous. You could slip and fall and crack your head on the tiles, or drive a piece of glass through your head. Or ... such silly things as taking your shoes off and running up to the dance floor, it's not a safe thing to do here, there's a lot of broken glass. And as much as we try and clean it up, we'll never get it all. (04: white male doorstaff)

Doorstaff typically show tremendous latitude when deciding on whether to remove someone for excessive drinking or doing drugs: "Drinking excessive amounts of alcohol is very acceptable here, which makes it hard because you've got to deal with a lot of people ... especially with a cabaret, because people come here and they've already been drinking all night, you've gotta deal with people who're loaded, and you can stay out and drink legally to like four in the morning. And you've got to deal with a lot of really drunk people who do a lot of stupid things" (19: white male doorstaff). One man was caught "snorting blow" in the men's washroom. He looked filthy as he was escorted out of the nightclub. The doorman indicated that he found him "so wasted that he had dropped in his own piss": "We'll just, usually if a guy's rolling a joint, or smoking a joint, or something like that, or even just they were doing some coke in the bathroom, we go on, 'Hey, buddy, you can't be doing this here. It's not cool. Get outside, you belong to the night, type of thing. But we don't care, the doormen are like, if I know a person's stoned I don't care. You know what I mean? Like I'll watch a person smoke a joint down the block, long as they put it down across the street and come in, I don't care, right?" (10: white male doorstaff).

It is only when patrons' behaviour undermines their own safety or the safety of others or when patrons challenge the authority of the bouncers that doorstaff are likely to react:

I was bitten – on the inner thigh by a guy. Again he was drug induced on some pretty serious stuff. He did this pushup with three bouncers sitting on him. It took about six cops to get him in the paddy wagon. After he bit me, I did what I, what was necessary to maybe possibly slow him down a little bit. It didn't work at all. He bit another doorman in the chest. He, again, punched [the] guy several times in the face, and the guy wasn't phased, he just looked at us both and just laughed. (02: white male supervisor)

Maybe it's not like the guy intended on rolling a joint when he came in. He just happened with the boys, "Hey, let's fuckin' roll a joint," like that, right? You bring a bottle in, you're intending to disrespect the staff and take money away from them, that kind of thing, right? So bottles, you know, I usually make it habit in, you know, I keep kicking them out, right? (04: white male supervisor)

You see what's going on in the washroom – I mean, there's people in there snorting cocaine. I mean all the time there's people in there and I mean … I didn't think that kind of stuff went on, but if we see it, we'll do something. They gotta be private. (15: visible minority doorstaff)

As a ruse to get inebriated patrons to leave, some doormen actually use a roadside sobriety test: "I'm very nice. I walk up, and say, I'll tap em on the shoulder and 'How ya doing, big fella? How's your night goin?' And say, 'I think you're, think you're pretty toast for the night. You mind steppin' outside, I'll give ya a little test.' And we'll get them to stand on one foot and they'll fall right over, and "Okay, you're finished.' If you can stand on one foot for about five seconds, 'Sorry, my mistake. Go back in. I just thought you were too messed up.' Sometimes you get people just fall right in the wall, and "Okay, okay, you're finished, man" (13: white male doorstaff). Such tactics create an aura of objectivity. A "failed test" can serve to diffuse the ignobility of being thrown out. A little show of respect in an otherwise degrading episode can go a long way to avoid an escalation in violence, because the incident avoids a crisis by not undermining the patron's dignity.

This chapter has examined the phenomenon of "getting noticed" in a nightclub – the compulsion to see and be seen, to desire and be desired, to join the spectacle of consumption. This spectacle is as alienating as it is seductive. The synoptic frenzy of the nightclub fuses surveillance and aesthetic consumption. It fetishizes bodies and amplifies social capitals, producing manifold forms of optic violence and crises of respect bolstered by alcohol-induced "liquid courage." Having navigated the synoptic frenzy of the nightclub, we move in the next chapter to describe our trip home.

7

Getting Home

After a night of seeing and being seen, of being churned through the synoptic frenzy, it's time to head home. This can be a dangerous and chaotic time. Most patrons will exit the nightclub doors, nod to police officers and doorstaff, and stagger their way into a taxi, oblivious to the potential violence around them. A surprising minority, however, will bear witness to an array of transgressional behaviours ranging from minor incivilities to brutal and bloody violence. Those who have had their night end prematurely are far more likely to fall into the latter group. I mentioned (in chapter 1) that as the field observations progressed, my research assistants and I were much more likely to see violence arriving later in the evening – the time when the majority of incidents took place. Patrons had ample opportunity to drink throughout the night and bouncers more time to assess and react to troublesome individuals.

If the nightclub is a seductive spectacle of consumption, nightly banishments are a brutal reminder of its private, exclusionary nature, no matter how liberal the codes of dress or conduct. Removal is a crisis of respect of the highest order. It is embarrassing, degrading, and disempowering. After 1 A.M., violent removals are more frequent, liquid courage is in high supply, and resistance to doormen is more common. This chapter examines the trip home from the nightclub, both in terms of being "bounced" and leaving of one's own accord.

The nightclub at closing time projects a rather vacuous and sickly ambience. The lights are turned on, the spectacle turned down and the night's excesses revealed: spilt beer, vomit, bloodshot eyes, sweaty shirts, matted hairstyles, and an assortment of aesthetic unpleasantness formerly obscured by the flashing lights, mob, music, and managed mayhem. After dealing with those patrons being "bounced," I analyze the transition of bodies moving into the early-morning darkness of downtown Halifax well after the "last waltz" has been played. Next, I examine the transition of private spectacle to public nuisance and the close interrelationship between bouncers and police officers at closing time. The interpenetration of the public and private spheres is fascinating for its choreographed transitioning of social control. Finally, this chapter examines theoretically the consumption and risk involved in the context of policing public urban spaces filled with drunken revellers – a predictable binge and purge ritual within the night's late capitalist market flow.

Bounced

> It has been a long night. A busboy emerges from the nightclub with two ten-gallon buckets of soapy water. He splashes the sidewalk and a nearby parked car bearing the evidence of a vicious fight earlier in the evening. The blood-soaked sidewalk and spattered vehicle are rinsed as onlookers watch in disgust and morbid curiosity. Before long, there is no physical evidence remaining of the recent violence. I watch pedestrians stagger past the wet sidewalk, oblivious to the night's brutality. (fieldnotes)

Getting thrown out of a nightclub is humiliating. People don't like being unwanted. They do not like being overpowered, and they become angry and panicked when they realize their nightclub experience is ending prematurely. It was a strangely consistent curiosity to witness patron after patron apparently acquiescing to demands by doorstaff, only to become irate and violent when they reached the exit doors. Was it their state of intoxication? Their inability to register what was happening to them until the very last instant? Was it the fact that they were still part of the synoptic frenzy up until they reached the doors? Were they holding out hope they could negotiate their way out of their predicament and back into the club? It was never clear. But over and over again, patrons targeted for removal would start their kicking, punching, and flailing at the exit. It was like a violent awakening, as if they had swallowed Morpheus's red pill and resented it. As they were degraded and temporarily stripped of any subcultural value, their recourse was the nightclub's natural optic product, a truthful representation of the nightclub's heated residue, its social tax for creating throwaways rendered now even more transparent, an obvious clarification of social capital through the exercise of violence.

Always boiling under the surface, this violent, steam-like pressure finally burst through the front door. For me, the desperate, bloodied, and enraged faces screaming back at the bouncers, denigrating the nightclub, vomiting on the sidewalk, and spitting forth a tirade of frustration was the ultimate manifestation of the nightclub's power to cultivate, indeed, produce violence: "We'll call him and tell him he has to leave and he'll start to go, and he might walk right out by himself and we'll just walk side by side with him. But if he starts wrestling and stopping and cursing and swearing, we'll just each hold onto an arm and … most times we'll still come with him. Sometimes you have to kind of pull them with you. But anyway, they come to the door and you bring them outside. Then the guys outside have to listen to them threaten, 'Aww, I'm gonna come back here and get you' and this and that." (13: white male doorstaff)

One removal started off "cool" but became so heated and physical that the patron being removed actually ripped the door from its hinges.

We had a guy a few Wednesdays ago … the doorman who talked to him first was being really cool with him. Like you know, just being relaxed, and "You don't have to get in a fight, it's cool." Like "You go this way, and you go this way and don't, you know, [start] arguing with each other." And the guy freaked out and started pushing the doorman. So he hooked up his arms and his girlfriend got in our face and was screeching, "Let go of him, you're hurting him! Let go, let go!" So the guy who had him hooked up let go of him. And as soon as he let go of him, the guy grabbed a glass and swung the glass at us. Then we hooked him up, and he was trying fight us the whole way out the door. Swinging at us with whatever. Like if he could get an arm free, he'd take swings, he was trying to kick us, trying to headbutt us. Trying to bite us. Tryin' to grab onto things. So we pin him down inside the front hallway, then we're like "Jay, relax, relax." And he's like, "Yeah, I'm relaxed, I'm relaxed. You guys are hurting me!" So we let him up, then he came at us again and ended up getting thrown out the door. The door ended up off its hinges. Outside he went after us again. And we let him go again and he charges up again. We ended having to hold him for the police, like up the street. (19: white male doorstaff)

In another case the patron only resisted once he was outside and had the help of a friend: "He got kicked out, then he was trying to come in, and he tried to fight a doorman. His other buddy went out to the car and got pepper spray and then started hosing guys down. Crazy … So I had to like aggressively pin my elbow or my forearm against his head, hold him down, put my knee in his lower back. He was a pretty big guy, I was trying to pound, get his arm behind his back and hold him there until the cops came in because there was no way – if I let him up, he was going hit somebody else or run away or whatever. But he was being real aggressive. He tried to bite my hand" (10: white male doorstaff).

Once banned individuals are outside, doormen are not particularly concerned with what happens to them. They are typically left to their own devices, and bouncers are loath to interfere. They prefer to "let the police handle it," because drunken revellers on city streets are "no longer a nightclub issue" – a strange declaration, considering the nightclub produced them, excited them, frustrated them, and then abandoned them. It is generally considered unnecessary and unwise for doormen to intervene in incidents that do not immediately concern the nightclub and its property. Indeed, I watched one evening as a group of young men walked past the entrance to the Beacon, trailing blood. One man I recognized as a Saint Mary's student had a large cut on his forehead, another cut near his eye, and a gash on his arm. He was dazed and had difficulty walking. His friends surrounded him and talked loudly as they passed the nightclub. One of the doormen at the entrance muttered, "Whoa, that's a lot of blood," but they all just watched them walk on by, ensuring that the group did not enter the nightclub.

There are, in fact, innumerable instances of patrons challenging one another or getting involved in fights after they have left the nightclub: "The week before, there was two or three fights out front there between customers at the end of the night. The police came down" (06: white male doorstaff). Typically, doormen look on but do not intervene. I observed:

Things are winding down for another night outside of the Beacon. A heavily intoxicated black male was not allowed in the club because he had been previously banned. He instead decides to hover outside the bar entrance talking to doorstaff and hitting on every woman that leaves the bar. Having been banned for punching someone in the face, he tells the doorstaff that he now realizes that they are just doing their jobs. He continues chatting to women who largely ignore him on their way out about the nightclub … Finally, he turns his attention to a young white man from Cavendish, P.E.I. He begins mocking the young man's attire and his hometown. Luckily, the young out-of-towner is far too drunk to realize he is being challenged. He jumps into a cab, and I decide to do the same.

Other respondents justified the idea of non-intervention:

You see in other clubs doormen out in the middle of the streets
fighting with people, outside the range. Or inside the bar these guys
are kicking and screaming and punching on people. And here, like I
said, it's basically you're restrained and taking them out the doors as
quickly and as quietly as possible kind of idea. (15: visible minority
male doorstaff)

It's your job to stop them from fighting and get them out of the
bar. Make sure they're okay … he's not beating up your family
member, or your best friend. It's not your problem. Get them out
of the bar. Don't make it a personal fight between you and the guy
who just won. You know, it has nothing to do with you, you just
gotta do your job … We're not trying to make personalities, we're
not the police. And we are not trying to solve society's ills. We're
trying to make sure the bar is running smoothly, and a lot of that is
to keep drugs out of it. So if we catch them doing drugs we just ask
them to leave. We catch them selling drugs, we bar them, but if
they just have it for personal use, we just ask them to leave. It's not
my responsibility to turn this person in to the police. (06: white
male supervisor)

We have already covered this ethic of noninterference in incidents that
occur off nightclub property (chapter 4), but it is important to remember that bouncers do intervene from time to time to restore order in the
downtown Halifax night. They are, after all, its primary policers simply
by virtue of their spatial concentration and the size of populations under
their purview.

Say some guy's freakin' out on his girlfriend, like we had the other
night. He was just goin' right off and like, you know, we try to keep
ourselves out of the parking lot and off the streets, and like we keep
it in the building. But if we gotta step up, we'll step up. You know
what I mean? Like if the guy was gonna start swinging at her, then
of course we'd run down and take care of what we have to do, put
him down or whatever. (04: white male supervisor)

Going off the property to help someone out – 'cause I, we don't like
bullies, I don't like people pickin',' you know, three or four beatin'
up one guy – we'll go out there. (05 white male supervisor)

Everybody knows the Gottingen Street area is, quote unquote, "a rough area," known for a rough area. And a lot of people claim they have been intimidated when they come here. Right? A bit leery? That's why often females come up to me asking me can they get a cab, blah blah blah, can you come outside and make sure I get a cab and stuff. And I often do go outside and help them. Help them, assist them to get a cab, right? And I like that part of it. Not from the viewpoint of females coming up to me, but just for the fact that, hey, they want to come here and have fun, they shouldn't be in threat of their lives. (16: white male doorstaff)

There is admittedly still a residual tendency among even certain neo-Marxian thinkers to romanticize the criminal acts of some rather unsavoury characters who purportedly share a "proto-revolutionary" consciousness. I too am risking romanticizing nightclub pugillists by suggesting those thrown out of nightclubs are entitled to their violence, that this violence is truthful, natural, that it is the obvious product of a relentless synoptic frenzy that ignites social friction and produces heat (Quinney 1997); by further suggesting that this violence is an amplification of inequities based on race, class, and gender; by arguing these things and suggesting that resistance in the face of being bounced is the ultimate manifestation of the nightclub's power to cultivate alienation by extolling the surface, and by producing a spectacle of consumption and its attendant "lonely crowds." Truth be told, these folks are probably not proto-revolutionaries challenging the nightclub because it is the ultimate postmodern symbol of aesthetic production. But their anger is seething, deep, and very resilient and it can even result, as we have already seen, in spontaneous group efforts against doorstaff – in a veritable union of the night's dispossessed.

One incident a guy … was involved in a domestic dispute and he smashed his girlfriend, just smashed her in the head and knocked her down. A patron coming through … hit him in the head with a bottle and cut him quite badly. I separated them. The guy with the bottle was grabbed [and then I] grabbed the guy [who] was hit with the bottle. Identified myself as staff, and he struggled with me, just was in a rage. So as a result he went out in a choke, and, you know, was placed on the sidewalk. And he looked terrible and his friends were outside, you know, assuming that we did it to him … On a Saturday night five or six people [may still be waiting] outside that had been told they can't come in, and, you know, they're upset with you. You might have two or three people who've been kicked outside. And they'll all band together, you know, in a common cause, and so you'll get a large group of people out there attacking the bouncers. (white male supervisor)

Enraged and drunken patrons will attack doormen and even police at closing time. I observed:

Another man is now hurriedly being pushed toward the door by two bouncers. Only moments ago a patron had been removed for hitting a man over the head with a beer bottle. His victim is bruised from the jaw to the temple and the offender now sits on the curb between two police cruisers as the officers take statements. When the tall man sitting on the curb sees the other patron being removed, he jumps up and attacks the bouncers. A scuffle between five doormen and the two men they removed begins. The scrum is joined by other patrons who were ejected for unrelated incidents.

The police officer taking statements runs over to the fracas looking a bit overwhelmed by its intensity and size. He situates himself between the two groups but is hit by the tall man who was the first to be ejected for using a beer bottle. The officer is infuriated and grabs the man while he is being restrained by the bouncers. He throws him up against the car and then over the hood of the other vehicle just as the paddy wagon with three other officers arrives on the scene. The other officers open the doors of the wagon while the enraged police officer drags the man by the shirt along the street. He literally throws the man into the back of the wagon, slamming his knees on the bumper. "Get the fuck in there!" yells the police officer. The doormen are watching the officer in amazement. One of them blurts out: "Someone HIRE that cop!" The officer is livid, cursing during and after he rolled the man off two vehicles and into the back of the paddy wagon ...

More patrons spill out into the early morning night. They look like the walking wounded. I count four patrons with blood and other injuries including broken glass injuries. One man had several slashes on the outside of his right arm. Blood is dripping onto the sidewalk and trailing off in different directions. The police have now arrested two men from the bottle-breaking incident, and an ambulance has come to attend to the battered man in the rear of the police van. The bouncers are licking their wounds but everyone's adrenalin level still seems high. Several of the doormen have bloodstains on their white shirts. Their arms and hands are also spattered with blood, and they head off downstairs to clean up. The front of the nightclub seems to clear surprisingly quickly, but there are still doormen milling around, retelling their side of the story and commenting on what an "action-packed night" it has been. One doorman turns to me and says, "There hasn't been a night like this for a while," but says that "it was good, because it keeps you on your toes."

We must remember too that, for bouncers, closing down and going home – by their own admission – is the riskiest time. They often remove their security T-shirts and move in groups before venturing to other night-clubs, restaurants, or their cars. "The crowds, like I said, they generally react negatively towards us, especially when we use physical force to put someone out, so we try to lay low when we leave" (05: white male doorstaff). The night's army of the culturally dispossessed make this a dangerous trip. The power of the gaze is inverted, bouncers hiding rather than standing out, troublesome revellers now less confined, roaming, predatory …

The Last Waltz: Private Spectacle to Public Nuisance

When the last waltz is played, when the lights are turned on, when the night's rubbish is revealed, all eventually goes quiet except for the buzzing of eardrums and the muffled laughs and yelps of those still left behind. Perhaps it's the afterglow of the nightclub's optic assault, or perhaps it is a symptom of whatever unfulfilled aspiration the night is still withhold-ing from the last of the punters. Patrons now will be reluctant to leave, and the bouncers will increasingly become irritated. As the last waltz is played, the strangeness of the evening becomes even more transparent. "That's what I like to hear. Slow that music down. Get 'em all horny and run them home," said one doorman. As the lights came up, he added, "That's what I like to see."

My least favourite part of the job, actually, if you'd pick a specific thing, is asking people to leave the bar once the music shuts off and the lights come on … 'Cause for some reason people refuse to want to go home. You have to practically shove them out the door kick-ing and screaming. (01: white male doorstaff)

But at the end of the night you're just asking these people to get out, and they don't listen to you. And ... you know what I mean, you've been here for six, eight hours, and that's when, that's just the shitty part. Because people are drunk, they don't wanna stop partying, and you're the guy that's stopping their party and telling them to get the hell out of there. And they look at you like you're the mean guy, which you're really not. You just want to go home. That's probably the worst part about my job. (18: white male doorstaff)

It would be inaccurate to describe the transition of the private spectacle of the nightclub to a public nuisance for policing in terms of some neat territorial shift. There is, instead, deep interpenetration. The state does not merely passively absorb the night's bodies, its swoops in to oversee their movement, to regulate their flow, to actively assist in the flow of patrons by partaking in the turning down of the spectacle itself. Police officers who were working on a paid-duty basis for a nightclub would enter and stand by the exit during closing time. I observed:

It is after 3:30 A.M. and the bar begins to shut down as the lights are turned on upstairs. Somehow, everything looks more grotesque, somehow more unfortunate. The police are inside at the box-office area and I stand next to them as they observe people leaving. Patrons leave slowly but in a steady flow. Once in a while a patron will pause next to a doorman and say, "Have a good night, thanks." The doorman responds, "Hey, no problem, goodnight." One of the police officers turns to me and says, "There's lots of dope in here, man. I mean, half the people here are fried. Just look at them!" He's exaggerating. There have been an inordinate number of people leaving and returning throughout the night ...

Once the upstairs has been cleared, all of the doormen proceed downstairs and start to corral the remaining patrons out the back door. Some stragglers are allowed to remain at the bar, and it appears that they are friends of the bar staff or doormen. "Time to go home folks, bar's closed, time to go home!" P. complains that some "friends" think they have the run of the place and "don't know when to take the party elsewhere." As the doormen clear the upstairs area, Halifax police officers fall in behind them. It is an interesting sight to see public law enforcement officers working alongside doormen to clear a private site of consumption, then flush clean the spectacle. As the doormen corral patrons downstairs, the police stand at the top of the stairs to make sure no one sneaks back to the cleared area.

All the nightclubs we researched had policies against bottles or glasses leaving the club. At least in this sense the private consumption of alcohol was banned from entering the public sphere. At closing time, Halifax Regional Police vans have already taken their place at strategic posts throughout the downtown core, one van outside the Mansion, sometimes two outside the Beacon, and always another either stopped or idling just past the Galaxy. "Everyone falls out, and there could be three, four, five hundred kids just all out there, and then a fight breaks out, and the police don't like coming into a big crowd like that" (06: white male doorstaff). Patrons are transitioned from private to public policing with a concrete showing of state presence. In some cases, police can be seen roughly handling belligerent patrons, showing them into paddy-wagons. Others look on, some scatter down the street.

Between 2 A.M. to 4 A.M. the city appears as if abandoned to its drunken youths and their police overseers – a potentially combustible and unpredictable cocktail. But the night's ritual migration of bodies has been managed, routinized, and, over time, its hot spots mapped and accounted for. Epicentres of trouble (Grafton and Blowers, Gottingen and Portland) are saturated with uniformed officers and HRM vehicles. Incivilities and minor transgressions are given ample latitude lest the criminal justice system become clogged. Staggering steps and meaningless howls echo down deserted sidestreets trawled by taxis, police cars, and a creeping ambulance slowly collecting up revellers or seeing them off as they stumble home.

Binge and Purge

This is the third time during the field research that I have gone directly from a nightclub to my favourite urban vantage point, seated comfortably on a retaining wall on the southwest corner of Grafton and Blowers. It is the only neutral corner at the intersection, the only curb not hosting a fast-food pizzeria. Halifax's famous "pizza corner" surely achieved its notoriety from the throngs of nightclub partiers that clog the intersection after 1 A.M. Tonight, clutching my monstrous Donair pizza slice with extra sesame sauce, I have arrived just in time to avoid the lineup. As I fold over the slice to stuff it in my mouth, I watch as large groups of inebriated revellers stagger their way to one of the three pizza parlours. Two Halifax Regional police cars are idling on opposite sides of Blowers Street. In one cruiser, two constables are writing reports, occasionally raising their heads to survey the scene around them. Officers from the other police vehicle are standing out on the street, intermittently instructing people to "move back on to the sidewalk." When a vehicle makes its way towards the intersection, the constables once again remind oblivious partygoers to make way.

In one of the pizzerias, five young men – one of them shirtless – begin a bellicose rendition of the Canadian national anthem for no particular reason. Another in the group starts to sing half of the anthem in French, much to the delight and applause of his mates and others watching in the queue. An unimpressed teenaged male in a Red Sox cap hurls out the obligatory slight from his vantage point on the southeast corner: "You suck!" he yells and is immediately congratulated by backslapping laughter from three drunken supporters. Luckily, inside the pizzeria our Canadian nationalists are too busy ordering their slices to notice. Police officers momentarily eye both groups. On the northeast corner four more young men are talking in close quarters. They are loud and boisterous, and appear to be challenging one another. After a few seconds, however, they are shaking hands and two of them are embracing. I actually hear one of them say, "I love you, man."

I bite once again into my hot, tasty slice, pleased that the sheer volume of customers at this late hour has forced the proprietor to bake fresh pizza. My absorption with the savoury Donair slice, however, is broken. "Are you a reporter?" I look up to see a teetering young man with bloodshot eyes and a large lump on his forehead pointing in my direction. Damn my notepad! My mouth is stuffed with pizza. He is held upright by a friend. "A bouncer shoved me to the ground," he slurs. "The fucking guy's an asshole!" I can barely make out what he was saying. To my left is a large garbage bin, now overflowing with aluminum cans, napkins, pizza crusts, and an assortment of other rubbish. Before I have a chance to finish chewing, he leans over the pile of garbage and begins to coat it in a long stream of saliva. I instinctively guard my pizza slice against any collateral spit from his dry heaving. His friend holds him in place.

"You better take him home," I finally say after swallowing. The bruised man's perturbed buddy simply nods in my direction as he hauls him down the street: "Come on, man, let's go."

The pizza shop on the northeast corner turns up the volume on its sound system. There is now techno music flowing into the street, and the nightclub's buzz has moved onto the intersection. Customers start bobbing their heads, and two are even dancing inside the pizzeria. An older woman in a green dress surprises me as she bends down to collect a discarded aluminum can. She has a large plastic bag and is gingerly collecting cans as she walks by. A young woman in a white shirt pulls away from her friends to temporarily assist the older woman who thanks her. When the young woman finally rejoins her confused friends, I notice in her eyes and smeared makeup that she must have been crying sometime during the evening. It's a rather strange sight.

I've almost finished my pizza. In the middle of the street two pairs of men begin grappling with one another. Someone yells: "Fight! Hey, there's a fight!" and is soon joined by others. Heads turn to watch the prospect of a melee. The police move immediately, roughly shoving their way through the gathering horde of spectators. The two constables filling out reports in their cruiser also jump from their vehicle to assist in breaking up the fight, although I haven't seen a single punch thrown yet. More partiers begin to encircle the police and pugilists. "You can go home right now or you can go to jail!" one constable offers forcefully. Another now begins inspecting the identification of the separated combatants. They are instructed to walk away in opposite directions. The young men look stunned but somewhat relieved. On this occasion they make no challenging gestures toward the police, and both sides quietly slink into the night.

The couple sitting on my right have edged toward me in order to make room for some friends. They begin kissing deeply, oblivious to those around them. I am accidentally elbowed by the amorous young woman and decide against shifting even closer to the garbage can on my left. I hop off my perch and head home. I walk slowly but nearly step into a pile of vomit complete with unchewed pepperoni slices. Its depositor must have literally inhaled his pizza. A tricked-out, metallic blue Honda Civic with neon runners signals its approach with a thumping bass heard two blocks away. It has twice already crept through the intersection, turning heads on both occasions. This time a petite woman in a plaid shirt chants out loudly: "You're a fucking loser!" punctuating each syllable by pointing to the car. She is joined by one of her friends, and three others also begin to applaud in support. A police officer steps off to the side of the car and motions the driver to turn down the volume. He obliges and is now able to hear more clearly the jeers coming from the plaid-shirted woman and her supporters.

"Hey Gino, you're a fucking loser!" He makes eye contact with the woman and her friends, gives her the finger, and spins out the Civic's front tires as he screeches the vehicle toward Spring Garden Road. A police constable shrugs into his epaulet-mounted radio, and I surmise that he may be notifying other police to stop the car. As I continue back to my own vehicle, I notice that those cars parked at or near the intersection are often being used as sitting areas and leaning posts by drunken revellers. A blue Mercedes now sports two soft-drink cans on its hood.

I have my own secret parking spot in the downtown core, not far from the pizza corner, thanks to a friend and colleague who has been renting a downtown apartment for the last few months. The spot is in a dark, tiny lot. As I turn into the lot, I notice two men and a woman smoking what smells like marijuana. As I get closer to them, I make eye contact. They smile and nod, "Hey man, what's up?" As I get even closer I notice that one of the two men is urinating close to my car. "Don't piss on my car, buddy!" I say in a stern voice. "Sorry, man," he replies as he realigns his trajectory. "When you gotta go, you gotta go! Right?"

"I guess so," I concede. I toss my pizza crust on the passenger seat and slowly back my rusty Ford LTD out of the cramped lot. Manoeuvring away from the unruly crowd and toward Quinpool Road, I start to make my way home … it's 3:50 A.M.

In the *Exclusive Society*, Jock Young (1999, 57) described the process by which societies have had both "swallowing and injecting aspects" that often exist concurrently. These are, in the parlance of Lévis-Strauss (1992), anthropophagic and anthropoemic tendencies. For Young (1999, 159), this cannabilistic and bulimic tendency, this odd "anthropoemic machine of late modernity," creates an "exclusion throughout its structure with the main motor being the rapidly developing pitch of market relations." Contemporary urban dwellers are nonetheless more tolerant despite the tremendous cultural and subcultural varieties that exist in our cities. But while the "late modern world celebrates diversity and difference, which it readily absorbs and sanitizes," it nonetheless builds elaborate defences against "different people and dangerous classes" not only by distinguishing between "insiders and outsiders, but throughout the population" (159).

The "cannabilistic" and "bulimic" tendency of late capitalism described by Young seems omnipresent in late-night city centres such as Halifax:

> An intoxicated young blond woman asks if she can "sit on the curb and wait for her roommate" to leave the nightclub. It is closing time at the Beacon, and the patrons are beginning to be herded towards the door. She looks rather dazed and disoriented. The bouncer responds, "No problem." Her need for fresh air and separation from the crowd is not realized as the nightclub begins to empty and people spill out onto the sidewalk and congregate around her. Quickly, she becomes a topic of conversation as she moans now with her head between her legs. The nauseous young woman has become an angry young woman. She suddenly launches herself to her feet to confront her antagonizers and begins yelling at patrons who are making fun of her. Her sudden movement and impassioned defence is ill-advised as she wobbles and grabs onto the nearest support. The crowd around her gives her the space she always wanted. The crowd winces as she doubles over to expel. The doorman laughingly exclaims, "Oh shit, all over [M.'s] truck!"

It is in this sense that even once outside the nightclub the "spectator feels at home nowhere, for the spectacle is everywhere" (Debord 1995, 23).

In the nighttime economy, patrons flow from the nightclub to the city streets, from private spectacle to public nuisance. The synoptic frenzy of the nightclub mirrors the general late capitalist compulsion to binge and purge, to consume perfectly by not leaving a trace. From dancing girls to shooters and pizza slices, this consumption is bracketed within a risk market linking consumption to risk and security. The frenzied and desirous consumption of the nightclub produces a myriad of unfulfilled courtiers of the night, spilling out of one spectacle and immediately into another, the former nightclub's optic and violent excesses merely an alibi for the latter society of the spectacle.

Conclusions

If this book has made one central argument, it is that nightclubs cannot be understood outside the consumption-security-risk nexus, a risk market that operates to illuminate the nightclub as a site of aesthetic consumption in late capitalism. The spinning gears of the nightclub's machinery, well lubricated by alcohol, process stylistic genres and subcultures, hierarchies of distinction, and the unceasing desire to be desired. Bakhtin's (1984, 5) analysis of the ritual spectacles described in Rabelais's medieval world – the "carnival pageants" and "comic shows of the market-place" – lead him to conclude, "While carnival lasts, there is no other life outside it" (7). Unlike the medieval carnival, however, in the nightclub the outside world is not mocked or challenged. On the contrary, it is valorized and made hyperreal. Rather than the "suspension of all hierarchical rank, privileges, norms, and prohibitions" (10), we have the crude reassertion and re-emphasis of class, race, and gender. Instead of the development of a "special type of communication impossible in everyday life," we have the intentional stunting of depth of dialogue in deference to surface and superficiality. In the place of liberation from the "norms of etiquette and decency imposed at other times" (ibid.), we instead have a very bounded and predictable transgressionalism policed by bouncers and circumscribed by the vigilant gaze of CCTV cameras and ID-card readers. In lieu of standing "opposed to all that was ready-made and completed, to all pretense" (10–11), we have contrived dramas and ceremonial reassertions of this even more extreme form of pretense, of cool, and of competing social capitals. As opposed to a "gay relativity of prevailing truths and authorities" (11), we have the fixity of symbolic capital and the channelling of dissent through aesthetic rebellion. Indeed, the life outside the nightclub today actually serves as an alibi (Baudrillard 1995). Its grotesque hierarchies make seem extreme what is already daily lived.

On MuchMusic's "Electric Circus,"[1] the unlucky, unwashed, uncool masses queued outside but never got in. They were essential for the broadcaster to signify how extra-special, extra-sexy, and extra-hip the insiders really were. Whereas the medieval carnival laughed at and flouted pastoral power, extolled individual expression, parodied official regalia, embraced the ridiculous, and purportedly created space for rebellion, the nightclub today feigns the same dynamic yet symbolically reinforces and retrenches established cleavages. Through its "rebel sell" (Heath and Potter 2005), it plays at reshuffling existing power relations, ameliorating alienation, promising "anything goes," but is instead already an integral part of late capitalism's regurgitative desire to remake and refigure identity.

Symbolically, at least, this enterprise is productive. Each act of individual differentiation, each subdivision of cool, each expression of laughter, every ribald and shameless display, indeed, each act of aesthetic rebellion in a nightclub must therefore already be pre-coded to be nothing more than the ceremonial worship of capital. "Even the aesthetic activities of political opposites are one in their enthusiastic obedience to the rhythm of the iron system" (Adorno and Horkheimer 2000, 3). The nightclub is thus teeming with drug-induced fantasy, competition, status degradation, and humiliation. If the nightclub dehumanizes, objectifies, amplifies cleavages, re-fabricates inequities and stunts communication, it is no wonder that violence, in its various forms, becomes as natural a recourse as revolution. It is no wonder that looks of disapproval or callous indifference to the position of another patron (both physical and symbolic) can be grounds for assault. And finally, it is no wonder that it often takes a humanizing voice, a sympathetic pat on the back, or a show of respect to re-establish dignity. In this way, a bouncer can often effortlessly usher a belligerent patron from a bar because such an act is perhaps among the most unnatural and jarring occurrences possible in the context of a nightclub. Indeed, the nightclub's primary fuel is rebellion. Counter-culture is its culture (as it is everywhere else for consumption).[2] These abstractions are both managed dutifully and valorized fetishistically through the synoptic frenzy that the nightclub (re)produces. A spectacle of consumption awash with symbolic and material exclusion, competition and alienation, it is navigated and structured by the circulating cultural and social capitals of its constituent players as both objects and subjects of commodification. Nightclubs are just as constraining and alienating as they are ostensibly liberating and communal. Bouncers, I have argued, are essential policing agents in the nighttime economy, often overlapping in function and territory with the public police but nonetheless maintaining their own bounded interest and well-defined subculture born out of the structural violence they are charged with keeping a lid on. Doormen, on average, experience more workplace violence than police officers and report higher levels of alienation from those outside their occupational group.

In another theoretical vein, it would serve us well when analyzing nightlife, nightclubs, raves, or other supposedly counter-cultural or transgressional activities (now largely theme nights) to temper our exuberence about their challenging the status quo, no matter how "alternative." Rather, nightclubs further reify and glamorize hierarchies of cultural capital. Nightclub participation is neither escapism nor revolution, in the former case no matter how blunted by alcohol or drugs our senses become, and in the latter case no matter how freaky our costume or how many fights we pick with the bouncer in order to "stick it to the man." There is, indeed nothing like the ironic sight of hundreds of similarly dressed partiers "raging against the machine" and pogoing to "Killing in the Name," raising their fists and defiantly screaming out in unison "Fuck you, I won't do what you tell me!" only to change mood as soon as a DJ fades to another track. But these revellers are no more robots than they are possessed of some proto-revolutionary consciousness. They are just part of the spectacle of consumption.

Aside from the self-servingly profound (Marxian) question of understanding the place of the nightclub and bouncer in late capitalism, there is the more practical (but perhaps more important) concern about what is to be done about nightclub violence. Legislative changes are being touted that in the next few years would ostensibly revolutionize the nightclub industry. Recently, proposed amendments to provincial legislation governing security guards and private investigators in Nova Scotia and Ontario will be expanded to include doorstaff, making licensing and minimum training mandatory. Eventually this stands to have a significant impact on the industry since licensing of each security provider in nightclubs (including in-house and contract security agencies) opens them up to a more penetrating form of provincial oversight and the auditing of their practices. If a nightclub security department loses its licence, the nightclub will have to shut down. This is even more likely now that municipalities are forcing nightclub owners to provide a security plan and employ a fixed number of trained doorstaff as a condition of their licence. The licensing of each doorman, moreover, will surely result in fewer bouncers with criminal records being hired. If the same provincial standards used for contract security guards are extended to bouncers, then any applicant with a criminal record will not be licensed (pending successful appeal).

The cronyism and infiltration of nightclubs by organized crime has already likely been reduced due to the encroachment of large corporate entertainment agencies buying up nightclubs in urban centres around the world. Corporate risk management has responded to judicial admonitions about potential liability (see chapter 3), resulting in standardized bouncer training, operating procedures, and use-of-force policies. Oversight even includes "secret shoppers" to catch bouncers who are on the take or particularly violent.

The climate thus seems ripe for the once-reticent contract private security industry to enter the nightclub market, and there are indications that this is already underway. These changes may have significant effects on bouncer culture and especially inter-nightclub rivalry (as bouncers begin to work in multiple locales) but will also largely serve to further accelerate the standardization of risk management and the proliferation of surveillance technology in nightclubs. On the other hand, and perhaps this is more wishing than prognosticating, state regulation may also have the effect of finally facilitating the unionization of doorstaff either within contract security providers or across such organizations. There are grounds to believe that bouncers would welcome such a development. A union could ensure that doorstaff receive enhanced medical attention including physiotherapy when they are injured. Long-term dental care is also a concern: one punch to the mouth can produce significant medical and aesthetic damage. Moreover, general safety is an ongoing concern. A union could ensure that threatened bouncers receive a ride to transit, their home, or car by van with their union brothers and sisters.

Of course, how this will develop is anyone's guess, but it would be a shame if bouncers, who may be seen as an emergent but neglected proletarian force, are left out of the labour movement. Far from being a reactionary presence, I believe that an international doorstaff union would be on the cutting edge of progressive urban planning and politics. I often wondered what would happen if all the city's bouncers walked off the job one Saturday night. Would the political economy of the urban night be laid bare? Who would dare cross the picket lines? How would an international doorstaff union be greeted at demonstrations?

Fantasies of a radicalized bouncer movement aside, it bears repeating that in cityscapes across the world, the most prolific gatekeepers of contemporary cool, of distinction, of in and out, the new physical labourers of postmodernity's ritual nocturnal spectacle, are yet to be organized.

Epilogue:
Confessions of a "Playa Hata"

About three months into my field research I found myself sitting alone at my usual position by the bar in another noisy and smoky dance and entertainment club in downtown Halifax. As I scrawled on my notepad, I occasionally paused for a gulp of Mexican beer, squinting through the dim lighting to make out what I had written only a few moments earlier. My furrowed brow and curious appearance attracted the attention of a young coat-check girl, who surprised me with a tap on the shoulder as she saddled up onto the stool next to me. "What are you doing?" she asked.

I sighed and went through my well-rehearsed routine, throwing out terms that had been firing in my grey matter – terms such as such as *hypermasculine, hyperfeminine, consumption, security, optic violence* – until I was certain she was sorry she had asked and that I had bored the both of us. I only took a minute or so, but that's an eternity for a nightclub conversation. More importantly, as I listened to myself talk about nightclubs, I realized that I was becoming as disgusted by my objects of analysis as I felt *laboured* at having to explain myself.

Finally, I summarized: "Basically, I'm a university professor from SMU studying nightclub security and what goes on in nightclubs. You know? Like, what makes them work." I was practically screaming in her ear to be heard over the bleating chorus of t.A.T.u's "All the things you said, all the things you said. Running through my head, running through my head …"

"That's cool!" she nodded. "I have a friend at SMU. So what are you going to write about?"

"I don't know," I responded, frustrated by the common expectation that I should be able to answer such a question in thirty seconds or less. "But how do *you* work in here?" I asked. "Don't you get sick of the posturing, the fighting? Look at the big guy in the blue baseball cap over there. He's ready to fight somebody. Why? What's his problem? People act like idiots in here. The women too, you know. It's as if feminism never happened."

That was only the beginning of my rant. I implicated everybody in sight: bouncers, dancers, drunkards, big guys, small guys, blonds and brunettes. My arguments were as superficial and puerile as my milieu, but I counted on the fact my young interlocutor couldn't tell the difference. It was the first time that I blew up about nightclubs. Today I can rant about them at the drop of a hat. I had spent way too much time in bars from Halifax to Vancouver, sitting apart, taking notes, asking questions, patrolling with bouncers, and even taking them aside, and in my best Howard Cosell impersonation, asking them how they "felt" after a fight.

I was winded after my tirade, finally letting my vocal chords take a break from screaming and my hands from gesticulation. I recall thinking it curious that my gestures grew wilder the louder I had to scream over the music.

The coat-check girl settled back on her barstool and took a sip of cola. No response. She must have eyed me with a smirk of self-satisfaction. That would only be fitting. Finally, after a long drag from her cigarette, for dramatic effect, I am sure, she slowly leaned back in. "You know what I think?"

Great, I thought.

"You know what I think *you* are?" she added.

"Me? What about me?"

"You're just a playa hata."

"A what?"

"A play*er* hat*er*." She smiled.

"What the hell is that?" I asked, although even at the time I think I had some idea.

The coat-check girl never answered my question. She was called back to her station by a manager, and I think the timing suited her just fine. She spun out of her chair, collected her drink, and never looked back. I watched her hustle to her post, turned to my notepad and wrote "11:38 – player hater(???)"

I was scribbling away. I diligently collected data throughout the evening, but it really couldn't be undone. The anonymous coat-check girl had symbolically drop-kicked me off my perch. Many months later as I began to write this book, that entry popped back into my head. Part of the reason was because I found myself falling into a familiar trap. I had critiqued some British colleagues because in their analysis of night-club security, "bar patrons [had] a propensity to be cast as little more than drunken 'idiots,' 'trouble-makers,' and 'arseholes'" (Rigakos 2004). When it came time to compose this book, I had a hard time avoiding hypocrisy. The problem was that after a while I really didn't connect with drunken revellers either. My review of Hobbs, Hadfield, Lister, and Win-low's (2003) illuminating work, *Bouncers*, reflected my general concern for understanding the attraction of consumption in a nightclub – hope-fully tackled with some success in this book. I thought that such an analy-sis would suffer if conducted in a normatively derogatory context. How can we understand why people go to nightclubs if we don't appreciate what they do or become? So, in my review of *Bouncers*, I wrote at the time: "For all the repeated reference to the allure, seduction and experi-ential lustre of this new night-time economy we have no notion as to why it survives aside from the (lack of) imagination of city planners and some important but rather broad material economic transformations." The point herein was to combat this tendency, but I was already branded an outsider, someone who didn't get it. The words stared up at me from my notes again: *player hater*.

What is a player hater, anyway? That I had not come across this epi-thet in the new millennium is amazing. Contrary to popular myth, aca-demics and especially those in the social sciences are usually more up to date on popular argot. Cultural criminologists like to think they're well ahead of the curve. Academics watch television too, and we're around young adults all the time. But I hadn't heard this one before.

Today, alert to its usage, I hear "player hater" everywhere, from music videos to the plethora of afternoon exploitation talk shows. In many ways, the term is self-explanatory: someone who hates players. But the key is in understanding "player" in context. The term can mean many things, depending on the circumstances, but outside a sports-related context, "player" almost invariably refers to one who is able to persuade and ma-nipulate others and especially the opposite sex in a heterosexual context. This is the only meaning in a nightclub setting. For both genders, being a player can be boiled down to the ability to seduce – to create desire and be able to take advantage of that feeling in others.

The idea is hardly new, and popular culture is replete with descrip-tions of "playboys": men who were essentially womanizers, leading liberated or "jet-set" lifestyles. Successive generations since at least the decadent Thirties produced their playboys both real and fictional: Great Gatsbys, the Kennedys, even "Bond, James Bond." These were supposedly sophisticated, worldly, mysterious, and flamboyant men. To symbolic interactionists (e.g., Blumer 1986; Goffman 1961), the idea of play, any play, is hardly a revelation. Everybody does it. Everyone represents, deceives, negotiates their identities. This is ongoing. There is always a backstage, and of course there are always ulterior motives.

But the playboy is something more than this. In the early Sixties, Hugh Hefner attempted no less than a "playboy philosophy" (Hefner 1963). His editorials sought to recast sexual history, defend his magazine against moral crusaders, and articulate a counterpoint to feminist critiques. In the process, Hefner became part of popular culture and a protagonist for the sexual revolution. In 1963, he encouraged his critics to reappraise their negative views about playboys. Citing his own declarations on the topic years earlier (*Playboy*, April 1956), he asked whether a playboy was really "a wastrel, a ne'er-do-well, a fashionable bum?" "Far from it," he responded: "He can be a sharp-minded young business executive, a worker in the arts, a university professor, an architect or engineer. He can be many things, providing he possesses a certain *point of view*. He must see life not as a vale of tears, but as a happy time; he must take joy in his work, without regarding it as the end and all of living; he must be an alert man, an aware man, a man of taste, a man sensitive to pleasure, a man who – without acquiring the stigma of the voluptuary or dilettante – can live life to the hilt. This is the sort of man we mean when we use the word *playboy*" (Hefner 1963: part 1: 3, his emphasis).

Hefner's discriminating playboy is about more than a *bon vivant* worldview. At its core is the notion of an insider – someone who understands and sees the world in a particular way and is able to enjoy its pleasures. Obviously, access to such pleasures depends on material and social capital as well as a presupposed natural charisma. By implication, those who are not playboys are not in the game – they are outsiders. Critics seized on Hefner's playboy as all "style and polish," someone who is a "consumer … who knows how to spend with flair" and "is a skilled and sophisticated lover, who knows how to avoid anything resembling a permanent attachment with his paramours" (see Crane, as cited in Hefner 1963, part 2, 1). The playboy here is either a sexually aware Renaissance man or a scandalously superficial usurer. Women, for the playboy, are at best equal partners in sensation-seeking and experiencing "life to the hilt" or simply "the grandest of all consumer goods." For us the keys here are again consumption and desire. And if I truly disliked players, if the coat-check girl was correct, then I was obviously making judgments about a form of consumption too.

While the nightclub clearly caters to many men who at least try to fashion themselves as Hefner-style playboys, the most important players are women. First, this is because within our theoretical theme of consumption, their presence makes the nightclub. There is no heterosexed nightclub without an abundant supply of women – they are a central symbolic commodity, the nightclub's key aesthetic labourers. Second, women are hardly passive objects of desire. They are just as likely to be players, and throughout this book I have described this process. It rests with the idea that women desire bounded and orderly attention – desire to be *safely* desired. Women are obviously and unavoidably the crux of the nightclub atmosphere. They are advertised, projected on screens, and targeted for marketing and inclusion.

As far as I can gather, female and male players in an ostensibly heterosexual context differ mostly in their desired end goals. Women players want to "play" men for attention and material gain. Men players want to "play" women for sex. Both genders use manipulation, seduction, and deceit. Often, for some players just the presumption that "if I want him, I can have him" is enough. As a derogatory epithet, a player hater is more than someone who dislikes players; imbued in the meaning is that a player hater feels this way because of deep-seated jealousy. According to my interpolation of its usage in nightclubs and popular culture, it is tantamount to, in more common parlance, a jealous loser. So, the coat-check girl was calling me a jealous loser. Her interpretation of my negative analysis of the fights, machismo, shameless displays, and clumsy courting was that I wished I could have been a player myself. I truly wanted to be a playboy.

Why raise all of this in an epilogue? For two reasons. First, this book adds up to a more worthwhile sociological analysis with the inclusion of some reflection on the research experience and particularly the author's place within it. I wrote this epilogue before the book was finished in an attempt at achieving some analytic catharsis. My intention was to either temporarily hold in abeyance my relatively negative frame of mind about the nightclub scene or at least wrestle with the reasoning behind such a negative mind-set. I was to do this by seizing on the idea of the player hater and reckoning with its normative implications. But in looking back over the book and revisiting this section, it seems to me that I accomplished neither of these aspirations and it was probably a rather naïve aim to begin with. As it stands, this epilogue adds and clarifies rather than *re-*

veals my own critical outlook during the research. In any case, perhaps this sentiment should not have been such a concern in the first place.

The second reason for this epilogue is to illustrate the power of place that a nightclub represents. To the coat-check girl, my attempted mastery over the nightclub setting, my derisive commentary about its players, and my slapdash, thirty-second rendition of a critical sociology of the bar scene was no mastery at all. Mastery and success could have only been achieved through active participation, by being a player. I have already equated the nightclub with the prison through a discussion of panopticism and even some of the crises of respect that prompt young men to engage in scowls, name-calling, abuse, profuse apologies, and violence because someone stepped on their shoe, bumped into them, or looked at them the wrong way. In what other site outside of a prison would such behaviour constitute grounds for assault? Now, obviously, prisons and nightclubs are very different. The prison is a punishment factory, the nightclub closer to a pleasure factory. But in my mind, the coat-check girl was reinforcing the spatial, aesthetic, and sensory power that the nightclub produces – smoke, flashing lights, perfume mixed with the smell of beer and sweat, waves of deafening percussion vibrating through our organs, the synoptic frenzy of hyper-sex and desire all washing over alcohol-blunted senses. Did my mere presence make me part of the machinery of the nightclub? Did I become part of its sea of spectacle?

From a sociological perspective, what was my place in the nightclub? Can I really describe myself as observer-participant or participant-observer? Within the synoptic frenzy, how meaningful are these distinctions? Everyone was watching everyone. Everyone was being categorized. Everyone carried around his or her own cluster of consumable aesthetics. The sounds, smells, and sights of the nightclub saturated everyone, and everyone saturated the nightclub. Just because I carried a notebook did not excuse me from being implicated in its production. Was I just one more set of eyes feasting hungrily and voyeuristically at this contrived nightly spectacle? Was I one more oddity of aesthetic consumption? At the risk of imbuing my mischievous coat-check girl with far more analytic power that she deserves, she nonetheless reminded me that I was just as easily consumed, just as easily part of the scene. On an aggregate social level, the nightclub had already analyzed me. I could not pretend to transcend the nightclub through analysis because, from the moment I walked in the door, it had already swallowed me (and spit me out).

Appendix

Observation Template: Bar Ethnography, Halifax

Surveillance and Panoptics
- What are the physical surveillance technologies? (Including CCTV, observation posts, door entry and exit configuration, etc.)
- How are these physical surveillance technologies staffed? (How many personnel, their rotation, and special surveillance systems, etc.)
- What are the modes of circumventing this system? (Usually gleaned from talking to those stationed there or by observation.)
- What is the historical dialectic of physical security deployment? (Why have certain surveillance techniques been implemented? Why and how have they been improved? How have they failed in the past? How has this been rectified?)
- How do bouncers communicate about dangers – both to each other and other bar employees? (Comment on the effectiveness of this method.)
- Is there a panoptic architecture present? (Are there blind-spots? If so, how are these managed? e.g., washrooms.)

Risk
- How are risk identities managed at the point of entry? (Observe what patrons are excluded and why. Pay specific attention to race, gesturing, attire, etc. Discuss the relevancy of identification cards, fake ID, etc.)
- Comment on those individuals previously banned. (Are they successful in negotiating access? How is this attempted? Describe the language of deference and re-interpretation used to re-classify oneself as less dangerous.)

- How do patrons assess and manage risk in the nightclub? (Examine movements, threatening gestures, impositions on others' space.)
- How do bouncers target risky persons?
- What acts are most likely to elicit the attention of bouncers? (Are these instigated by complaining patrons?)
- What techniques are used by bouncers to minimize risk to themselves and other patrons? (Look out for "fire brigade" policing.)
- Do bouncers follow a protocol? (Are there standing orders or procedures that are used? Are there experiential "recipe rules" that are used?)

Masculinity and Femininity
- How do underage women negotiate access to the nightclub or bar?
- How do male bouncers constitute their masculinity? (Listen to conversations between bouncers concerning female patrons, sexual prowess, physical toughness, machismo. Record reactions to personal masculinity crises or challenges, e.g., being called cowardly or feminine.)
- How do male bouncers deal with female patrons and bouncers? (Is there a notion of deserving and undeserving victims? How is this constructed?)
- How do male bouncers deal with male and female patrons differently?
- How do female bouncers deal with male and female patrons differently?

Violence and Crime
- How do bouncers use violence or the threat of violence to gain compliance?
- Is there any criminal activity by patrons, bouncers, bar staff? (What Criminal Code offences? Describe any illicit activity.)
- Are unruly patrons legally detained or arrested? Take detailed notes on the removal of patrons.

Notes

CHAPTER 1

1 This is not a pseudonym for the Lighthouse Tavern popular with some Halifax pub-goers. This establishment was not included in our sample.
2 It is admittedly uncomfortable for me to label some of these visits as "ethnographic" since they often coincided with my own social life. Often, I would take no notes at the nightclub and later make revisions to some of my arguments from memory.
3 Andrew Dunn and David MacDonald did splendid ethnographic work. Dunn was a former DJ in the Halifax nightclub scene, and MacDonald is now a Calgary police officer.
4 Listed alphabetically, they are: Jillian Cameron, Neera Datta, Andrew Dunn, and David MacDonald.
5 I arrived at an estimate of one hundred doorstaff based on responses to my initial canvassing of bar managers and owners for their inclusion in this study. While asking them if they were willing to participate, I also inquired as to how many bouncers they maintained on their employment roster and how many would work on a given Saturday night.

CHAPTER 2

1 Rage against the Machine, from their eponymous album, 1992.
2 Note that Baudrillard comes to this problematic understanding only in his later works, *The System of Objects* (1996) and *Simulations* (1983). In *Consumer Society* (1998, 152; 1970 in the original French), he holds theoretically

fast to the material and symbolic distinction between use and exchange-value (except for the notion of time) when he argues: "Of most objects, one can still say that they have a certain use-value, which is in theory dissociable from their exchange-value."

Baudrillard's rejection of Marx is based on his critique of two of Marx's foundational theoretical concepts: use-value and exchange-value. Baudrillard argues that Marx uncritically accepted conservative economic notions of value by imbuing use-value with some implicit, inherent, natural, or "true" value outside human apprehension of a given object. According to Baudrillard (1996), Marx may have understood the symbolic importance imbued in objects at the realm of exchange (i.e., exchange value) – what he powerfully described as commodity fetishism (see Marx 1976, 163–77) – but failed to theorize the fact there is no inherent ontological value in an object at *any* level of circulation. In other words, there is no "use-value," as Marx would have it – this is only a guise, an illusion, a theoretical economic construction, in Baudrillard's parlance, an alibi: "[We] have to be more logical than Marx himself ... Use-value is an abstraction. It is an abstraction of the *system of needs* cloaked in the false evidence of a concrete destination and purpose, an intrinsic finality of goods and products" (Baudrillard 1981, 130–1).

3 Indeed, in certain sections Marx seems to argue for a natural value outside exchange: "The *exchangeable values* of commodities are only *social functions* of those things, and have nothing at all to do with their *natural* qualities." (Marx 1935, 30, his emphasis). But as Jhally (1990, 41) reminds us, this so-called "mystery of fetishism is false. The symbolism of use-value not necessarily so. Use-value can ... be seen as a result of social mediation," and commodity fetishism can form a core part of a Marxian analysis of consumption "without contradiction." Indeed, Marx does not argue the inherent value of objects outside their malleability in the minds of humans. This is repeatedly demonstrated as a basis for *Capital* where Marx begins with the commodity on the very first page: "The commodity ... satisfies human needs of whatever kind. The nature of these needs, whether they arise, for example, from the stomach, or the *imagination*, makes no difference." He goes on to emphasize, "Nor does it matter here how the thing satisfies man's need, whether directly as a means of subsistence, i.e., an object of consumption, or indirectly as a means of production." Thus, for Marx, "Every useful thing is a whole composed of many properties; it can therefore be useful in various ways." In fact, in the final analysis, Marx insists that "the *manifold uses all things* is the work of history" (Marx 1976, 125, emphases added).

CHAPTER 3

1 Proposed legislative amendments to Nova Scotia's *Private Investigators and Security Guards Act* would include such provisions for bouncers.

2 It would have been extremely difficult to successfully negotiate acceptance of a research instrument by nightclub owners and police executives that would have revealed their employees' use of physical and non-physical violence.

3 *Brien et al. v. Astoria Hotels Ltd.*, [1939] 1 W.W.R. 641 (B.C.S.C.).

4 In this action, Brien had been injured while being ejected from a beer parlour. Although asked to leave, he did not comply and was forcibly removed from the premises. In her civil suit for damages, the judge ruled: "It is lawful for the occupier and for any other person with the authority of the occupier to use a reasonable degree of force in order to prevent a trespasser from entering or to eject him after entry. A trespasser in the circumstances of this case cannot be ejected until requested to leave the premises and a reasonable opportunity of doing so peaceably has been afforded" (*Brien et al. v. Astoria Hotels Ltd.*, [1939] 1 W.W.R. 641 (B.C.S.C.) at 641).

5 *R. v. Franke*, [2002] A.J. no. 786 (Alta. Prov. Ct. (Crim. Div.)) (QL, C.L.).

6 *R. v. Franke*, [2002] A.J. no. 786 (Alta. Prov. Ct. (Crim. Div.)) (QL, C.L.), paras 63, 64.

7 *Cullen v. Rice*, [1981] A.J. no. 614 (Alta. C.A.) (QL, C.L.), para. 11.

8 *C.P.R. v. Anderson*, [1936] S.C.R. 200 at 203–204.

9 *Latham v. Johnson*, [1913] 1 K.B. 398 [U.K.] at 410.

10 *Cullen v. Rice*, [1981] A.J. no. 614 (Alta. C.A.) (QL, C.L.), paras. 12, 13.

11 *R. v. Giles*, [1989] N.S.J. no. 341 (N.S.C.A.) (QL, C.L.) at 7.

12 Section 41 (1) states: Everyone who is in peaceable possession of a dwelling-house or real property, and everyone lawfully assisting him or acting under his authority, is justified in using force to prevent any person from trespassing on the dwelling-house or real property, or to remove a trespasser therefrom, if he uses no more force than necessary; and Section 41 (2) states: A trespasser who resists an attempt by a person who is in peaceable possession of a dwelling-house or real property, or a person lawfully assisting him or acting under his authority to prevent his entry or to remove him, shall be deemed to commit an assault without justification or provocation.

13 [2003] 2 S.C.R. 3, 2003 SCC 38.

14 *R. v. Swenson*, [1993] S.J. no. 586 (Sask. Ct. Q.B.) (QL, C.J.), para. 35.

15 *O'Tierney v. Concord Tavern Ltd.*, [1960] O.W.N. 533.

16 In *Cottreau*, where the bouncer "used more force than was reasonable," he "rendered himself ... and [the owner] liable for damages for assault and battery." Inherently, "reasonableness" is subjective and determined by myriad circumstances surrounding each instance. And within each case, multiple contingencies can arise that will determine reasonableness within the context of an owner's property rights.

17 The original basis for using force to prevent unauthorized assault comes from the *Ritter* (*R. v. Ritter* (1904), 8 c.c.c. 31 (N.S.S.C.) (QL) at 44) doctrine, which states that "Everyone so assaulted is justified, though he causes death or grievous bodily harm, if he causes it under reasonable apprehension of death or grievous bodily harm from the violence with which the assault was originally made, or with which the assailant pursues his purpose, and if he believes on reasonable grounds that he cannot otherwise preserve himself from death or grievous bodily harm."

18 Criminal Code, ss. 34(1).

19 Criminal Code, ss. 34(2).

20 *R. v. Reilly* (1984), 15 c.c.c. (3d) 1 (s.c.c.).

21 Kent Roach, *Criminal Law*, 2nd ed. (Toronto: Irwin Law, 2000) (QL) at C3, quoting *R. v. Reilly* (1984), 15 c.c.c. (3d) 1 (s.c.c.).

22 Ibid., at C5.

23 *Thompson v. Celebration Saloons Ltd.* (1992), 12 L.W. 1232 (Man. Ct. Q.B.) (QL).

24 (1994), 91 c.c.c. (3d) 541 (Sask. c.a.) (QL) at 8.

25 *Cole v. California Entertainment Ltd.* [1989], B.C.J. no. 2162 (B.C.C.A.) (QL, C.J.).

26 The judge noted: "From the foregoing evidence I conclude that this fight, organized by Wolf, was not a personal vendetta or just his uncontrolled animosity that led him to attack Cole but, rather, this whole ugly affair developed when [the club manager] Mr. Lalli directed the three bouncers to clear the entrance to the club. It was not just Wolf's doing, it was the hastily conceived plan of all three bouncers who perceived that they were fulfilling the mandate given to them by Mr. Lalli to clear the ingress and egress routes to the front door of the club by whatever means or methods were necessary. Unfortunately for Mr. Lalli, instead of supervising his three bouncers in the delicate task he left matters entirely within their collective wisdom or discretion" (*Cole v. California Entertainment Ltd.* [1989], B.C.J. no. 2162 (B.C.C.A.) (QL, C.J.) at 8).

27 *Downey v. 502377 Ontario Ltd.* (1991), 10 L.W. 1043 (Ont. Ct. J. (Gen. Div.)) (QL).

28 Ibid., at 2.

29 Ibid.

30 *Renaissance Leisure Group Inc. (c.o.b. Muskoka Sands Inn) v. Frazer* [2001], O.J. no. 866 (Ont. Sup. Ct.) (QL, C.J.).

31 Ibid.

32 *Occupiers' Liability Act,* R.S.O. 1990, C. O-2.

33 *Pereira v. Airliner Motor Hotel (1972) Ltd.* [1997], M.J. no. 424 (Man. Ct. Q.B.) (QL, C.J.) at 1.

34 Ibid.

35 The judge stated clearly: "On all of the evidence before me, I have no hesitation in being satisfied on a balance of probabilities that the defendant, on the particular night in question, and bearing in mind all of the circumstances, failed in its duty to care to the plaintiff, Blaine Dombowsky." The judge even spoke about response time, finding that the employees should have intervened in the ensuing incident: "In my view the defendants could have reasonably foreseen what happened. There was, over a 15 to 20 minute span, a number of indicia that should have easily alerted the defendants to the likelihood of an altercation." Negligence was further manifested through a failure to secure the area and remove the persons, so that a third assailant ended up causing bodily harm to Dombowsky (*Dombowsky v. Argyll Triple Five Place Ltd. (c.o.b. Goose Loonies Party & Playhouse*), [1993] A.J. no. 1311 (Alta. Ct. Q.B.) (QL, C.J.) at 25 and 26).

36 *Sweet v. Paramount Investments Ltd.* [1990], O.J. no. 2342 (Ont. Ct. Gen. Div.) (QL, C.J.).

37 *Evaniuk v. 79846 Manitoba Inc.* (1990), 68 Man. R. (2d) 306 (Man. Ct. Q.B.) (QL).

38 *McCarthy v. Pupus Entertainment Ltd.* [1996], B.C.J. no. 967 (B.C.S.C.) (QL, C.J.).

39 *R. v. 1300378 Ontario Ltd. (c.o.b. Tonic the Nightclub)* [2002], O.J. no. 2246 (Ont. Ct. J. (Prov. Off. Ct.)) (QL, C.J.).

40 Ibid., para. 1.

41 Ibid., para. 2.

42 Ibid., para. 26.

43 Ibid., para. 27.

44 *R. v. Sault Ste. Marie* (1978), 40 C.C.C. (2d) 353 (S.C.C.). The test of due diligence for employers of doorstaff is twofold: first, that the acts committed by the bouncers took place without its direction or approval and, second, that in the balance of probabilities, it took reasonable care to institute a system to prevent the offence and took reasonable steps to ensure its effective operation or undertaking.

45 N.J. Strantz, "Beyond R. v. Sault Ste. Marie: The Creation and Expansion

of Strict Liability and the 'Due Diligence' Defence," 30:4 *Alta. L. Rev.* 1233 at c [referenced in *R. v. 1300378 Ontario Ltd. (c.o.b. Tonic the Nightclub)*, [2002] O.J. no. 2246 (Ont. Ct. J. (Prov. Off. Ct.)) (QL, C.J.), para. 39.].

CHAPTER 4

1 Internal consistency reliability (coefficient alpha) was reported by Spector and Jex (1998) to average .74 across thirteen studies.
2 It is a domain specific locus of control scale that correlates about .50 to .55 with general locus of control. Internal consistency (coefficient alpha) generally ranges from .80 to .85 in the English language version. Test-retest reliability for a year was reported as .60 by Moyle (1995). The scale has been shown to relate to several work variables including job performance and job satisfaction. It also relates to counterproductive behavior and organizational commitment. Details of scale development can be found in Spector (1985) and Spector and Jex (1998).
3 In comparison, Lipkus's (1991) scale was designed to distinguish among belief in a just world for the domains of the self, for others, and in the socio-political realm. It has been found that individuals who have a low belief in a just world may be troubled by the realization that their world is not orderly and people do not always get what they deserve or deserve what they get.
4 Not shown.
5 Later in this section I consider the role of experience and its direct effect on workplace violence for bouncers.

CHAPTER 5

1 If such a phenomenon actually exists (see Heath & Potter, 2004).
2 Contrary to the aspirations of counter-cultural hipsters, the rave scene, like the hippie scene before it, never "sold out," because regardless of the style, "there will always be merchants lined up to sell it." It is in this sense that consumption *needs* new subcultures. They reflect yet another stylistic distinction, another basis for keeping ahead of the Joneses. Restless, cool-hunting hipsters are merely the "shock troops" of mass consumption. "It's not that the system 'co-opted' their dissent, it's that they were never really dissenting" (ibid., 150).
3 While the flouting of gender norms, androgynous dress, and the celebration of transgendered, lesbian, and gay cultures have surely had an impact on nightclubs, the establishments selected for this book focused entirely on mainstream, heterosexed sites.

CHAPTER 6

1 It is usually at this point in the discussion that some in my audience are tempted to protest, "But I'm not there to be seen. I just want to dance ... to have a good time." My response to the many students who raise this protest is always: "If you just want to dance, why not stay home and turn on the stereo? Why not dance alone in the basement?"
2 My own research experience with masculine subcultures in public policing (Rigakos 1996) and aggressive private policing, or parapolicing (Rigakos 2002), is the basis of this observation.
3 Indeed, a wide range of technical risk research on alcohol, nightclubs, and violence has produced consumption protocols for doorstaff and bartenders to assist in the avoidance of corporate risk and liability as well as harm to patrons and third parties.

CONCLUSIONS

1 A live Canadian television program that aired on CityTV and MuchMusic from 1988 to 2003 featuring guest DJs, musicians, and rappers who entertained a select group of dancers. Outside the nightclub, large groups gathered to watch through floor-to-ceiling windows, enduring all types of inclement weather as cameras pitilessly scanned them. Dancers on the show also developed devoted fan bases dependent on their moves and style.
2 See Heath and Potter's (2005) scathing and insightful critique of the impossibility of "culture jamming" and the structurally naïve claims of leftist counter-culture pundits. The authors are wrong, however, about Marxian notions of overproduction, erroneously connecting this materialist idea to the rationale for campaigns such as "Buy Nothing Day" for which there exists no reasonable Marxist economic basis. Moreover, they adopt a classical (and therefore conservative) political economy by reasserting the maxim that all commodities are sold at their value and repeatedly obfuscate labour-time, by extension denying the existence of surplus-value and the exploitation of labour. They make these claims even though one of their two guiding morality questions is: "Is my individuality creating more work for other people?" (244).

Bibliography

Adam, Frane, and Borut Ronāeviç. 2003. "Social Capital: Recent Debates and Research Trends." *Social Science Information* 42: 155–83.

Adorno, Theodor W., and Max Horkheimer. 2000. [1944.] "The Culture Industry: Enlightenment as Mass Deception." In *The Consumer Society Reader*, edited by Juliet B. Schor and Douglas B. Holt, 3–19. New York: New Press.

Altmeyer, Robert. 1988. *Enemies of Freedom: Understanding Right-Wing Authoritarianism*. San Francisco, Calif.: Jossey-Bass.

— 1996. *The Authoritarian Spectre*. Cambridge, Mass.: Harvard University Press.

Arendt, Hannah. 2000. [1958.] "The Public and Private Realm." In *The Portable Hannah Arendt*, edited by Peter Baehr. London: Penguin.

Armoore, Louise. 2006. "Biometric Borders: Governing Mobilities in the War on Terror." *Political Geography* 25: 336–51.

Bakhtin, Mikhail. 1984. [1931.] *Rabelais and His World*. Translated by H. Iswolsky. Bloomington: Indiana University Press.

Basu, A.K., and R. Kenyon III. 1972. "Causality and Typology: Alternative Methodological Solutions in Theory and Practice." *Pacific Sociological Review* (October): 425–41.

Baudrillard, Jean. 1981. *Critique of the Political Economy of the Sign*. St Louis: Telos Press.

— 1983. *Simulations*. New York: Semiotext(e).

— 1995. *Simulacra and Simulation*. Ann Arbor: University of Michigan Press.

— 1996. *The System of Objects*. New York: Verso.

– 1998. [1970.] *The Consumer Society: Myths and Structures*. Thousand Oaks: Sage.

Beattie, J.M. 1986. *Crime and the Courts in England, 1660–1800*. Princeton: Princeton University Press.

Beck, Ulrich. 1992. "Modern Society as a Risk Society." In *The Culture and Power of Knowledge*, edited by N. Stehr and Richard V. Ericson, 199–214. Berlin: de Gruyter.

– 1997. "A Risky Business." In *LSE Magazine*: 4–6.

– 1999. *World Risk Society*. Malden, Mass.: Polity Press.

Becker, Howard S. 1967. "Whose Side Are We On?" *Social Problems* 14: 239–47.

Bell, Daniel. 1973. *The Coming of Post-Industrial Society: A Venture in Social Forecasting*. New York: Basic Books.

Bentham, Jeremy. 1995. [1787.] *The Panopticon Writings*. London: Verso.

Bhaskar, Roy A. 1975. *A Realist Theory of Science*. London: Verso.

Bianchini, Franco. 1995. "Night Cultures, Night Economies." *Planning Practice and Research* 10: 121–6.

Blumer, Herbert. 1986. [1969.] *Symbolic Interactionism: Perspectives and Methods*. Berkeley: University of California.

Bogard, William. 1996. *The Simulation of Surveillance: Hypercontrol in Telematic Societies*. Cambridge: Cambridge University Press.

– 2000. "Smoothing Machines and the Constitution of Society." *Cultural Studies* 14: 269–94.

Bourdieu, Pierre. 1984. [1979.] *Distinction: A Social Critique of the Judgement of Taste*. Cambridge, Mass.: Harvard University Press.

– 1986. [1983.] "The Forms of Capital." In *Handbook of Theory and Research for the Sociology of Education*, edited by J.G. Richardson, 241–58. New York: Greenwood Press.

Brewer, J. 1989. *The Sinews of Power: War, Money and the English State, 1688–1783*. London: Unwyn Hyman.

Bryman, Alan E. 2004. *The Disneyization of Society*. Thousand Oaks: Sage.

Button, Mark. 2003. "Private Security and the Policing of Quasi-Public Space." *International Journal of the Sociology of Law* 31: 227–37.

– 2007. *Security Officers and Policing: Powers, Culture and Control in the Governance of Private Space*. Aldershot: Ashgate.

Callinicos, Alex. 1989. *Against Postmodernism: A Marxist Critique*. New York: St Martin's Press.

Campbell, Gayle, and Bryan Reingold. 1994. "Private Security and Public Policing in Canada." *Juristat* 14.

Cannon, Walter B. 1915. *An Account of Recent Researches into the Function of Bodily Changes in Pain, Hunger, Fear, and Rage*. New York: Appleton.

Castel, Robert. 1991. "From 'Dangerousness' to Risk." In *The Foucault Effect: Studies in Governmentality*, edited by Graham Burchell, Colin Gordon, and Peter Miller, 281–98. Chicago: University of Chicago Press.

Chan, Janet B.L. 1996. "Changing Police Culture." *British Journal of Criminology* 36: 109–34.

– 1997. *Changing Police Culture: Policing in a Multicultural Society*. Cambridge: Cambridge University Press.

Chan, Wendy, and George S. Rigakos. 2002. "Risk, Crime and Gender." *British Journal of Criminology* 42: 743–61.

Christie, Nils. 1986. "Suitable Enemies." In *Abolitionism: Toward a Non-Repressive Approach to Crime*, edited by H. Bianchi and R. Van Swaaningen, 42–54. Amsterdam: Free University Press.

Coleman, Roy. 2004. *Reclaiming the Streets: Surveillance, Social Control and the City*. Cullompton, U.K.: Willan.

Colquhoun, Patrick. 1800. [1795.] *Treatise on the Police of the Metropolis ...* London: Mawman.

Connell, Robert W. 1995. *Masculinities*: Berkeley: University of California Press.

Crank, John P. 1998. *Understanding Police Culture*. Cincinnati, OH: Anderson Publishing.

Dandeker, C. 1990. *Surveillance, Power and Modernity: Bureaucracy and Discipline from 1700 to the Present Day*. Cambridge: Polity Press.

Davis, M. 1990. *City of Quartz: Excavating the Future of Los Angeles*. London: Verso.

Debord, Guy. 1995. [1967.] *Society of the Spectacle*. New York: Zone Books.

– 2002. [1988.] *Comments on the Society of the Spectacle*. London: Verso.

Defert, Danial. 1991. "'Popular Life' and Insurance Technology." In *The Foucault Effect: Studies in Governmentality*, edited by Graham Burchell, Colin Gordon, and Peter Miller, 211–34. Chicago: University of Chicago Press.

Dennis, Norman, Fernando Henriques, and Clifford Slaughter. 1969. *Coal Is Our Life: An Analysis of a Yorkshire Mining Community*. London: Tavistock.

Denzin, N.K. 1978. *Sociological Methods: A Sourcebook*. New York: McGraw-Hill.

Douglas, M. 1986. *How Institutions Think*. Syracuse: Syracuse University Press.

Douglas, Mary, and Baron Isherwood. 1996. [1979.] *The World of Goods: Towards an Anthropology of Consumption*. New York: Routledge.

Doyle, Aaron, and Richard Ericson. 2004. *Uncertain Business: Risk, Insurance and the Limits of Knowledge*. Toronto: University of Toronto Press.

Egan, Danielle. 2004. "Eyeing the Scene: The Uses and (RE)Uses of Surveillance Cameras in an Exotic Dance Club." *Critical Sociology* 30:
299–319.

Eick, Volker. 2003. "New Strategies of Policing the Poor: Berlin's Neo-
Liberal Security System." *Policing and Society* 13: 365–79.

– 2006. "Preventive Urban Discipline: Rent-a-Cops and Neoliberal
Globalization in Germany." *Social Justice* 33: 1–19.

Emsley, Clive. 1991. *The English Police: A Political and Social history.* 2nd
ed. New York: Harvester Wheatsheaf/St Martin's Press.

Engel, Uwe, and Hermann Strasser. 1998. "Global Risks and Social Inequality: Critical Remarks on the Risk-Society Hypothesis." *Canadian
Journal of Sociology* 23: 91–103.

Ericson, Richard V. 1982. *Reproducing Order.* Toronto: University of
Toronto Press.

Ericson, Richard V., and Kevin D. Haggerty. 1997. *Policing the Risk Society.*
Toronto: University of Toronto Press.

Ericson, Richard V., Kevin D. Haggerty, and Kevin D. Carriere. 1993.
"Community Policing as Communications Policing." In *Community
Policing: Comparative Aspects of Community Oriented Police Work*, edited
by Dieter Dölling and Thomas Feltes, 37–70. Holzkirchen: Felix-Verlag.

Ewald, Francois. 1991. "Insurance and Risk." In *The Foucault Effect: Studies
in Governmentality*, edited by Graham Burchell, Colin Gordon, and
Peter Miller, 197–210. Chicago: University of Chicago Press.

Faludi, Susan. 1999. *Stiffed: The Betrayal of the American Man.* New York:
W. Morrow.

Feeley, Malcolm, and Jonathan Simon. 1994. "Actuarial Justice: The
Emerging New Criminal Law." In *The Futures of Criminology*, edited by
David Nelken, 173–201. Thousand Oaks: Sage.

Fenstermaker, Sarah, and Candace West (eds.). 2002. *Doing Gender, Doing
Difference: Social Inequality, Power, and Resistance.* London: Routledge.

Ferrell, Jeff. 2004. "Boredom, Crime and Criminology." *Theoretical Criminology* 8: 287–302.

Foucault, Michel. 1977. *Discipline and Punish.* New York: Vintage Books.

– 1991. "Governmentality." In *The Foucault Effect: Studies in Governmentality*, edited by Graham Burchell, Colin Gordon, and Peter Miller,
87–104. Chicago: University of Chicago Press.

Fox, S, and Paul E. Spector. 1999. "A Model of Work Frustration-Aggres-
sion." *Journal of Organizational Behavior* 20: 915–31.

Furedi, Frank. 1997. *Culture of Fear: Risk Taking and the Morality of Low
Expectation.* Harrison PA: Continuum Publications.

Garland, David. 1997. "'Governmentality' and the Problem of Crime: Foucault, Criminology, Sociology." *Theoretical Criminology: An International Journal* 1: 173–214.

Gavendo, Michael. 2006. "Toronto Public Policing for Hire: The Effects of Commodification of Policing Services in the Downtown Yonge Business Improvement Area." Master's thesis, Carleton University, Ottawa.

Giddens, Anthony. 1990. *The Consequences of Modernity*. Cambridge: Polity Press.

– 1991. *Modernity and Self-Identity: Self and Society in the Late Modern Age.* Cambridge: Polity Press.

Gladwell, Malcolm. 2005. *Blink*. New York: Little, Brown.

Goffman, Erving. 1959. *The Presentation of Self in Everyday Life*. New York: Doubleday Anchor.

– 1961. *Asylums: Essays on the Social Situations of Mental Patients and Other Inmates.* New York: Anchor.

Gordon, Colin. 1991. "Governmental Rationality: An Introduction." In *The Foucault Effect: Studies in Governmentality*, edited by Graham Burchell, Colin Gordon, and Peter Miller, 1–52. Chicago: University of Chicago Press.

Gough, Brendan, and Gareth Edwards. 1998. "The Beer Talking: Four Lads, a Carry Out and the Reproduction of Masculinities." *Sociological Review* 46: 409–35.

Haggerty, Kevin. 2003. "From Risks to Precaution: The Rationalities of Personal Crime Convention." In *Risk and Morality*, edited by Richard Ericson and Aaron Doyle, 193–214. Toronto: University of Toronto Press.

Hall, Tim, and Phil Hubbard. 1998. "The Entrepeneurial City and the 'New Urban Politics.'" In *The Entrepreneurial City: Geographies of Politics, Regime and Representation*, edited by Tim Hall and Phil Hubbard, 1–28. Chichester, U.K.: Wiley and Sons.

Hannah-Moffat, Kelly. 1999. "Moral Agent or Actuarial Subject: Neoliberal Governance in Canadian Women's Prisons." *Theoretical Criminology* 3: 71–94.

Hardt, Michael, and Antonio Negri. 2001. *Empire*. Cambridge, MA: Harvard University Press.

Harre, Rom. 2001. "How to Change Reality: Story v. Structure – A Debate between Rom Harre and Roy Bhaskar." In *After Postmodernism: An Introduction to Critical Realism*, edited by Jose Lopez and Garry Potter, 22–8. New York: Athlone Press.

Hayward, Keith. 2004. *City Limits: Crime, Consumer Culture and the Urban Experience*. London: Glasshouse Press.

Heath, Dwight. 1987. "Anthropology and Alcohol Studies: Current Issues." *Annual Review of Anthropology* 16: 99–120.

Heath, Joseph, and Andrew Potter. 2005. *The Rebel Sell: Why the Culture Can't Be Jammed.* Toronto: HarperPerrenial.

Hefner, Hugh. 1963. *The Playboy Philosophy, Volume I.* Beverly Hills, CA: Playboy.

Hobbs, Dick, Philip Hadfield, Stuart Lister, and Simon Winlow. 2002. "Door Lore: The Art and Economics of Intimidation." *British Journal of Criminology* 42: 352–70.

– 2003. *Bouncers: Violence and the Night-Time Economy.* Oxford: Oxford University Press.

Huey, Laura, Richard Ericson, and Kevin Haggerty. 2005. "Policing Fantasy City." In *Re-Imagining Policing*, edited by Dennis Cooley, 140–208. Toronto: University of Toronto Press.

Hunt, Alan. 1996. *Governance of the Consuming Passions: A History of Sumptuary Law.* New York: St Martin's Press.

– 2003. "Risk and Everyday Life." In *Risk and Morality*, edited by Richard Ericson and Aaron Doyle, 165–92. Toronto: University of Toronto Press.

Hutton, Fiona. 2004. "Up for It, Mad for It? Women, Drug Use and Participation in Club Scenes." *Health, Risk and Society* 6: 223–37.

Jackson, Phil. 2004. *Inside Clubbing: Sensual Experiments in the Art of Being Human.* New York: Berg.

Jameson, Fredric. 1984. "Postmodernism, or the Cultural Logic of Late Capitalism." *New Left Review* 146: 59–92.

Jensen, Sune Qvotrup. 2006. "Rethinking Subcultural Capital." *Young* 14: 257–76.

Jhally, Sut. 1990. *The Codes of Advertising: Fetishism and the Political Economy of Meaning in the Consumer Society.* New York: Routledge.

Joh, Elizabeth E. 2004. "The Paradox of Private Policing." *Journal of Criminal Law and Criminology* 95: 49–131.

Jones, Trevor, and Tim Newburn. 1995. "How Big Is the Private Security Sector?" *Policing and Society* 5: 221–32.

– 1999. "Urban Change and Policing: Mass Private Property Re-considered." *European Journal on Criminal Policy and Research* 7: 225–44.

Jones, Trevor, and Tim Newburn (eds.). 2006. *Plural Policing in Comparative Policing.* London: Routledge.

Keat, Russell, and John Urry. 1982. *Social Theory as Science.* London: Routledge, Kegan and Paul.

Kellogg, Paul. 1987. "Goodbye to the Working Class?" *IS* 36: 108–10.

Kemshall, Hazel. 2003. *Understanding Risk in Criminal Justice.* Berkshire: Open University Press.

Klein, Naomi. 2000. *No Logo: Taking Aim at the Brand Bullies*. Toronto: Vintage Canada.

Kneal, James. 1999. "'A Problem of Supervision': Moral Geographies of the Nineteenth-Century British Public House." *Journal of Historical Geography* 25: 333–48.

Knemeyer, Franz-Ludwig. 1980. "Polizei." *Economy and Society* 9: 172–96.

Lash, Scott, and John Urry. 1994. *Economies of Signs and Space*. London: Sage.

Law Commission of Canada, ed. 2005. *Law and Risk*. Vancouver: UBC Press.

Leadbeater, David. 1985. "The Consistency of Marx's Categories of Productive and Unproductive Labour." *History of Political Economy* 17: 591–618.

Lefebvre, Henri. 1991. *The Production of Space*. Oxford: Blackwell.

Lerner, Melvin J. 1980. [1965.] *The Belief in a Just World: A Fundamental Delusion*. New York: Plenum Press.

Lerner, Melvin J., and D Miller. 1978. "Just World Research and the Attribution Process." *Psychological Bulletin* 85: 1030–51.

Lévis-Strauss, Claude. 1992. [1955.] *Tristes Tropiques*. New York: Penguin.

Levy, Ron, and Mariana Valverde. 2001. "Knowledge on Tap: Police Science and Common Knowledge in the Legal Regulation of Drunkenness." *Law and Social Inquiry*: 819–46.

Lin, Nan. 1999. "Building a Network Theory of Social Capital." *Connections* 22: 28–51.

Lindman, R.E., and A.R. Lang. 1994. "The Alcohol-Aggression Stereotype: A Cross-Cultural Comparison of Beliefs." *International Journal of the Addictions* 29: 1–13.

Linebaugh, Peter. 1991. *The London Hanged: Crime and Civil Society in England*. London: Allen Lane.

Lipkus, Isaac. 1991. "The Construction and Preliminary Validation of a Global Belief in a Just World Scale and the Exploratory Analysis of the Multidimensional Belief in a Just World Scale." *Personality and Individual Differences* 12: 1171–8.

Lippert, Randy, and Daniel O'Connor. 2006. "Security Intelligence Networks and the Transformation of Contract Private Security." *Policing and Society* 16: 50–66.

Liska, Allen. 1974. "Strategies for Typology Construction." *Sociological Focus* 7: 21–36.

Lister, Stuart. 2002. "Violence as a Commercial Resource." *Journal of Forensic Psychiatry* 13: 245–49.

Loader, Ian. 1999. "Consumer Culture and the Commodification of Policing and Security." *Sociology* 33: 373–92.

– 2002. "Policing, Securitization, and Democratization in Europe." *Criminal Justice* 2: 125–53.

Lofland, John. 1974. "Styles of Reporting Qualitative Field Research." *American Sociologist* 9: 101–11.

Lovatt, Andy, and Justin O'Connor. 1995. "Cities and the Night-Time Economy." *Planning Practice and Research* 10: 127–33.

Lyng, Stephen (ed.). 2005. *Edgework: The Sociology of Risk-Taking*. New York: Routledge.

Maclean, Brian D., and Dragan Milovanovic, eds. 1997. *Thinking Critically about Crime*. Vancouver: Collective Press.

Malbon, Ben. 1999. *Clubbing: Dancing, Ecstasy and Vitality*. London: Routledge.

Mandel, Ernest. 1975. *Late Capitalsim*. London: NLB.

– 1995. [1980.] *Long Waves of Capitalist Development: A Marxist Interpretation*. London: Verso.

Mandel, Ernest, and George Edward Novack. 1970. *The Marxist Theory of Alienation: Three Essays*. New York: Pathfinder Press.

Manicas, Peter T., and Paul F. Secord. 1983. "Implications for Psychology of the Philosophy of Science." *American Psychologist* 38.

Manning, Peter K. 1997. *Police Work: The Social Organization of Policing*. 2nd ed. Prospect Heights: Waveland Press.

– 2001. "Theorizing Policing: The Drama and Myth of Crime Control in the NYPD." *Theoretical Criminology* 5: 315–44.

Manning, Peter K., and John H. Van Maanen, eds. 1978. *Policing: A View from the Street*. Santa Monica: Goodyear.

Marx, Karl. 1935. *Value, Price and Profit*. New York: International Publishers.

– 1972. *Theories of Surplus-Value, I*. London: Lawrence and Wishart.

– 1973. *Grundrisse*. New York: Penguin.

– 1976. *Capital, I*. New York: Penguin.

– 1977. [1933.] *Wage-Labor and Capital*. New York: International Publishers.

Mass Observation. 1943. *The Pub and the People*. London: Gollancz.

Mathiesen, Thomas. 1997. "The Viewer Society: Michel Foucault's 'Panopticon' Revisited." *Theoretical Criminology* 1: 215–34.

McKinney, John C. 1966. *Constructive Typology and Social Theory*. New York: Appleton-Century-Crofts.

McMullan, John L. 1996. "Policing, Lawlessness, and Disorder in Historical Perspective." In *Post-Critical Criminology*, edited by Thomas O'Reilly-Fleming, 111–40. Scarborough: Prentice Hall Canada.

– 1998. "Social Surveillance and the Rise of the 'Police Machine.'" *Theoretical Criminology* 2: 93–117.

Measham, Fiona. 2004. "Play Space: Historical and Socio-Cultural Reflections on Drugs, Licensed Leisure Locations, Commercialization and Control." *International Journal of Drug Policy* 15: 337–45.

Melbin, Murray. 1978. "Night as Frontier." *American Sociological Review* 43: 3–22.

Menzies, Robert. 1992. "Beyond Realist Criminology." In *Realist Criminology: Crime Control and Policing in the 1990s*, edited by John Lowman and Brian MacLean, 139–56. Toronto: University of Toronto Press.

Messerschmidt, James W. 1993. *Masculinites and Crime: Critique and Reconceptualization*. Lanham: Rowman & Littlefield.

– 1997. *Crime as Structured Action: Gender, Race, Class and Crime in the Making*. Thousand Oaks, CA: Sage.

Micucci, Anthony J. 1994. "The Changing of the Guard: A Case Study of Professionalization in a Campus Security Force." In *Department of Sociology Journal*. North York: York University.

Miller, Peter, and Nikolas Rose. 1997. "Mobilizing the Consumer: Assembling the Subject of Consumption." *Theory, Culture, & Society* 14: 1–36.

Mills, C. Wright. 1959. *The Sociological Imagination*. New York: Oxford University Press.

Mopas, Michael. 2005. "Policing in Vancouver's Downtown Eastside." In *Re-Imagining Policing in Canada*, edited by Dennis Cooley, 92–139. Toronto: University of Toronto Press.

Murphy, Christopher, and Curtis Clarke. 2005. "Policing Communities and Communities of Policing: A Comparative Study of Policing and Security in Two Canadian Communities." In *Re-Imagining Policing in Canada*, edited by Dennis Cooley, 209–59. Toronto: University of Toronto Press.

Mythen, Gabe. 2004. *Ulrich Beck: A Critical Introduction to the Risk Society*. London: Pluto Press.

– 2005. "Employment, Individualization and Insecurity: Rethinking the Risk Society Perspective." *Sociological Review* 53: 129–49.

Neocleous, Mark. 2000a. "Against Security." *Radical Philosophy* 100: 7–15.

– 2000b. *The Fabrication of Social Order: A Critical Theory of Police Power*. London: Pluto Press.

Newman, Oscar. 1973. *Defensible Space: Crime Prevention through Urban Design*. New York: Macmillan.

Newton, Tim J., and Anthony Keenan. 1985. "Coping with Work Related Stress." *Human Relations* 38: 107–26.

O'Connor, Daniel, Randy Lippert, Kelly Greenfield, and Phil Boyle. 2004. "After the 'Quiet Revolution': The Self-Regulation of Ontario Contract

Security Agencies" *Policing and Society* 14: 138–57.

O'Malley, Pat. 1991. "Legal Networks and Domestic Security." *Studies in Law, Politics, and Society* 11: 171–90.

– 1992. "Risk, Power and Crime Prevention." *Economy and Society* 21: 252–75.

– 1996. "Risk and Responsibility." In *Foucault and Political Reason: Liberalism, Neo-liberalism and Rationalities of Government*, edited by Andrew Barry, Thomas Osborne, and Nikolas Rose, 189–207. London: UCL Press.

– 2001. "Discontinuity, Government and Risk: A Response to Rigakos and Hadden." *Theoretical Criminology* 5: 85–92.

– 2004. *Risk, Uncertainty and Government*. London: Glasshouse Press.

O'Malley, Pat, Lorna Weir, and Clifford Shearing. 1997. "Governmentality, Criticism, Politics." *Economy and Society* 26: 501–17.

Palmer, Bryan. 2000. *Cultures of Darkness: Night Travels in the Histories of Transgression (from Medieval to Modern)*. New York: Monthly Review Press.

Palys, Ted. 1992. *Research Decisons: Quantitative and Qualitative Perspectives*. Toronto: Harcourt Brace Jovanovich.

Pasquino, Pasquale. 1991. "Theatrum Politicum: The Genealogy of Capital – Police and the State of Prosperity." In *The Foucault Effect: Studies in Governmentality*, edited by Graham Burchell, Colin Gordon, and Peter Miller, 105–18. Chicago: University of Chicago Press.

Perrott, Stephen B. 1991. "Social Identity Patterns in the Police: Attitudinal and Performance Implications." In *Psychology*. Montreal: McGill University.

Perrott, Stephen B., and E. Kevin Kelloway. 2006. "Workplace Violence in the Police." In *Workplace Violence in the Police*, edited by Julian Barling, E. Kevin Kelloway, and Stephen B. Perrott, 211–29. Thousand Oaks, CA: Sage.

Perrott, Stephen B., and Donald M. Taylor. 1994. "Ethnocentrism and Authoritarianism in the Police: Challenging Stereotypes and Reconceptualizing Ingroup Identification." *Journal of Applied Social Psychology* 24: 1640–64.

– 1995. "Crime Fighting, Law Enforcement and Service Provider Role Differentiations in Community-Based Police Officers." *American Journal of Police* 13: 173–95.

Presdee, Mike. 2000. *Cultural Criminology and the Carnival of Crime*. London: Routledge.

– 2004. "Cultural Criminology: The Long and Winding Road." *Theoretical Criminology* 8: 275–85.

Priest, George L. 1990. "The New Legal Structure of Risk Control." *Daedulus* 119: 207–27.

Putnam, Robert D. 1988. Foreword. *Housing Policy Debates* 9: v–vii.

– 1993. *Making Democracy Work: Civic Traditions in Modern Italy*. Princeton, N.J.: Princeton University Press.

– 2000. *Bowling Alone: The Collapse and Revival of American Community*. New York: Simon & Schuster.

Quinney, Richard. 1997. "Socialist Humanism and Critical/Peacemaking Criminology: The Continuing Project." In *Thinking Critically about Crime*, edited by Brian MacLean and Dragan Milovanovic, 114–17. Vancouver: Collective Press.

Reiner, Robert. 1992. *The Politics of the Police*. 2nd ed. Toronto: University of Toronto Press.

Rigakos, George, and Jon Frauley. 2007. "The Promise of Critical Realism: Toward a Post-Empiricist Criminology." In *The Criminological Promise*, edited by Aaron Doyle, Kevin Haggerty, and Dawn Moore. Toronto: University of Toronto Press.

Rigakos, George S. 1995. "Constructing the Symbolic Complainant: Police SubCulture and the Nonenforcement of Protection Orders for Battered Women." *Violence and Victims* 10: 227–47.

– 1999a. "Hyperpanoptics as Commodity: The Case of the Parapolice." *Canadian Journal of Sociology* 23: 381–409.

– 1999b. "Risk Society and Actuarial Criminology: Prospects for a Critical Discourse." *Canadian Journal of Criminology* 41: 137–50.

– 2000. "Bubbles of Governance: Private Policing and the Law in Canada." *Canadian Journal of Law and Society* 15: 145–86.

– 2001. "On Continuity, Risk and Political Economy: A Response to O'Malley." *Theoretical Criminology* 5: 93–100.

– 2002a. *In Search of Security: The Roles of Public and Private Agencies*. Ottawa: Law Commission of Canada.

– 2002b. *The New Parapolice: Risk Markets and Commodified Social Control*. Toronto: University of Toronto Press.

– 2004. Review of *Bouncers: Violence and Governance in the Night-Time Economy*, by Dick Hobbs, Philip Hadfield, Stuart Lister and Simon Winlow, Oxford University Press, 2003." *Theoretical Criminology* 8: 114–17.

– 2006. "Beyond Public-Private: Toward a New Typology of Policing." In *Re-Imagining Policing in Canada*, edited by Dennis Cooley, 260–319. Toronto: University of Toronto Press.

Rigakos, George S., and Richard W. Hadden. 2001. "Crime, Capitalism and the Risk Society: Towards the Same Olde Modernity?" *Theoretical Criminology* 5: 61–84.

Rigakos, George S., and Alexandra Law. Forthcoming. "Risk, Realism and Resistance." *Critical Scoiology.*

Rintoul, Scott, and Christy MacKillican. 2001. *Designer Drugs and Raves.* 2nd ed. Ottawa: Addictive Drug Information Council and the RCMP "E" Division Drug Awareness Service.

Rubin, Zick, and Letita Anne Peplau. 1975. "Who Believes in a Just World?" *Journal of Social Issues* 31: 65–89.

Ruppert, Evelyn. 2006. *The Moral Economy of Cities: Shaping Good Citizens.* Toronto: University of Toronto Press.

Rustin, Michael. 1994. "Incomplete Modernity: Ulrich Beck's *Risk Society.*" *Radical Philosophy* 67: 3–19.

Sahlins, Marshall. 1976. *Culture and Practical Reason.* Chicago: University of Chicago Press.

Salmond, J.W. *Salmond on the Law of Torts.* 17th ed. London: Sweet & Maxwell 1977.

Sanders, Trevor. 2003. *Rise of the Rent-a-Cop.* Ottawa: Law Commission of Canada.

Shearing, Clifford D., and Richard Ericson. 1991. "Culture as Figurative Action." *British Journal of Criminology* 42: 481–506.

Shearing, Clifford D., and Philip C. Stenning. 1983. "Private Security: Implications for Social Control." *Social Problems* 30: 498–505.

– 1987. "SAY 'CHEESE:' The Disney Order That Is Not So Mickey Mouse." In *Private Policing,* edited by Clifford D. Shearing and Philip C. Stenning, 317–23. Newbury Park: Sage.

Skolnick, Jerome. 1966. *Justice without Trial.* New York: Wiley and Sons.

Skolnick, Jerome H., and James J. Fyfe. 1993. *Above the Law: Police and the Excessive Use of Force.* New York: Free Press.

Smith, Adam. 1937. [1776]. *The Wealth of Nations.* New York: Random House.

Somers, Margaret R. 2005. "Let Them Eat Social Capital: Socializing the Market Versus Marketizing the Social." *Thesis Eleven* 81: 5–19.

South, Nigel. 1984. "Private Security, the Division of Policing Labor and the Commercial Compromise of the State." *Research in Law, Deviance and Social Control* 6: 171–98.

Spector, Paul E. 1985. "Measurement of Human Service Staff Satisfaction: Development of the Job Satisfaction Survey." *American Journal of Community Psychology* 13: 693–713.

Spector, Paul E., and Steve M. Jex. 1998. "Development of Four Self-Report Measures of Job Stressors and Strain: Interpersonal Conflict at Work Scale, Organizational Constraints Scale, Quantitative Workload Inventory, and Physical Symptoms Inventory." *Journal of Occupational Health Psychology* 3: 356–67.

Spitzer, Stephen. 1987. "Security and Control in Capitalist Societies: The Fetishism of Security and the Secret Thereof." In *Transcarceration: Essays in the Sociology of Social Control*, edited by John Lowman, Robert J. Menzies, and Ted S. Palys, 43–58. Aldershot: Gower.

Spitzer, Steven, and Andrew T. Scull. 1977. "Privatization and Capitalist Development: The Case of the Private Police." *Social Problems* 25: 18–29.

Stanko, Elizabeth A. 1997. "Safety Talk: Conceptualizing Women's Risk Assessment as 'Technology of the Soul.'" *Theoretical Criminology* 1: 479–99.

Swol, Karen. 1999. "Private Security and Public Policing in Canada." In *Juristat Reader*, 15–25. Toronto: Thompson Educational Publishing.

Thomas, Jim. 1993. *Doing Critical Ethnography*. Newbury Park: Sage.

Thompson, E. 1963. *The Making of the English Working Class*. London: Victor Gollancz.

Thomsen, Stephen. 1997. "A Top Night: Social Protest, Masculinity and the Culture of Drinking Violence." *British Journal of Criminology* 37: 90–102.

– 2005. "'Boozers and Bouncers': Masculine Conflict, Disengagement and the Contemporary Governance of Drinking-Related Violence and Disorder." *Australian and New Zealand Journal of Criminology* 38: 283–97.

Thornton, Sarah. 1995. *Club Cultures*. Cambridge: Polity Press.

Urry, John. 2002. [1990.] *The Tourist Gaze*. London: Sage.

Valverde, Mariana. 2003. "Police Science, British Style: Pub Licensing and Knowledges of Urban Disorder." *Economy and Society* 32: 234–52.

Van Katwyk, Peter T., S. Fox, Paul E. Spector, and E. Kevin Kelloway. 2000. "Using the Job-Related Affective Well-Being Scale (JAWS) to investigate affective responses to work stressors." *Journal of Occupational Health Psychology* 5: 219–30.

Van Maanen, John. 1978. "Kinsmen in Repose: Occuptional Perspectives of Patrolmen." In *Policing: A View from the Street*, edited by Peter K. Manning and John Van Maanen. Santa Monica, CA: Goodyear Publishing.

Veblen, Thorstein. 1902. *The Theory of the Leisure Class: An Economic Study of Institutions*. New York: Macmillan.

Wagner, David G. 1984. *The Growth of Sociological Theories*. Beverly Hills: Sage.

Wakefield, Alison. 2006. "Private Policing: A View from the Mall." Unpublished paper. London: City University.

Wallerstein, Immanuel. 1979. *The Capitalist World-Economy*. Cambridge: Cambridge University Press and Edition de la Maison de l'Homme.

Weiss, Robert. 1978. "The Emergence and Transformation of Private Detective Industrial Policing in the United States, 1850–1940." *Crime & Social Justice* 9: 35–48.

Westley, W. 1970. *Violence and the Police*. Cambridge: MIT Press.

Wilson, Brian. 2006. *Fight, Flight, or Chill: Subcultures, Youth, and Rave into the Twenty-First Century*. Montreal: McGill-Queen's University Press.

Winlow, Simon. 2001. *Badfellas: Crime, Tradition and New Masculinities*. Oxford: Berg.

Young, Jock. 1997. "Left Realism: The Basics." In *Thinking Critically about Crime*, edited by Brian MacLean and Dragan Milovanovic, 28–36. Vancouver: Collective Press.

– 1999. *The Exclusive Society: Social Exclusion, Crime and Late Modernity*. Thousand Oaks, CA: Sage.

Index